# THE GEORGIAN REVOLT

# The Georgian Revolt

RISE AND FALL OF A POETIC IDEAL
1910–22

Robert H. Ross

FABER AND FABER
24 Russell Square, London

*First published in England in mcmlxvii*
*by Faber and Faber Limited*
*24 Russell Square London WC1*
*Printed in Great Britain by*
*Latimer Trend & Co Ltd Plymouth*
*All rights reserved*

# To MARY
*who helped even more than she knew*

# Contents

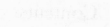

# Illustrations

# Preface

'You start a question, and it's like starting a stone,' said Robert Louis Stevenson. If we were always knowledgeable enough to ask the right questions at the beginning, writing a literary history would be much less hazardous. The question which led me to undertake this book arose from an anomaly I thought I observed while teaching an undergraduate course in modern British literature. In the age of Bennett and Wells, Shaw and Galsworthy, when most English non-poetic literature was oriented towards a sober, serious representational realism, it seemed a curious anachronism that poetry should have turned to little nature lyrics, pastoral effusions on the beauties of certain rural counties, or unconsidered trifles about moonlight and nightingales. Why should such poetry —Georgian poetry—have flourished precisely at the time that it did?

Like many historical questions, this one carried with it an un-examined critical premise. I quickly discovered that my too easy assumption about the nature of Georgian poetry was ridiculously oversimplified and, in most cases, downright wrong. My initial question, moreover, soon became only a first step into the laby-rinth of other, anterior questions. Who, in fact, were the Geor-gians? Was the word to be used denotatively, as a historical tag, that is, to describe those poets who wrote by and large in the second decade of the century? Or should it be used connotatively, to describe a poetic school? Critics had used it both ways, with confusing results. If the word described a coterie and not an age, what, then, made a Georgian a 'Georgian'? What poetic canons did the 'Georgian' poet subscribe to? Again, since Edward

Marsh's anthology included poetry published as early as 1910 and as late as 1922, was it not reasonable to assume that over a thirteen-year span—which included the cataclysmic years of the First World War—Georgian poetry should have experienced several mutations? Did the word 'Georgian' connote the same thing, then, in 1912 as, say, in 1919 or 1922? Finally, was the relationship of the Georgian poets to their age as tidy as some subsequent critics had made it out to be? Were the Georgians only misty-eyed lark-lovers, belated pastoral poets, or escapists who, in the alien twentieth century, pursued the chimera of 'Beauty and Certainty and Quiet kind'? Or did they too reflect something of the temper of their age? What, indeed, was the age of the Georgians? Did they perhaps live and write not in one but in two very different literary ages, the pre-war and the post-war?

I hope my initial wrong question led me finally to ask a few of the right ones. At any rate, I was impelled from the beginning to undertake an essentially historical study of the Georgians and their age. To the reader who finds my critical conclusions too slight I can only assert that my aim in this book has been not so much to evaluate as to explain, not so much to colonize as to explore. Therefore, I have not attempted any formal, systematic critical assessment of the achievement of the Georgian poets. Obviously, some critical judgments have been necessary; the line of demarcation between literary history and literary criticism is not as easily definable in practice as it sometimes appears to be in theory. But even in those places where I have felt required to express a few critical opinions, I have been guided, I hope, by an overriding historical purpose. Least of all have I used Georgian verse as an excuse for an exercise in the explication of poetry. Close textual explication is perhaps the most useful tool the modern critic possesses, but the kinds of insights it affords are, I believe, largely irrelevant to my purpose in this particular book.

What I have tried to do is neither complex nor abstruse. I have attempted to place the Georgians in the perspective of their time; to reconstruct some of the conditions under which Edward Marsh's anthology was born, flourished, and died; to describe and define—loosely, I fear, for that is the only way it can be defined—the Georgian poetic temper; to describe the changes which occurred in Georgian poetry from 1912 to 1922; and to account for the downfall of the Georgian poetic ideal.

This kind of approach was required by the fact that this book is the first attempt at an extended study exclusively of the Georgians and their age. The Georgian fields have never been really systematically tilled. An incidental spadeful of earth turned up here, a haphazard furrow there; a snippet or two, a few isolated pages, a small chapter at best: the literary histories of twentieth-century poetry have been remarkably incomplete on the Georgians. And so when a unique set of tools was offered me, I took the opportunity to begin digging. Others who follow will, I hope, turn their efforts towards evaluating the Georgian achievement in the light of our contemporary critical norms; with our perspective of fifty years, it is time the process was begun. But I have attempted little here beyond some of the first, rough historical spade-work.

I hope that this book has succeeded in avoiding the extremes of special pleading on the one hand and of undue harshness on the other. For some years the collective reputation of the Georgians has been at a low ebb. Indeed, perhaps no group of poets since the Pre-Raphaelites has suffered more, or more ignominiously, from the widespread acceptance of oversimplified stereotypes and critical half-truths, even among readers who should know better. Often the Georgians have been misrepresented because of the ignorance of their subsequent critics, but even more often they have been the victims of pure critical spleen. Many of the major Georgian poets surely deserve rescue from the almost universal obloquy which the weaknesses of a few of the brethren have drawn down upon the heads of the entire body. The law of poetic averages alone—to say nothing of careful reading—would suggest to an unbiased observer that not every poet published in the five volumes of *Georgian Poetry* was a glib, pseudo-pastoral lark-lover.

Nevertheless, Georgian poetry undeniably demonstrates certain characteristic weaknesses. The Georgian renascence was not, after all, the Elizabethan Renaissance. And W. H. Davies was not William Wordsworth nor was meant to be; the sonnets of Rupert Brooke are not to be confused with those of John Keats, nor his metaphysical poetry with the best of John Donne. And so the temptation to start a literary crusade must be resisted, especially by the literary historian. Experience too often demonstrates that the caparisoned charger which he pictures himself mounting in such situations appears to the alert reader to be no more than a spavined literary hobby-horse. What is required is neither the over-praise of the zealot nor the wholesale depreciation of the cynic. An indiscriminate condemnation of the Georgian muse is wholly undeserved, but equally unsupportable is an indiscriminate panegyric.

R. H. R.

# Acknowledgements

One does not have to read very far into my text to become aware that my indebtedness to other persons who helped bring this book into being is both wide and deep. The most significant source of information which I have been permitted to use is the Edward Marsh Letter Collection. When Sir Edward Marsh, editor of *Georgian Poetry*, died in 1953, he was found to have preserved a voluminous body of letters written to him over a span of more than fifty years not only by countless public figures but also by almost every British poet of consequence in the twentieth century. During his lifetime Sir Edward had allowed only a few of his letters from the poets to be published: those from D. H. Lawrence appeared in Aldous Huxley's edition of the Lawrence letters (1932); most of his letters from Isaac Rosenberg were printed in *The Collected Works of Isaac Rosenberg* (1937); and a small amount of his correspondence from Rupert Brooke appeared in Arthur Stringer's *The Red Wine of Youth* (1948) and in Sir Edward's own memoir, *A Number of People* (1939).

Upon his death Sir Edward willed all his papers to the late Christopher Hassall, a close friend of the later years. Mr. Hassall drew upon many of the Marsh letters as a major source for his *Edward Marsh: A Biography* (1959). In 1957 Mr. Hassall sold almost all the letters to the Berg Collection of the New York Public Library, where they now reside. Obviously, no significant history of the Georgian movement was possible without taking into account the Marsh papers, and so, having received a leave of absence from teaching duties in 1954–55, I went to London to see them.

To Mr. Hassall I owe a debt which I cannot now repay nor even

adequately acknowledge. He not only gave me access to the Marsh
Letter Collection but also gave abundantly of his knowledge,
assistance, and influence in many other ways. Without his initial
generosity and continuing interest, my work, as it is here em-
bodied, would have been impossible. His detailed comments on an
early draft of my manuscript were indispensable. In 1956 Mr.
Hassall edited a collection of Rupert Brooke's prose, in 1959 he
published his exhaustive and scholarly biography of Sir Edward
Marsh, and only a few weeks before his shocking, untimely death
from a thrombosis in April 1963, he had sent to the publisher his
completed manuscript of the official biography of Rupert Brooke.
To the memory of one who did so much directly to ensure a more
enlightened understanding of the Georgians, my work may serve,
I hope, as an indirect tribute. To my sorrow, he cannot see this
book he helped produce.

 I am also indebted to several other English friends, chief among
them Mr. Bertram Rota, at whose bookshop in Vigo Street I
examined most of the Marsh papers in 1955. I often relied on Mr.
Rota's encyclopaedic knowledge of twentieth-century literature,
and I am as grateful for his never-failing hospitality and friendship
as I am for his judicious, balanced appraisal of the Georgian
poetic achievement and his constructive, detailed comments upon
my manuscript.

 Among the Georgian poets I am particularly indebted to the
late Wilfrid Gibson, who received me graciously in his home in
West Byfleet, Surrey, and, in the course of a long afternoon's
conversation, as well as several subsequent letters, gave me new
insights into Georgian verse and the close friendships which
existed among many of the Georgian poets in the pre-war years.
Mrs. John Drinkwater and Mrs. Harold Monro also received me
cordially, and their complete and candid answers to my questions
about their husbands' associations with Sir Edward Marsh and the
*Georgian Poetry* series have contributed significantly to my understanding of the pre-war Georgian movement. Although, unfortunately, I had no opportunity to meet Mrs. Lascelles Abercrombie
while I was in England, we have corresponded frequently over the
past several years, and her letters have been not only informative
but immensely encouraging as well.

 There are few visiting scholars in Britain who are not indebted
to the staff of the Reading Room of the British Museum. I am no

exception. To the staff of the Bodleian Library I also owe thanks. But my special gratitude goes to the staff of the London Library and to the Director (in 1955), Mr. Simon Nowell Smith, who were uncommonly helpful in facilitating my research into Georgian periodicals and little magazines.

Among other friends who helped with this book in various ways while I was in England, both in 1954–55 and 1961, are Mr. and Mrs. Ronald A. Brett, Mrs. Bertram Rota, Mr. Anthony B. Rota, Mr. Anthony Newnham, Miss Sheila and the late Miss Elaine Wardlaw Turner, the Reverend and Mrs. Daniel Jenkins, and Mr. and Mrs. Nicholas Hackett.

As this book progressed many of my American colleagues gave me excellent advice as well as more active forms of assistance. I am uniquely obliged to Professor Richard D. Altick of the Department of English at The Ohio State University; the suggestions which ensued from his characteristically thorough reading of my manuscript in its early stages were indispensable. I also acknowledge the considerable help of Professors John Harold Wilson and Edwin W. Robbins of The Ohio State University and Professors Roy Harvey Pearce and Andrew H. Wright of the University of California at San Diego. Finally, I owe a good deal more than I can say to Professor Benjamin T. Spencer, my former Chairman in the Department of English at Ohio Wesleyan University. I am particularly grateful to him for undertaking the final line by line reading of my manuscript immediately before it went to print. No colleague should ever be called upon to do such a brain-deadening job. But Professor Spencer did it as a friend.

Ohio Wesleyan University helped bring this book to fruition by granting me leaves of absence necessary to pursue my research in England. Naturally, many American libraries assisted me in a variety of ways, especially the Houghton Library at Harvard University, the Library of The Ohio State University, and the Slocum Library at Ohio Wesleyan University. Mr. J. Herrold Lancaster, Librarian, Mr. John Reed, Reference Librarian, Mrs. Lawrence Wick, at my own University, and Miss Patricia J. Delks, the Reference Librarian of the Smith College Library, Northampton, Massachusetts, were extraordinarily helpful.

I gratefully acknowledge the permission of the New York Public Library to quote from those letters to Sir Edward Marsh which are now part of the Henry W. and Albert A. Berg Collection. For

allowing me to quote from letters in the Marsh Collection I am
also grateful to the following of Sir Edward Marsh's correspon-
dents or their literary heirs, executors, or trustees: Professor
Claude Colleer Abbott (for Gordon Bottomley); Mrs. Lascelles
Abercrombie; Professor Edmund Blunden; Lord Bridges (for
Robert Bridges); Mr. Spencer Curtis Brown (for A. A. Milne);
Mrs. W. H. Davies; Mr. Richard de la Mare, on behalf of the
Literary Trustees of Walter de la Mare; Mrs. John Drinkwater; the
Misses Joy and Catharine Freeman (for John Freeman); Mr.
Michael Gibson (for Wilfrid Gibson); Mr. A. V. Moore, on behalf
of Mr. Ezra Pound; Miss Jennifer Gosse (for Sir Edmund Gosse);
Mr. Robert Graves; the late Christopher Hassall (for letters written
by Sir Edward Marsh); Sir Geoffrey Keynes, on behalf of the
Rupert Brooke Trustees; the Hon. Lady Maclean (for Maurice
Baring); Mr. John Masefield; Mrs. D. M. Mewton-Wood (for W.
J. Turner); Mrs. Harold Monro; Miss Riette Sturge Moore (for
T. Sturge Moore); Mrs. John Middleton Murry; Messrs. Laurence
Pollinger Ltd., the Estate of the late Mrs. Frieda Lawrence and
Messrs. William Heinemann Ltd. (for D. H. Lawrence); Mrs. B.
F. G. Richards (for Maurice Hewlett); Mr. William Rathbone (for
Sir Bruce Richmond); the Literary Executors of Isaac Rosenberg,
Messrs. Chatto and Windus Ltd., and Mr. Ian Parsons (for Isaac
Rosenberg); Mr. Siegfried Sassoon; Mrs. Edward Shanks; The
Society of Authors and the Estate of James Stephens; and Mr.
Raglan Squire (for Sir John Squire).

For allowing me to quote from various poems in my text I am
happy to make the following acknowledgements:

LASCELLES ABERCROMBIE, 'The Sale of St. Thomas' and
'The End of the World': by permission of Mrs. Lascelles Abercrombie.

GORDON BOTTOMLEY, 'King Lear's Wife': by permission of Professor Claude Colleer Abbott.

RUPERT BROOKE, 'Channel Passage', 'Dining-room Tea', and
'Menelaus and Helen': by permission of Sir Geoffrey Keynes, on
behalf of the Rupert Brooke Trustees.

W. H. DAVIES, 'Confession', 'Days Too Short', 'Down Under-
ground', 'The Truth', and 'Wasted Hours': by permission of Mrs.
W. H. Davies and Jonathan Cape Ltd., publishers of *Collected
Poems* (1928) by W. H. Davies.

WALTER DE LA MARE, 'Full Moon': by permission of the

Literary Trustees of Walter de la Mare and The Society of Authors as their representative.

H. D[oolittle], 'Oread': from *H. D. Selected Poems*, copyright © 1957 by Norman Holmes Pearson, published by Grove Press Inc., by permission of Professor Pearson.

JOHN DRINKWATER, 'Moonlit Apples': by permission of Mrs. John Drinkwater.

JOHN FREEMAN, 'I Will Ask' and 'Happy Is England Now': by permission of the Hutchinson Group for Selwyn and Blount, publishers of *Poems Old and New* (1920) by John Freeman.

WILFRID GIBSON, 'Hoops' and 'The Parrots': by permission of Mr. Michael Gibson.

DOUGLAS GOLDRING, 'Post-Georgian Poet in Search of a Master': by permission of Mrs. Douglas Goldring.

RALPH HODGSON, 'The Bull': by permission of St. Martins Press Inc., publishers of *Collected Poems* by Ralph Hodgson.

E. V. KNOX, 'Companions', 'Go', and 'The Snail': from *Parodies Regained* (1921) and *These Liberties* (1923), by permission of Methuen and Company Ltd.

D. H. LAWRENCE, 'Grief': by permission of Messrs. Laurence Pollinger Ltd., the Estate of the late Mrs. Frieda Lawrence, William Heinemann Ltd., and The Viking Press Inc.

JOHN MASEFIELD, 'Biography' and 'The Everlasting Mercy': reprinted with permission of the Society of Authors and Dr. John Masefield, O.M.

HAROLD MONRO, 'Week-end' and 'The Nightingale Near the House': by permission of Mrs. Harold Monro and Gerald Duckworth and Company Ltd., publishers of Harold Monro's *Collected Poems* (in preparation).

ROBERT NICHOLS, 'The Assault': by permission of Mr. Milton Waldman, Literary Executor of the late Mr. Nichols.

EZRA POUND, 'L'Art', 'Monumentium Aere', 'Salutation the Third', 'Women Before a Shop', 'The New Cake of Soap', and 'Meditatio': from *Personae* by Ezra Pound. Copyright 1926, 1954 by Ezra Pound. All rights reserved. Reprinted by permission of New Directions, Publishers, and A. V. Moore Esq.

ISAAC ROSENBERG, 'Returning, We Hear the Larks': reprinted by permission of the Literary Executors of Isaac Rosenberg and Chatto and Windus Ltd., from *The Collected Poems of Isaac Rosenberg*, edited by Gordon Bottomley and Denys Harding.

21

Siegfried Sassoon, 'Attack' and 'They': by permission of the author.

Sir Osbert Sitwell, 'Te Deum': by permission of the author.

Sir John Squire, 'The Birds' and 'The Lily of Malud': from *Collected Poems* (1926) by Sir John Squire, by permission of Mr. Raglan Squire and Macmillan and Company Ltd.

W. J. Turner, 'Romance' and 'The Princess': by permission of Mrs. D. M. Mewton-Wood.

For granting me permission to quote extensively from copyrighted books, critical articles, reviews, and other works, I acknowledge my indebtedness to the following:

George Allen and Unwin Ltd., for quotations from *Old and New Masters* (1919) by Robert Lynd.

Chapman and Hall Ltd., for quotations from *Thus To Revisit: Some Reminiscences* (1921) by Ford Madox Ford.

Chatto and Windus Ltd., for quotations from *A Critical History of English Poetry* (1947) by H. J. C. Grierson and J. C. Smith.

Stanley K. Coffman for quotations from his book *Imagism: A Chapter for the History of Modern Poetry* (University of Oklahoma Press, 1951).

Professor Arundel del Re for quotations from a series of articles entitled 'Georgian Reminiscences' appearing in *Studies in English Literature* (1932, 1934).

Mrs. John Drinkwater for quotations from critical articles by John Drinkwater in *Poetry Review* and from his *Discovery: the Second Book of an Autobiography* (Ernest Benn Ltd., 1932).

Gerald Duckworth and Company Ltd., for quotations from *Aspects of Modern Literature* (1934) by Dame Edith Sitwell.

The late Mr. T. S. Eliot for quotations from articles he wrote for the *Times Literary Supplement*, the *Egoist*, and *To-day*.

Faber & Faber Ltd. for quotations from *The Literary Essays of Ezra Pound* (1950), edited by T. S. Eliot.

Mrs. Douglas Goldring for quotations from *Reputations* (Chapman and Hall Ltd., 1920), *The 1920's* (Nicolson and Watson, 1945), and articles from *Chapbook* and *Art and Letters* by Douglas Goldring.

Mr. Robert Graves for quotations from *Contemporary Techniques of Poetry. Hogarth Essays*, No. 8 (1925) and critical articles in the *Times Literary Supplement* and the *Owl*.

The late Christopher Hassall and Longmans, Green and Company Ltd., for quotations from *Edward Marsh, Patron of the Arts: A Biography* (1959) by Christopher Hassall; and the late Mr. Hassall for quotations from his book *The Prose of Rupert Brooke* (Sidgwick and Jackson Ltd., 1956).

William Heinemann Ltd., and Hamish Hamilton Ltd., joint publishers of the English edition, for quotations from *A Number of People* (1939) by Sir Edward Marsh.

William Heinemann Ltd., for quotations from *More Books on the Table* (1923) by Sir Edmund Gosse.

Holt, Rinehart and Winston Inc., for quotations from *Life Is My Song* (1937) by John Gould Fletcher.

Holt, Rinehart and Winston Inc. for a portion of a letter from Robert Frost to Sidney Cox reprinted from *Robert Frost: The Trial by Existence* by Elizabeth Shepley Sergeant. Copyright © 1960 by Elizabeth Shepley Sergeant. Reprinted by permission of Holt, Rinehart and Winston Inc.

E. Hulton and Company Ltd., for quotations from Alan Pryce-Jones's Introduction to *Georgian Poets* (The Pocket Poets, 1959).

The Hutchinson Publishing Group for quotations from *The Georgian Literary Scene* (1934) and *Background With Chorus* (1956) by Frank Swinnerton.

Sir Geoffrey Keynes, on behalf of the Rupert Brooke Trustees, for quotations from a critical article by Rupert Brooke in the *New Statesman* (1914).

Sir Shane Leslie for quotations from his *End of a Chapter* (William Heinemann Ltd., 1916).

Mrs. Wyndham Lewis for quotations from articles written by Wyndham Lewis for *Blast*.

Mrs. Harold Monro for quotations from Harold Monro's book *Some Contemporary Poets* (Leonard Parsons, 1920) and from critical articles Mr. Monro wrote for *Poetry Review*, *Poetry and Drama*, and the *Egoist*.

Mr. A. V. Moore and Faber & Faber Ltd., for quotations from *The Letters of Ezra Pound*, 1907–1941, edited by D. D. Paige.

Mr. Thomas Moult for quotations from a critical article in the periodical *Voices* (1919).

Mrs. John Middleton Murry for quotations from John Middleton Murry's autobiography *Between Two Worlds* (Jonathan Cape Ltd., 1935) and from critical articles Mr. Murry wrote for *Rhythm*, the *Blue Review*, and the *Athenaeum*; Mrs. Murry and A. P. Watt and Son, on behalf of the Trustees of the Estate of the late John Middleton Murry, for quotations from 'The Present Condition of English Poetry', which originally appeared in the *Athenaeum* (1919) and was reprinted in *Aspects of Literature* (W. Collins' Sons Ltd., 1920).

Messrs. Laurence Pollinger Ltd., and the Estate of the late Mrs. Frieda Lawrence for quotations from a review entitled 'The Georgian Renaissance' by D. H. Lawrence, which appeared in *Rhythm* (1913).

Mr. James Reeves for quotations from his Introduction to *Georgian Poetry* (Penguin Books Ltd., 1962).

Mrs. Michael Roberts for quotations from *T. E. Hulme* (Faber and Faber Ltd., 1938) by Michael Roberts.

Charles Scribner's Sons Inc., for a portion of a letter from Henry James to Mrs. Humphry Ward reprinted from *The Letters of Henry James* (1920), edited by Percy Lubbock.

Mrs. Edward Shanks for quotations from 'New Poetry, 1914–1925', from *Second Essays on Literature* (W. Collins' Sons Ltd., 1927) by Edward Shanks.

The Author's Representatives and the publishers, Sidgwick and Jackson Ltd., for quotations from Henry James's preface to *Letters from America* (1916) by Rupert Brooke.

Sir Osbert Sitwell and the C. W. Daniel Company Ltd., for quotations from *Who Killed Cock Robin?* (1921) by Sir Osbert Sitwell; and Sir Osbert Sitwell for quotations from *Laughter in the Next Room* (Macmillan and Company Ltd., 1949).

Mr. Raglan Squire for quotations from *Water Music* (William Heinemann Ltd., 1939) and critical articles in *Land and Water*, the *London Mercury*, and the *New Statesman* by Sir John Squire.

Dame Rebecca West for quotations from an article she wrote in the *New Freewoman* (1913).

Finally, I acknowledge that to the members of my own family I owe a very special kind of debt. I have not always found it easy to be simultaneously a parent and a scholar, and my children, Susan, Robert, and Carolyn, were too frequently required to exercise an uncommon degree of forebearance and tolerance for a father often preoccupied with problems which they could not share. With incredible patience, a good deal of tact, and a fine ear for a slushy sentence, my wife endured the horrors of authorship with me page by page, chapter by chapter. Nor did her assistance stop there: she not only read proof for me but also searched out copyrights and undertook the long, onerous task of writing the hundreds of letters necessary to obtain permissions to reproduce large amounts of protected materials in this book. Thanks are scarcely adequate.

ROBERT H. ROSS

# I

# The Literary Scene: 1911

*This volume is issued in the belief that English poetry is now once again putting on a new strength and beauty. . . .*

*This collection, drawn entirely from the publications of the past two years, may if it is fortunate help the lovers of poetry to realize that we are at the beginning of another 'Georgian Period' which may rank in due time with the several great poetic ages of the past.*

EDWARD MARSH, Preface to *Georgian Poetry*, 1911–1912

By his brief preface to the first volume of *Georgian Poetry*, written in October 1912, Edward Marsh achieved several remarkable results. It is ironic that literary history should record the chief among them to be the launching of a new school of poetry, for if Marsh initiated a new poetic movement in 1912, he did so almost by accident. Intensely certain that English poetry stood on the threshold of a new age, convinced that vital new voices were not getting the hearing they deserved, Marsh set out to secure for several promising young poets an adequate and, if possible, enthusiastic audience. Though that was his aim (and in the beginning his only aim), he achieved more. He gave the new poetic age a name. 'Georgian', it would be called. But by 'Georgian' Marsh did not intend to describe, strictly speaking, a new school of poetry much less launch a coterie. His proud adjective was more connotative than denotative. It was intended to distinguish his own poetic era from the Edwardian decade which had preceded it and, in its context, to suggest the widely held assumption that by 1912 poetry was beginning to strike out on new and exciting paths. It was intended to suggest, moreover, that the new age dawning would be somehow more vital, more stimulating, more 'modern', than the Edwardian era. It was the consciousness of a poetic renaissance which, more than anything else, Marsh intended to connote by his preface to *Georgian Poetry* 1.*

Edward Marsh did not claim either to have begun the renaissance or to have been the first to call attention to it. Subsequent critics who claim for him either honour pay him an unsolicited and undeserved compliment. English poetry had begun to quicken with new vigour over a year before the publication of *Georgian Poetry* 1, a fact which contemporary critics and poets alike were quick to discern and announce to any who would listen. By the happy choice of a word, however, Edward Marsh succeeded in epitomizing the feeling for newness which he perceived all around him in 1912. He gave the chief tendencies of his new age a name; and by so doing he gave his age, for the first time, self-consciousness.

Unfortunately, in his preface Marsh also set himself up as something of a prophet. To suggest that the new 'Georgian Period' might rank 'in due time' alongside such notable eras of poetic achievement as the Renaissance or the Romantic Age seems pretentious or, in the light of subsequent events, ironic. But Marsh was expressing a conviction which, in his time and place, was being subscribed to on every side. By 1912 old men were dreaming dreams and young men were seeing visions. The Edwardian decade was passed; the time was spring, they thought; the air was fresh, the morning at seven. For a brief moment not even the faintest premonitory wind presaging the coming storm of the First World War had arisen to ruffle the euphoria of Edward Marsh's generation. In such an innocent dawn it did indeed seem bliss to be alive. Nostalgically, Frank Swinnerton recalled the temper of the age:

> We had been taught by Ibsen that the compact Liberal majority was always wrong, by Butler and Shaw that the old were always ridiculous, by Wells and Henry Ford that history was bunk, by Galsworthy that the poor and the suffering had moral right on their

* For the sake of brevity and clearness, throughout this study I shall refer to the volumes of *Georgian Poetry* in this fashion, i.e. by adding the appropriate Roman numeral suffix to the title. The full title of the first volume is *Georgian Poetry, 1911–1912*. The second volume of the anthology covered the years 1913 through 1915; the third, 1916–1917; the fourth, 1918–1919; and the fifth, 1920 through 1922. Volumes I, III, and IV were biennial, volumes II and V triennial. The entire anthology covered a period of twelve years.

side, and by Arnold Bennett that there was beauty in ugliness. It had not entered our heads that deliberately organized evil would be the chief menace of an anxious future. . . .

Life stretched before the poorest as almost unlimited opportunity. A shilling theatre gallery or Promenade Concert, a trip to the Continent on five or ten pounds without passport or visa, the best books at a shilling a time, free unlectured strolls in the London art galleries, and all of Henry James's 'pedestrian gaping' at command. Sun, moon, and stars, brother, not yet part of a finite universe, not yet to be bombarded by atoms. And never, anywhere, the tyranny of the party line. . . .

You must imagine us as completely unsuspicious of the likelihood of war. We were impressed by Norman Angell's book, *The Great Illusion*, which prophetically showed war as inevitable loss to the victor; and we felt with Robert Louis Stevenson that:

The world is so full of a number of things
I'm sure we should all be as happy as kings.[1]

Edward Marsh, like most of his contemporaries, may understandably be pardoned if he thought he saw the coming of a new age. The comments in his preface to *Georgian Poetry* I erred, if at all, on the conservative side. To say that English poetry seemed once again to be 'putting on a new strength and beauty' was to understate the facts as they appeared to most observers in 1912. Most of Marsh's contemporaries were willing to use far more dramatic language to describe what was happening at the turn of the decade. A 'revolt', many called it, or a 'revival'. And by 1912 such phrases as the 'new era', the 'new age', and the 'boom in poetry' had become clichés in the literary journals. What did these phrases describe? Did English poetry suddenly begin to flower in late 1911 or 1912 ? Was English poetry in fact 'putting on a new strength and beauty'?

In 1911 British poetry had almost no place to go but upwards. 'There can seldom have been so flat a period of writing as that through which the poets were stumbling' at the end of the Edwardian age, as Alan Pryce-Jones observed; 'what in Tennyson and Browning had once seemed eloquent or provoking, what, in the *Yellow Book* period, had taken on a brief but dashing Continental glow, now fell away into a set of standardized attitudes'.[2] However nostalgically one may look back on the uncomplicated Edwardian days of the bicycle and bloomers, feminism, Fabian Socialism, and ta-ra-ra-boom-de-ay, surely one cannot claim that the age produced, with one or two obvious exceptions, any but mediocre verse. In the history of English poetry the Edwardian age appears as a hiatus, a time comparable perhaps to the period between the death of Byron and the first mature verse of Tennyson. By 1900 the mighty voices of the Victorian poet-prophets had been silenced: Arnold had died in 1888, Browning in 1889, and Tennyson in 1892. Both Swinburne and Meredith lived long enough to publish their last volumes of poetry in the twentieth century before they died in 1909, but neither Meredith's *Reading of Life* (1901) nor Swinburne's *Channel Passage* (1904) opened any new vistas for English poetry. Kipling was turning in the new century to prose fiction as a more popular and acceptable medium than poetry. Francis Thompson, though he lived until 1907, published no more verse after *New Poems* (1897). Henley published yet one more volume of poetry, *Hawthorn and Lavender* (1901), and died in 1903.

By the turn of the century the Decadence had passed into history. Beardsley had died in 1898, and as if to mark the end of an era finally and dramatically, both Wilde and Dowson died in 1900. Lionel Johnson survived them only two years. With *Kathleen ni Houlihan* (1902), Yeats began a new phase of his career with the Abbey Theatre; and Arthur Symons, after publication of his *Poems* (1901), turned away from poetry to literary history and criticism. Among the considerable poets of the Rhymers' Club, only John Davidson continued producing important poetry well into the new Edwardian decade. His five *Testaments* appeared from 1901 to 1908. To put a fitting coda to the melancholy nineties, Davidson drowned himself in 1909 before an incipient cancer could kill him.

Robert Bridges was doing important work during the Edwardian decade, but the poetry-reading public paid scant attention to the scholarly recluse at Boar's Hill until he was appointed Laureate in 1913. There was of course one poet whose work alone could be said to redeem the time: Thomas Hardy. *The Dynasts* (1903-1906-1908) stands out like a brilliant beacon over the monotonous flatlands of mediocrity and worse. But though the *Dynasts* was 'almost unanimously considered to be the most majestic poetic creation of the age' by discerning contemporary critics, the Edwardian public could scarcely have been expected to take Hardy's poetry to its heart.[3] Its message was too austere, and the crabbed, unsonorous verse grated too harshly on ears long accustomed to

the music of Tennyson or the triolets and ballades of the Deca-
dents.

In 1911 the future of English poetry seemed to rest in the hands
of poets like Stephen Phillips and William Watson.* Conservative
to the core, with a 'disconcerting fragrance of Wordsworth and
Arnold about them',[4] these men carried over into the new century
some of the less happy aspects of the old: the tone and diction of
Tennyson in the 'Ode on the Death of the Duke of Wellington';
the ornateness and sentimentalism of Coventry Patmore; the Car-
lylean conception of the poet as *vates*, but shorn of Carlyle's power
and fervour; the high seriousness of Arnold, but without Arnold's
understanding of the grand style; and a pseudo-Wordsworthian
concept of nature, but lacking both Wordsworth's majesty and his
philosophic mind. In Watson and Phillips the flame of the great
tradition which had produced Keats and Tennyson, Shelley and
Browning, Wordsworth and Arnold, finally guttered and died. In
the twentieth century the verse of Watson and Phillips seemed
little more than decorated rhetoric, ironically redolent of the past
glories of English poetry. One must agree with the critic who, in
1912, summed up Watson's modest contribution to poetry in
terms which apply equally to both poets. 'In a turbulent and
unmannerly age,' he wrote, 'Mr. Watson provides a soothing
draught for well-bred, contemplative, unprogressive, peaceable
persons who have a regard for the decencies of language and a
respect for the limitations of form.'[5]

It is startling to recall, however, that the age of Watson and
Phillips in poetry was also the age of Wells, Bennett, Galsworthy,
and Shaw in the novel and drama. How can one account for the
apparent vitality and popularity of the Edwardian novel and
drama and the corresponding decline of poetry? One explanation
is simply that, historically speaking, the die had been cast during
the last two decades of the nineteenth century. By 1900 the trend
towards realism in prose fiction and on the stage had been firmly
established. Ibsenism had come in the late eighties and nineties
with the successful assault upon the moribund English stage by
Archer, Pinero, Jones, and Shaw. When Galsworthy turned to the

---

* Watson deserves to be held in memory primarily as the elegist of two great
Victorians in whose tradition he followed. His elegies to Tennyson ('Lachrymae
Musarum', *Poems* [1905], I, 3–8) and to Arnold ('In Laleham Churchyard', *Poems*,
II, 27–30) say noble things nobly. Stephen Phillips never recovered from the over-
praise accorded his first volume, *Poems* (1897).

drama of ideas towards the end of the Edwardian decade, he was already, so to speak, a second-generation Ibsenite. And so in the novel: the realism of Arnold Bennett, politely Edwardian though it was, had its antecedents not only in the militantly naturalistic French models of Zola and the brothers Goncourt but also in the work of Bennett's nineteenth-century British predecessors in naturalism, Moore and Gissing.[6] Both of these men had struck their most effective blows in the realistic cause by the mid-nineties. And so the dramatists and novelists had made some attempt to adjust their art to the world they lived in by means of social protest or the techniques of representational realism.

Not so the poets. In the closing years of the old century, poetry, having turned a nobly resolute back on 'the troughs of Zolaism', had succeeded in isolating itself from the world of men and ideas and had withdrawn into its aesthetic cloister, there to burn with the gem-like flame of its brief moments of ecstasy. As the nineties drew to a close, the *fin de siècle* spirit had so attenuated English verse that the once vital Romantic-Victorian poetic stream had dwindled to a mere trickle of ennui and languor, of inert pessimism or spiritless hedonism, and exquisitely chiselled small verses on the vanity and nothingness of human existence. Aestheticism was well nigh dead of its own anaemia, and the slender verses that were wrung from the phosphorescence of decay were as remote from the attitudes of the would-be poetry reader of the Edwardian age as Cynara was from a Floradora Girl. Despairing of a poetry which had despaired of itself, the literate Edwardian was almost forced to turn to stage and novel for literary sustenance.

A second and perhaps more compelling reason for the flowering of the novel and drama and the withering of poetry lies in the fact that the novel and drama gave the Edwardian reader precisely what he demanded. In the Five Towns novels or *Tono-Bungay*, in *Major Barbara* or *Strife*, he was getting an essentially literal, representational art which made him think but put no severe tax on his imagination; he was getting an art which, in its themes and subject matter, often reflected his own social, political, and ethical liberalism. Above all, he was getting a serious, straightforward art, uncluttered by any aesthetic cant and produced not by questionable dandies who ate green carnations for breakfast but by real 'gentlemen' who took their craft seriously and did not waste time talking about 'Art' but knew how to show a chap what they meant straight out. Though Shaw did his best to obscure the fact by his wit, his gleeful iconoclasm, and his innate sense of good theatre, his plays, pleasant or unpleasant, were obviously not designed solely to amuse. They were serious plays in which humour was the means to an end. And though the Edwardian theatre-goer often paid Shaw the compliment of violent antipathy, he came out of the theatre more thoughtful and sometimes even better informed than he was when he went in. Shaw's best plays were directly in the Ibsenite tradition of the drama of ideas, but Shaw had the wit to discern that to be serious one does not necessarily have to be solemn.

Realism as a fictional and dramatic mode was an almost perfect reflection of the timbre of the Edwardian mind. Like late Victorian England before it, Edwardian England, too, was in large part a literal-minded, middle-class society devoted to pursuit of the worldly. By the turn of the century the state of affairs foreseen by the great Victorian social prophets, Carlyle, Ruskin, and Arnold, had come to pass: in the rush to modernity the nation's cultural traditions had been allowed to atrophy. Culture had given way to anarchy. At the top of the social scale the Barbarians, moneyed or merely titled, had little cultural tradition and less taste. At the bottom were the Populace, the manual labourers, 'always in danger of sinking into the festering poverty of the slums'.[7] Between the extremes stretched the serried ranks of the Philistines ranging all the way from the new-rich to the small house-agent's clerk. Conservative in their literary tastes, suspicious of any poetry after *Idylls of the King*, the majority of the Edwardian middle class lived their lives innocent of the muses among the cricket clubs and garden societies of 'suburban villadom'.[8] To say they had no literary traditions would be incorrect. Worse, their norms belonged to a time long past, and their poetic tastes 'were overlaid by a thick veneer of conservatism that was at once academic and puritanical. Poetry was regarded as something inseparable from the worship of the classics, and especially the Victorian classics, Tennyson, Browning, and Arnold'.[9] Small wonder that the blank verse of Stephen Phillips or the would-be Wordsworthian odes of William Watson were received with as much favour as was accorded any poetry in Edwardian England, for poetic standards in the suburbs were unstrenuous, demands easily satisfied.

Poetry was expected to be 'the expression of a charming personality', or a metrical statement of poetical experience or of sentiments that were flattering to the reader. The minor poets of the day were certainly walking in Tennyson's shoes and wearing Byron's cloak: they turned up occasionally in Shakespeare's doublet and Swinburne's elastic-sided boots, but it was sometimes hinted that they had not quite the same insight and inspiration as their predecessors. There was nothing against the fancy-dress, but it did not of itself entitle them to a hearing. . . . In spite of the murmurs, however, most readers expected English poetry to follow the romantic tradition of Shelley and Byron, and as long as the vocabulary and rhythms of that tradition were retained they were not sharply critical of the actual content of the poems.[10]

No doubt the Edwardian age had glitter and brilliance aplenty. It was perhaps the last amusing age in history, an interlude before the grim decades of recurrent wars and crises. According to the evidence of one who experienced it, the Edwardian 'concert was a mad one while it lasted'.

In the midst Bernard Shaw sang solos in minor blasphemy, while Chesterton wrung fantastic fugues from a Gothic organ. . . . Belloc . . . became the herald of Philo-Gallicism. Masefield variegated the slum novel in heroic verse. Galsworthy wrote like a depressed Police Court Missionary, and Wells hoisted the Gonfalon of the Polytechnic. If readers remained sane, it was because they no more took literature seriously than the writers thereof. . . . They needed rest more than change, and it must be confessed that it was out of sheer vertigo that Kipling, Chesterton, and Belloc began to hymn such English simplicities as *Sussex*, *Chalk*, and *Beer*.[11]

But for all its glittering counterpoint, the Edwardian melody had gone stale; the dancers were wearying of the waltz. Beneath the surface brilliance the age was essentially barren; it was 'bright enough', as Edgar Jepson remarked, 'but rather jaded'.[12] It was for England a Hellenistic period, a time of endings, not beginnings.

One may hazard that even the vitality of the novel was perhaps more apparent than real. The Edwardian novel seemed to have come to a cul-de-sac from which there was no outlet except by a battering down of walls. On the one hand, representational realism had taken fiction perilously close to reportage. On the other, the rage for cleverness had resulted in a kind of Alexandrianism. In short, the Edwardian novel, for all its technical polish, lacked inspiration, or, in the phrase of a later critic, 'heart'.[13] Like the era out of which it came, Edwardian fiction was clever, amusing, and smart. Perhaps Henry James's familiar comment on Wells's *Marriage* may be allowed to stand as an adequate short summary of the major indictment against the Edwardian novel: 'Strange to me . . . the co-existence of so much talent with so little art, so much life, with (so to speak) so little living! But . . . I really think him more interesting by his faults than he will probably ever manage to be in any other way; he is a most vivid and violent object lesson.'[14] 'So much talent with so little art': the dead end reached by the novel, in spite of its apparent vitality, seems no less real than that reached by poetry in Edwardian England. In the case of the novel a revolt was brewing at the end of the first decade; new and exciting vistas both in technique and subject matter were shortly to be opened before the startled eyes of readers of Bennett and Wells. New writers, obscure, most of them unpublished in 1910, were shortly to revolutionize twentieth-century British fiction: James Joyce, D. H. Lawrence, Virginia Woolf, Katherine Mansfield. And two older men were to be recognized as prophets of the new schools, revolutionaries before their time: Joseph Conrad and Henry James.

In the closing years of the first decade, then, the time was ripe for a general literary revolt, for fresh starts, larger perspectives, new aims. And a revolt was brewing in poetry as well as in other genres. Beginning in late 1911, poetry set out to catch up to the novel and drama and to regain some of the audience it had lost during the nineties and the Edwardian decade. The result was a poetic renaissance which sent new lifeblood coursing through the enfeebled body of British verse.

The prevailing political liberalism of the Edwardian age cannot be discounted as one of the possible causes of the poetic renaissance of the Georgian. The middle class, conservative in literary tastes, succeeded in dissociating its artistic from its political convictions and became the mainstay of the Liberal Party from 1904 to 1914. The social reforms of the Campbell-Bannerman and the Asquith governments were made possible, in fact, only by the strong support of the middle class. Most of the young poets came down from the Universities around the turn of the decade enthusiastically pledged to Fabian Socialism—one thinks of Brooke, Flecker, and Monro, for instance. Many others not so fortunate in their formal education—Gibson, Hodgson, Davies—were equally liberal in their political views. Most of them were idealistic, dedicated Socialists; a few, like Monro, even tried to put some of their Fabian tenets into practice. But one recognizes, too, that the profession of Socialism had become almost *de rigueur* in Edwardian intellectual and artistic circles by 1910. As the *Times Literary Supplement* pointed out, during the first decade 'it was the happy fashion of clever undergraduates, "deadly serious" but "disreputably young", to profess an epigrammatic ardour for the tenets of Socialism; and where twenty years previously it would have been proper to play the aesthete, treasure a chaste copy of "Les Fleurs du Mal" as your bedside literature . . . public taste [now] decreed that you should attend Fabian summer schools with vegetarians and suffragettes, and sit at the feet of Nietzsche, Ibsen, and Mr. Bernard Shaw'.[15]

If political liberalism and poetic revival were not linked in a causal relationship—and evidence for such a claim is far from convincing—perhaps they had a fraternal relationship. They were children of the same parent, for a spiritual revival fathered both. 'The resurgence of liberal England', as one historian claims, 'was the political aspect of a spiritual awakening which [also] found expression in a remarkable literary revival.'[16] An anti-authoritarian spirit pervaded the age. The first decade had scarcely been free from political and social ferment. There had been serious strikes, suffragette agitation, and a recurrence of that perennial English problem, Irish tension. There was a general 'sense of rebellion in the air, against convention, against accepted codes of morals, and, with Bernard Shaw in the van, against almost every accepted idea'.[17]

For whatever reasons, by late 1911 the poetic pot had clearly begun to simmer. Two events, occurring almost simultaneously, put it beyond doubt that a poetic renaissance was beginning to take shape. The public's interest in poetry, long dormant, was beginning to reawaken. More important, the nature of poetry itself was undergoing drastic changes; a new, twentieth-century poetic was being created. The resurgence of the interest of the reading public in poetry can be termed the 'Georgian revival'. The attempts to change the nature of poetry itself can be called the 'Georgian revolt'.* In this semantically restricted sense of the

* The term 'Georgian', as it is used in this context and as I shall use it henceforth to the end of this chapter, has no implications of a poetic coterie or school. It is used

terms, both a revolt and a revival did in fact occur during the second decade of the twentieth century. The Georgian revolt, however, was predominantly a pre-war event whereas the revival assumed its most significant proportions only after the First World War had begun.

To be sure, the poetic revival had been well started before the war came. With the benefit of hindsight, one can even date its beginning with some accuracy: it started in late 1911 with the publication of Masefield's *Everlasting Mercy*, the seminal work of the new realistic school, which achieved almost instant, widespread popularity because it was the first book of verse since *Barrack Room Ballads* to succeed in titillating the British public by poetry which managed to be at once both ribald and respectable. Throughout 1912 and 1913 critics were hailing the revival, the public's curiosity had been aroused, 'people began to argue, and even to quarrel, about poetry as though it were really of some importance, and—what is always a significant sign—the charlatan began to lift an alert and interested head'.[18] But the extent of the revival during the pre-war years was frequently overstated by those who were too eager to take the wish for the fact. In spite of the perfervid claims of widespread interest in poetry in 1912 and 1913, the most dramatic spurt in the public's interest began only in early 1916 and lasted through 1919.* It occurred, in fact, largely as a result of the emotional impact upon the British public of the death of Rupert Brooke in the Aegean. The circumstances of his death, as of his life, made it almost inevitable that Brooke should have been presented 'to the popular imagination as a romantic figure', and so 'for many persons, in some queer way, his life and death seemed to rehabilitate poetry, to give it once again some

---

in its widest and most literal sense, i.e. as a historical tag to describe that poetry written after the accession of George V. Cf. 'Edwardian'. In this use of the term, obviously Ezra Pound and Richard Aldington are to be considered as much 'Georgian' poets as Rupert Brooke or W. H. Davies. As will be made clear below (Ch. 6), the term is susceptible of a more restricted definition, namely to describe those poets who were contributors to any of the five volumes of Edward Marsh's anthology.

* This assertion is based upon statistics gathered from the *Publishers' Circular*, the trade journal of British publishing houses, for the years 1910 to 1922. Though the figures are too lengthy and ponderous to reproduce here, they show, both in the total numbers of volumes of poetry published in England during the second decade and in the proportion of volumes of poetry to novels and plays, that the public's interest in poetry, as demonstrated by the numbers of volumes it was willing to buy, was unusually high from 1916 to 1919.

sort of standing as a serious, not a trivial, human activity'.*

But if the poetic revival was largely inspired by wartime conditions, there is evidence to show that the Georgian revolt was in fact a pre-war event. In the brief years from 1911 to about 1915, poetic fashions were undergoing rapid and drastic change. A new poetic suited to a new age was being forged. In its beginnings the Georgian revolt appeared to be more a spiritual than a poetic revolt. It began around 1911, that is, with a perceptible change in the spiritual climate. Though its sources were vague, the feeling was unmistakable. It was one of happy expectancy, as Sir Osbert Sitwell observed, the consciousness of a new release of energy within the arts, an intuition widespread among artists of all kinds that they were on the verge of something new and momentous.† There was 'a fresh breeze in the air . . . a general feeling of confidence', Middleton Murry wrote; and though, as he claimed, he took no personal part in the 'general exaltation', he was 'conscious of its existence . . . affected by the feeling of confidence, of faith in the future, which was general among [his] coevals at that time'.[19] Harold Monro experienced the same kind of exhilaration. By 1911, he declared, 'the numbing effect of the Victorian period [seemed] finally to have relaxed its pressure on the brain of the rising generation', and hopeful young poets foresaw the coming of a new age, one which would be related neither to the age of Tennyson nor to the *fin de siècle*.[20]

Though poet after poet among the rising generation testified to feeling the 'fresh breeze in the air', perhaps D. H. Lawrence gave most eloquent tongue to the pre-war spirit. Vigour was his cry, a spiritual vigour which, Lawrence claimed, had created a rich, and new, and energetic modern poetry, a poetry whose most characteristic tone was 'a note of exultation after fear, the exultation in the vast freedom, the illimitable wealth that we have suddenly got'. Modern poets, he exclaimed, are casting off the ennui of the *fin de siècle*:

We are waking up after a night of oppressive dreams. The nihilists, the intellectual, hopeless people—Ibsen, Flaubert, Thomas Hardy—

* Edward Shanks, *Second Essays on Literature*, p. 109. On the further effects of Rupert Brooke's death, see below, Chapter 7.
† Sir Osbert Sitwell, *Great Morning* (London, 1948), pp. 235–6. Chapter 3 of Sir Osbert's book (which is vol. III of his autobiography, *Left Hand, Right Hand*) catches the pre-war spirit of exhilaration and renascence as perceptively and precisely as any other single secondary source.

represent the dream we are waking from. It was a dream of demolition. Nothing was, but was nothing. Everything was taken from us. And now our lungs are full of new air, and our eyes see it is morning, but we have not forgotten the terror of the night. We dreamed we were falling through space into nothingness, and the anguish of it leaves us rather eager.

But we are awake again, our lungs are full of new air, our eyes of morning. . . .

This great liberation gives us an overwhelming sense of joy, joie d'être, joie de vivre.[21]

Nor did the existence of new vigour escape the more perceptive among the older literary generation. Speaking specifically of Rupert Brooke and of the group of poets who surrounded him, Henry James clearly recognized the spirit which animated the young poets in the years before the war. 'They were all young together,' he wrote:

They were all fresh and free and acute and aware and in 'the world', when not out of it; all together at the high speculative, the high talkative pitch of the initiational stage of these latest years, the informed and animated, the so consciously non-benighted, geniality of which was to make [Brooke] the clearest and most projected poetic case . . . that it was possible to conceive. He had found at once . . . an England breaking out into numberless assertions of a new awareness, into liberties of high and clean, even when most skeptical and discursive, young intercourse; a carnival of half anxious and half elated criticism.[22]

The awareness of spiritual reawakening naturally fostered a vigorous self-consciousness among the young pre-war poets. For reasons never quite explicit they felt that the new age dawning would be different from any which had preceded it. It was to be 'modern'. 'What with modern science, modern philosophy, modern religion, modern politics, and modern business,' wrote Lascelles Abercrombie in 1912, 'the present is a time fermenting with tremendous change; the most tremendous of all changes, a change in the idealistic interpretation of the universe.' Abercrombie continued:

To any man with brain and spirit active and alert in him, the present is a time wherein the world, and the destiny of man in the world, are ideas different from anything that has ever been before. If there is any resemblance at all . . . the present resembles more the time of the pre-Socratic Greek philosophers . . . than any other time. These disturbing periods, indeed, seem to recur regularly, in vast pulsations, through man's history. They are exciting but fearfully exacting times for the poet.[23]

As one looks back upon it from a vantage point of over fifty years, the spiritual reawakening of the second decade seems to have arisen from almost inexplicable sources and to have occurred with a suddenness which surprised even those who experienced it. Whether it did actually occur so quickly or whether it was merely the florescence of a state of mind which had been building slowly through the Edwardian decade, is a moot question. What did arise with unmistakable rapidity at a point in late 1911 and early 1912 was, if not the reawakening itself, certainly the widespread conviction of one among artists of all persuasions. Among poets particularly there suddenly occurred, as J. C. Squire testified, a 'new exuberance and enthusiasm, in individuals and the generality. And you got a new generation of young men just before the war: an imperceptible alteration had taken place . . . and automatically preciousness, self-consciousness, poetic sectarianism, had largely gone, and you had a great crowd of youths all willing to expose the best and truest in them and spontaneously aware that they must do it in musical language'.[24]

Ultimately, however, the event that must be described is a poetic, not a spiritual, revolt. The Georgian poetic revolt must finally be explained in its own terms. What, then, were its lineaments? In the first place, seen in its broadest historical terms, the pre-war revolt of the younger generation against poetic standards which had governed since the Romantic Revival was part of a larger and more widespread intellectual revolt against Humanism. One of the most significant events in the intellectual history of the twentieth century and one which was to gather force and sweep across large areas of Western thought and art in the post-war years, the reaction against Humanism among modern artists and thinkers was essentially a revolt against 'that anthropocentric view of life which had supplanted the theocentric conception of the Middle Ages. The leaders of the revolt maintained that Western Europe had taken the wrong turn at the Renaissance, which made man, not God, the measure of all things, and had gone finally and fatally astray at the time of the French Revolution, when Rousseau cast adrift the last anchor that held men to the ancient faith, the doctrine, namely, of Original Sin'.[25]

Among the young pre-war rebels it was of course T. E. Hulme who put the case against Humanism most forcefully. 'More than anyone else in this period,' a recent biographer has written, Hulme 'was responsible for clearing away the debris left over from Victorian romanticism and for pioneering the new poetic ground upon which his successors have built.'[26] His assault upon Humanism and its literary offspring, Romanticism,* was aggressive, dogmatic, and direct: Humanism alone was responsible for 'the state of slush in which we have the misfortune to live', Hulme wrote; and contemporary Romantic poetry was insipid, 'like pouring a pot of treacle over the dinner table'.[27] For the new poets who followed Hulme's footsteps the Wordsworthian doctrine of the poetic had finally to be consigned to the dustbin. Poetry was not the 'spontaneous overflow of powerful feelings'; it did not originate from 'emotion recollected in tranquillity'. Poets could no longer contemplate the Grecian urn or strain after a fleeting vision of the white radiance of eternity. Indeed, in the modern world the quaint Romantic notion of straining after infinity was only—in Harold Monro's phrase—'harmlessly ridiculous'.[28] No longer required to attempt a feat which was not only positively harmful to the poet but also in the nature of things utterly unattainable, modern poetry, Hulme claimed, must limit its aspirations. It must deal with the thing itself; it must become hard, dry, sophisticated.[29]

Secondly, the pre-war poetic revolt was part of a general revolt in all the arts, especially the pictorial and the plastic, against the dead hand of 'Academism', a pejorative neologism used generically by young artists to describe the 'enemy' (i.e. almost any group which insisted upon even a modicum of formalism, convention, or tradition in art). The early Georgian era was one of those recurring periods in the history of English literature when the pictorial and the literary arts drew close together. For a brief while in the pre-war years, as Ford Madox Hueffer observed, 'the Fine, the Plastic and the Literary arts touched hands with an unusual intimacy and what is called one-ness of purpose.... The Sculptors, Painters and Poets and Prosateurs of that Movement happened to synchronize

* One might perhaps as well draw no distinction at all between Humanism and Romanticism. Cf. Hoxie Neale Fairchild, *Religious Trends in English Poetry*, IV (New York, 1957), 4, wherein Professor Fairchild argues that in the sense in which I am using the terms here they are virtually interchangeable because both 'describe man's desire for limitless expression or self-sufficiency'. I have preferred, however, to keep my essentially literary tag ('Romanticism') separate from an essentially metaphysical one ('Humanism').

in a discovery'.[30] Like the age of the pre-Raphaelites sixty years earlier, the pre-war Georgian era was a time in which new strains —as well as curious, ephemeral mutations—were created out of a healthy cross-pollination among the arts. Painting was perhaps the first to become infected with the rage for newness. At the turn of the second decade, both on the Continent and in England painters had been seized by 'a kind of fever, an almost exasperated craving for the violent, the elemental, the barbaric, for energy and self-assertion at all costs. Virility and vitality became the cant words of praise in criticism'.[31] This urge for self-assertion most clearly manifested itself among painters and sculptors in such movements as Post-Impressionism, Futurism, Cubism, or Vorticism. The one common denominator of all these *avant-garde* movements was a thorough-going revolt against representational art. 'We are educated in the appetite for fact. Our vision is thickened and confused,' cried Laurence Binyon. 'How long have we been sitting down before Nature and letting her impose herself upon us! Our imaginations have been schooled into passivity. Unconsciously enslaved, we were growing benumbed. And now we want to stretch our limbs, to move, to dance, to feel our life-blood running again. . . . Our art is dissatisfied with itself.' [32]

Modern art must not only be non-representational; it must also embody and express the artist's unique personality. The *fin de siècle* attitude that art was a delicate conjuration of Beauty was as abhorrent as the Victorian notion that art should be moral or didactic. The modern artist was required to fly in the face of both conventions; he had to affirm 'not only that the old beauty is as dead as the old ugliness, but that beauty and ugliness have nothing whatever to do with the creation of a work of art. The artist simply discusses life in whatever media he may work . . . apropos of himself'.[33] Far from suppressing their personalities in their work, then, modern artists must set out to advertise—even to dramatize —themselves.

> The Cubists, Vorticists, Imagists, Vers Librists . . . said simply: 'All this attempt to hypnotise the Public is a mere waste of time. An Artist attracts; gets a public or royalties for sales because he is a clever fellow . . .' Let him begin by saying: 'I am a clever fellow. . . .' And let him go on saying: 'What a clever fellow I am!' Conspuez the Subject! A bas all conventions of tale-telling! We the Vorticists, Cubists, Imagistes, Symbolists, Vers Libristes, Tapagistes, are fine,

young Cocks of the Walk! We and we only are the Playboys of the Western World. We and we only shall be heard.[34]

Seeing painters and sculptors like Epstein and Wyndham Lewis, Wadsworth, Fry and Gaudier-Brzeska noisily and successfully kicking their way out of the shackles of Academism, the poets, quite naturally, began to fashion a modern poetic to attempt to reproduce in their own medium the new effects which the artists were striving for. By late 1912 an agitation for newer, more striking forms was sweeping over British poetry. Such a movement naturally attracted the charlatans and invited extremes.

One experimentalist published a volume called Cubist Poems[35] and many more indulged in individual flourishes of the inane, crying on Picasso, Bomberg, and Mr. Roger Fry, by way of making it perfectly clear what they were about. But the matter was by no means as simple as it appeared. Too many of these poets saw no more in the new pictures than a startling difference from the old; and they believed that by writing verses absurdly at variance with what had hitherto been accepted as poetry, they would achieve a similar result. It did not matter whether they followed serious artists or charlatans; their verses betrayed too plainly the fact that they aimed at nothing but oddness.*

So strident and insistent had the young poets and *avant-garde* critics become by the end of 1912, in fact, that the *Times Literary Supplement* was moved to utter a few words of caution *ex cathedra*. Having seen 'Futurism, Post-Impressionism, Cubism, rousing rage, or laughter, or bewilderment', the journal admitted, poets naturally wanted to kick over the traces too. But was the contemporary situation in poetry entirely analogous to that in painting? 'Is it quite certain that nothing more can be got out of the means already at hand? What must strike any reader of modern poetry is this, that not the best use is being made of the myriad forms which the diverse poetical practice of ages has put at our disposal. . . . It is originality of character and thought, not of form, which modern poetry lacks.'†

Thirdly, the Georgian revolt, as the young poets themselves looked upon it, was a revolt against Victorianism. More precisely,

* *NS*, IX (1917), 594. Behind the anonymity of the article from which this passage was taken one can readily detect the tone of J. C. Squire.
† *TLS*, 12th Dec. 1912, p. 568. The volume which had invited the *TLS's* caveat was Ezra Pound's *Ripostes*.

they saw it as a repudiation of the unbroken chain of poetic history which had extended from the Romantic Revival through the Victorian age to the inevitable cul-de-sac of the nineties. The pre-war poetic rebel arraigned his Victorian predecessors on several counts. With the possible exception of Browning, he claimed, Victorian poetry was 'unthoughtful'. It was rather emotional. In Victorian poetry, 'wit, play of intellect, stress of cerebral muscle had no place: they could only hinder the reader's being "moved" —the correct poetical response'.[36] Moreover, he concluded that the Romantic-Victorian tradition had simply run its natural course. The great Victorian poets, he argued, had 'achieved a finish on which it would be ridiculous to attempt to refine. Had not the nineties tried with no satisfying result?'[37] Finally, even if it were possible to gild the lily, the Victorians had strayed too far from life as the proper subject matter for poetry. In the new twentieth century, poetry must either perish as anachronism or return whole-heartedly to strength and truth to life as it is lived. Poetry of the study must go. 'There was but one lesson the modern artist must learn and ponder' in 1912, declared John Gould Fletcher: 'the lesson already proclaimed by the Irish dramatist Synge, who had said that poetry, to be human again, must first learn to be brutal. In revolt against the elaborations of end-of-the-century aestheticism, against the romantic movement faltering in sentimental prettiness, against the genteel tradition in decay, artists everywhere were turning back to the primitively ugly, knowing that in primitiveness alone lay strength.'[38]

Against the time-honoured Romantic-Victorian tradition which had sung its last long roundelay in those too precious and languorous lyrics of the *fin de siècle* the young Georgian poets hoisted the banner of poetic sincerity. 'Sincerity is the grail of the modern quest,' one contemporary critic wrote; 'to be a poet is to be frank even unto brutality.'[39] The young pre-war poets were therefore characteristically aggressive. 'They were furiously impatient of the tradition, which had stuck [them] with the Royal Academy and the Blah-Blah school of British Verse.' It was not so much a case of 'the younger generation knocking at the academic door as the younger generation trying to batter the door down to make hay of everything inside'.[40] The results were numerous—not the least of them being the return to wit and humour to poetry—but perhaps the most important was a universal eagerness among the young poets to experiment with new forms and new subject matter.

The modern poet's task, then, as he conceived it at the turn of the decade, was before all else to achieve truth to life. 'Objectivity and again objectivity,' Ezra Pound exclaimed to Harriet Monroe; and 'no hind-side-beforeness, no straddled adjectives . . . no Tennysonianness of speech; nothing—nothing, that you couldn't, in some circumstance, in the stress of some emotion, actually say.'[41] A. C. Bradley wrote of Wordsworth: 'what he showed was what he saw'. And, as Alan Pryce-Jones points out, 'some such purpose' also moved the young pre-war poet.[42] He deliberately set out to be a realist, to reproduce faithfully and fearlessly what he saw. He tried 'to see nature and men as they are and honour them with all the resources of his understanding', not simply—as he conceived his predecessors of the nineties had done—'to feel vague personal emotions and spend all his intellectual powers in embellishing them'.[43]

In an age when truth became more sought-after than beauty, the too assiduous cultivation of the new had its obvious dangers. Sometimes the young poets confused mere novelty with genuine newness; sometimes their revolt against odious Victorian sentimentalism or the *fin de siècle* cult of Beauty led them to indulge in cleverness, or cynicism, or brutality merely for its own sake; and sometimes in their distaste for poetry which dealt with concepts and absolutes they never quite became poets at all, but remained mere recorders of private experiences personal to themselves. But to point out the weaknesses in imperfect human nature does not reflect upon the high objectives which the young pre-war poets set for themselves; it merely elucidates the perils of attempting to be poetically sincere and spiritually honest.[44]

These three general assertions can be advanced, then, partially to describe the pre-war poetic revolt: it was a part of the larger twentieth-century revolt against Humanism; in the beginning it was the poetic phase of a widespread revolt against Academism among all the arts; and, specifically in the field of poetry, it was a reaction against the dead hand of the Romantic-Victorian tradition. Almost all the young Georgian rebels of whatever coterie— realists or Vorticists, Futurists or Imagists, Ezra Pound or Rupert Brooke, Richard Aldington or Lascelles Abercrombie—can be said in varying degrees to exemplify these tendencies. Beyond such common ground, however, agreement became the exception rather than the rule, for the movement towards modernism took two divergent paths. It split into two warring factions which, to borrow political nomenclature, one may designate as the parties of the Left and of the Centre.*

By late 1911 the poetic Right Wing had become negligible. It comprised a group of traditionalists, like Watson and Phillips, who denied 'that there [was] anything seriously wrong with the tradition of English verse that [had] its roots in Ovid, Vergil, Sophocles, and Homer, and whose poetic charter was drawn up by Aristotle'. In their poetry emotion was only to be recollected in tranquillity; the True, the Beautiful, and the Good were inevitably and ultimately triumphant in a world of sin and error.† The Rightist was more or less violently opposed to new forms and subjects in art most frequently, one suspects, simply because they were new. Failing to adjust to his environment, he tended to become increasingly rare, until at the end of the second decade his species survived only in the sanctuaries afforded by the pages of a few of the conservative literary journals.

The really violent battles of the era raged between the poets of the Centre and the Left. The first battleground was subject matter. Both parties held in common abhorrence that outmoded creature whom they called, with some asperity, the 'cosmic poet'—that is, 'roughly, the fellow who had read something somewhere that someone had written about Darwin or about the Nebular Hypothesis, and had developed a diseased habit of writing in an inflated manner about these cosmic matters usually without having taken the trouble, or perhaps without possessing the intelligence, to understand them'. But in order to escape the onus attached to cosmic verse the poets devised two different methods: 'some decided to tolerate the old subjects, but to discover a new method of presenting, or representing them; others, not so satisfied, probed nervously the psychological recesses of the New World

* Though the terms are borrowed from political diction, they are intended here to convey only artistic, not political implications. They are intended only as useful terms more or less descriptive of the positions taken by various poets and poetic coteries vis-à-vis the literary revolution of the second decade. The poets' views on political revolution are irrelevant.

† Robert Graves, *Contemporary Techniques of Poetry: Hogarth Essays, No. 8* (London, 1925), p. 7. The terms Right, Left and Centre are by no means my own. They were commonly used by critics of the second decade and were developed to their fullest implications by Graves in the source cited here.

and dragged out all the strangest rags of fancy they could find, exhibiting them solely on account of their whimsical colours and shapes'.[45] Those who tolerated the old matter but sought the new manner were, roughly, the Centrists; those who sought novelty in both matter and manner were the Leftists. The two parties had a falling out, too, over technical matters: poetic diction, rhyme, metre, texture, and structure. The Centrist favoured poetry 'free from heroics and rant on the one hand, and from roughness and violence of expression on the other'.[46] He saw some value, aesthetic or personal, in retaining certain of the traditional poetic techniques, but was quite capable upon occasion of using new forms without experiencing either bad conscience or aesthetic nausea. He was attacked from both sides, by the Left for cowardice, by the Right for apostasy.

For all his interest in poetic diction, the Centrist kept his eye more consistently on the matter than on the manner of poetry. One frequently finds him advocating the use of contemporary speech in modern verse. Occasionally he approached the Leftist position so far as to argue, like Lascelles Abercrombie, that if poetry is cast in the contemporary idiom, then modern verse can dispense with nobility, for realistic diction is more important than fundamental brainwork.[47] But the Centrist's first concern was for truth to life, the quality which, for want of a more precise term, one is compelled to call realism. It is the quality most apparent in the verse of Masefield or Gibson, Abercrombie, Bottomley or Brooke, and it resulted in a vigorous poetry 'which avoided as its first enemy the insipid'.[48] The Centrist tried to walk the razor's edge between the poets of the old guard, who refused to recognize the fact of revolt, and those of the *avant-garde*, who refused to recognize anything except revolt. His was a difficult position— and, in the end, one doomed to failure—for he wished to 'transfuse into poetry new blood from the romance of actuality and nature, but, at the same time . . . try never to forget its high and noble traditions inherited from the great ones of the past'.[49]

It was from the curious coalition of parties which formed the artistic Left that most of the sound and fury, the bombs and the pyrotechnics, were erupting in the pre-war years. The factitious, insolent, brash and noisy coteries which formed the Left Wing defy easy classification; indeed, their liveliness and, paradoxically, their strength lay precisely in their splendid devil-may-care diver-

47

sity. Generically they were 'a number of small groups loosely bound by a dislike of the Right and a scorn of the Centre; agreeing amiably to rebel, but not agreeing as to the ultimate direction of their rebelliousness'.[50] That it was a spirited rebellion, full of scurrilous shouts, insolent laughter, and derisive sneers, was only to be expected, for to its banners the Left attracted such *enfants terribles* of the Georgian age as Ezra Pound, Wyndham Lewis, Filippo Marinetti, and countless other less strident but no less dedicated soldiers of literary fortune.

If realism was the informing spirit of the Centre, precision was the watchword of the Left.* The Leftist poet tended to concentrate more on purifying poetic technique than upon truth to life or upon expanding the subject matter of modern verse. He was more or less single-mindedly devoted to good craftsmanship, and he found the poets of the Centre damnworthy not, usually, because they were realists, but because of what he considered their sloppy craftsmanship. 'I believe in technique as the test of a man's sincerity,' wrote Ezra Pound; 'in law when it is ascertainable; in the trampling down of every convention that impedes or obscures the determination of the law, or the *precise* rendering of the impulse.' Among the conventions to be 'trampled' were traditional verse forms. A poem has a ' "fluid" as well as a "solid" content', Pound argued; 'some poems may have form as a tree has form, some as water poured into a vase'. And although the traditional 'symmetrical' forms can still be said to have 'certain uses . . . a vast number of subjects cannot be *precisely*, and therefore not properly rendered in symmetrical forms'.[51] The Leftist shared with the Centrist an abhorrence of archaic poetic diction. Ezra Pound, again, complained to Harriet Monroe about some of the poets she had published in *Poetry*: 'Good God! Isn't there one of them that can write natural speech without copying clichés out of every Eighteenth Century poet still in the public libraries? God knows I wallowed in archaisms in my vealish years, but these imbeciles don't even take the trouble to get an archaism, which might be silly and picturesque, but they get phrases out of just the stupidest and worst-dressed periods.'[52] Perhaps the diverse factions of the Left found their most extensive area of agreement, however, in

* The word 'precision' is Ezra Pound's. In a report to Harriet Monroe on the London poetic scene *c*. late 1912, he applied the term specifically only to the Imagists, but it is equally applicable to most of the pre-war Leftist factions (though to the Futurists perhaps least of all). See *Poetry*, I, no. 4 (Jan. 1913), 126.

Courtesy of the photographer, Alvin Langdon Coburn
Ezra Pound, October 1913

A caricature of Ezra Pound from
*The New Age*, 9 October 1913

## PREFATORY NOTE

THIS volume is issued in the belief that English poetry is now once again putting on a new strength and beauty.

Few readers have the leisure or the zeal to investigate each volume as it appears; and the process of recognition is often slow. This collection, drawn entirely from the publications of the past two years, may if it is fortunate help the lovers of poetry to realize that we are at the beginning of another "Georgian period" which may take rank in due time with the several great poetic ages of the past.

It has no pretension to cover the field. Every reader will notice the absence of poets whose work would be a necessary ornament of any anthology not limited by a definite aim. Two years ago some of the writers represented had published nothing; and only a very few of the others were known except to the eagerest "watchers of the skies." Those few are here because within the chosen period their work seemed to have gained some accession of power.

My grateful thanks are due to the writers who have lent me their poems, and to the publishers (Messrs Elkin Mathews, Sidgwick and Jackson, Methuen, Fifield, Constable, Nutt, Dent, Duckworth, Longmans, and Maunsel, and the Editors of *Basileon*, *Rhythm*, and the *English Review*) under whose imprint they have appeared.

E. M.

Oct. 1912.

Edward Marsh's declaration of the new Georgian age in the Preface to *Georgian Poetry, 1911–12* their common advocacy of free verse. In the Imagist movement particularly one sees the beginning of the battle for *vers libre* in the pre-war years. And although more or less violent arguments about the nature and the uses of free verse continued throughout the war years and even into the twenties, as early as 1915 the verslibrists were in full cry on the heels of the retreating traditionalists, and by 1920 they were in almost complete possession of the field.

The pre-war Leftist poet was frequently doctrinaire, sometimes supercilious, and more often than not derisive. But he was no reluctant warrior. 'I've got a right to be severe,' wrote Pound. 'For one man I strike there are ten to strike back at me. I stand exposed. It hits me in my dinner invitations, in my weekends, in reviews of my own work. Nevertheless it's a good fight.'[53] The Leftist was imbued with a sense of mission, even of destiny. He fought with the 'tendencies' on his side and he knew it. And so in 1912, on the brink, as he thought, of a new age, he could confidently predict, along with Pound, that in the next decade modern poetry 'will move against poppycock, it will be harder and saner, it will be . . . "nearer the bone". It will be as much like granite as it can be, its force will lie in its truth, its interpretive power. . . . I mean it will not try to seem forcible by rhetorical din, and luxurious riot. We will have fewer painted adjectives impeding the shock and stroke of it. At least for myself, I want it so, austere, direct, free from emotional slither'.[54]

# 2

# Sound and Fury

## REALISM

The realistic poets of the pre-war poetic renaissance established no recognizable school or coterie as did the Imagists, for example, of the Vorticists. Rather than a movement realism was only a tendency shared by poets of divergent persuasions. It deserves brief consideration nevertheless because an essentially realistic poem can be said to have begun the poetic renaissance in 1911 and because realism largely dominated the first two volumes of *Georgian Poetry*.

The beginnings of Georgian poetic realism can be seen in the early works of two young men, Wilfrid Gibson and Rupert Brooke. The very titles of Gibson's first volumes are perhaps enough to suggest the derivative Tennysonian vein in which the poet started his career: *Urlyn the Harper* (1902), *The Queen's Vigil* (1902), *The Golden Helm* (1903), and *The Nets of Love* (1905). But suddenly and inexplicably, around 1907, Gibson did an about-face and turned to the lowly, the poor, and the oppressed for his poetic themes. The result was *The Stonefolds* (1907) and *Daily Bread* (1910).* Because of the widespread public apathy toward poetry, and because some of the poems in these two volumes were realistic only in the sense that their subjects were drawn from the works

---

* In an interview in the spring of 1955 Mr. Gibson assured me that though he recognized it, he had no explanation for the sudden shift in his verse around 1907. That he lived on a very small private income in a garret in Glasgow—and therefore was in daily contact with the kinds of people who were to become the subjects of his verse—may have had some effect upon the shift. But Mr. Gibson could recall no conscious 'influence' at work upon him at this time.

and days of the labouring classes, Gibson's poetry in the new vein
can scarcely be said to have begun a trend in English poetry toward realism. Nor can that dubious distinction be claimed for
Rupert Brooke. His first volume, *Poems* (1911), contained several
poems which were a good deal more frank in their realistic details
than any of Gibson's mild-mannered sallies into social verse. They
therefore achieved what one suspects was their major reason for
being: they attracted public attention. With a fine insolence toward his conservative readers' sense of formal proprieties in verse,
Brooke used the sonnet to describe in realistic detail the querulous
old age of Menelaus and Helen: 'Menelaus bold', who 'waxed
garrulous, and sacked a hundred Troys/'Twixt noon and supper';
and Helen, whose 'golden voice/Got shrill as he grew deafer',
who 'weeps, gummy-eyed and impotent', and whose 'dry shanks
twist at Paris's mumbled name'. Or in 'Channel Passage' he used
a sestet of the same form to describe a young man aboard a channel steamer who suffers simultaneously from seasickness and love-
sickness:

> Do I forget you? Retchings twist and tie me,
> Old meat, good meals, brown gobbets, up I throw.
> Do I remember? Acrid return and slimy,
> The sobs and slobber of a last year's woe.
> And still the sick ship rolls. 'Tis hard, I tell ye,
> To choose 'twixt love and nausea, heart and belly.

'Sickly animalism', cried one reviewer; mere 'swagger and brutality', cried another.[1] But the effect of Brooke's *Poems* in 1911
was limited primarily to critics and reviewers; the British reading
public remained largely unperturbed.

It was John Masefield's *Everlasting Mercy* (1911) which can
fairly be said to have set the pre-war poetic renaissance in motion.
Published first in the *English Review* in October 1911, and then as
a separate volume, this poem was the seminal realistic work of
the renaissance. Masefield should have been no stranger to the
British poetry-reading public in 1911, nor should his colloquial
narrative verse have been particularly novel. It is difficult to
understand why *Salt Water Ballads* (1902), *Ballads* (1903), and
*Ballads and Poems* (1910) had not prepared British readers for *The
Everlasting Mercy*. But the public read the poem not only with surprise but with pleasure and a generous admixture of curiosity.

Recalling the effect of its publication ten years later, even Harold Monro, never a devotee of Masefieldian art, was forced to admit:

> Here was stuff that the general public could appreciate without strain-
> ing its intelligence. People who thought that English poetry had
> died with Tennyson suddenly recognized their error. The blank verse
> of Stephen Phillips was a mere echo of the Victorian manner, but the
> rapid free doggerel of 'The Everlasting Mercy', its modernity, its
> bald colloquialism, and its narrative interest awakened the curiosity
> of the public in 1911, and a revival of the dormant interest in poetry
> was at once assured.[2]

Over fifty years after the event, and at an incalculably distant spiritual remove, one finds it difficult now to understand the British public's reaction to *The Everlasting Mercy* in 1911. A long narrative cast in irregular, often doggerel, metre, the poem re-counts in some detail the activities of a drunken village poacher. The protagonist, Saul Kane, is allowed to state the bill of par-ticulars against himself: 'I drunk, I fought, I poached, I whored', he says. And Masefield is careful to include ample details to sub-stantiate Kane's claim to pre-eminence in each of the four fields of activity. But in its own inscrutable way the heaven in which he disbelieved reached down to save even the veriest of sinners, for in spite of his sins Kane was also possessed of a conscience—Victorian style. As he sat inside the ring being prepared to fight a grudge-match with a one-time friend, his eye hit upon the place where he had recently seduced 'poor Nell':

> My corner faced the Squire's park
> Just where the fir trees make it dark;
> The place where I begun poor Nell
> Upon the women's road to hell.
> I thought of't, sitting in my corner
> After the time-keeper struck his warner. . . .
> And while my seconds chafed and gloved me
> I thought of Nell's eyes when she loved me,
> And wondered how my lot would end,
> First Nell cast off and now my friend.

Goaded by his conscience, and having been led to a final vision of his own revolting state by the ministrations of a Quaker lady who made the rounds of the village pubs daily 'To bring the drunkards' souls to grace', Kane was converted to the ways of

high living and clean thinking and presumably ended his days
nobly tilling the soil.

The poem is interlarded with some implied social criticism as
Masefield allows the drunken Kane to expatiate to the parish priest
on the evils of the social and economic system as seen from the
lower classes. It also contains several lengthy and would-be bitter
comments upon the evils of organized religion and the hypocrisy
engendered by middle-class social conformity. In the social sphere,
however, Masefield allows the measured liberalism of the clergyman clearly to win the day over Kane's drunken radicalism. 'You
think the Church an out-worn fetter,' says the priest;

> Kane, keep it till you've built a better.
> And keep the existing social state;
> I quite agree it's out of date,
> One does too much, another shirks,
> Unjust, I grant; but still . . . it works.

And he sums up his argument against Kane in one of the most
incredible couplets in English poetry: 'Put these two words beneath your hat,/These two: securus judicat.' In short, *The Everlasting Mercy* contains a moralistic flavour, a kind of sentimental
liberalism, even didacticism, which makes it more redolent of
Tom Hood than of the twentieth century.

The feature which caught the public eye in the poem was not
so much the matter as the manner. In *The Everlasting Mercy* Masefield 'called a new tune which set the muse dancing, not very
classically, in full view of the man in the street for the first time
since the days of Tennyson'.[3] It was not only the rapid free metres
but also Masefield's colloquial poetic diction and the mild oaths
with which his poem was studded that attracted the attention of
the public. Such a passage as the one in which Saul Kane en-
counters a fellow-poacher was certainly new—and to some degree,
one supposes, even daring—in 1911, though a multitude of
shocked voices quickly arose to point out that it was not 'poetic'.

> By Dead Man's Thorn, while setting wires,
> Who should come up but Billy Myers,
> A friend of mine, who used to be
> As black a sprig of hell as me,
> With whom I'd planned, to save encroachin',
> Which fields and coverts each should poach in.

Now when he saw me set my snare,
He tells me 'Get to hell from there.
This field is mine,' he says, 'by right;
If you poach here, there'll be a fight.
Out now,' he says, 'and leave your wires;
It's mine'
    'It ain't'
        'You put.'
            'You liar.'
'You closhy put.'
'You bloody liar.'
'This is my field.'
'This my wire.'
'I'm ruler here.'
'You ain't.'
'I am.'
'I'll fight you for it.'
'Right, by damn.'

At this late date it requires an almost impossible stretch of the critical imagination to conceive of what the British reading public found shocking in such a piece of folk poetry. Even the profanity seems too obviously forced. As Robert Lynd observed, 'one may amuse oneself by fancying that there is something of the manner of St. Francis even in Mr. Masefield's attitude to his little brothers the swear-words. He may not love them by nature, but he is kind to them by grace. They strike one as being the most innocent swear-words in literature'.[4]

Moreover, Masefield was neither the first nor the only practitioner of realistic verse in modern times. By 1911 both Alfred Noyes and Henry Newbolt had had their fling at the kind of verse Masefield was attempting; and of course he had been long anticipated by Kipling. Compared to Kipling's realistic verse, indeed, Masefield's seems too obviously sprung from the forcing house, too self-conscious, too clearly contrived. 'When Mr. Kipling repeats a soldier's oath, he seems to do so with a chuckle of appreciation. When Mr. Masefield puts down . . . oaths . . . he does so rather as a melancholy duty. He swears, not like a trooper, but like a virtuous man. He does not, as so many realists do, love the innumerable coarsenesses of life which he chronicles; that is what makes his oaths often seem as innocent as the conversation of elderly sinners echoed on the lips of children.'[5]

Why, then, the almost instant and widespread popularity of *The Everlasting Mercy*? Perhaps the reasons alleged by Harold Monro are as sound as any. For the first time in many years, in Masefield the general reader found verse which he could 'appreciate without straining his intelligence'. Moreover, to the public delight Masefield stretched traditional poetic forms to the breaking point. No more exquisitely jewelled lyrics, no more triolets or double ballades on the nothingness of things; rather, the 'rapid, free doggerel', the 'bold colloquialism', and the 'narrative interest' of *The Everlasting Mercy*.[6] Perhaps an even more compelling reason for the poem's startling success lay in its timing. It was published at precisely the right moment to act as a catalyst for some of the new forces of discontent stirring beneath the surface of British poetry in late 1911. Finally, like the naturalistic novel and the realistic drama, *The Everlasting Mercy* suited its age. In the liberal though not radical social ethos with which the poem was infused, in its racy, colloquial diction, in its rigorous avoidance of traditionally 'poetic' subject matter, the English reading public saw tangible evidence that poetry had finally caught up, so to speak, with the contemporary novel and the stage.

For whatever reasons, publication of *The Everlasting Mercy* may be said to mark the beginning of the pre-war poetic renaissance, for, as Edmund Blunden observed, Masefield's poem 'energized poetry and the reading of it, no matter what extremes of feeling it then aroused or now fails to arouse'.[7] Masefield followed up the success of *The Everlasting Mercy* with other narrative poems of the same order, *The Widow in the Bye Street* (1912), *The Story of a Roundhouse* (1912), and *Dauber* (1913). And in 1915, when Edward Marsh staked the considerable critical reputation of *Georgian Poetry* on two long works in the realistic tradition—Abercrombie's 'End of the World' and Bottomley's 'King Lear's Wife'—he made amply evident what was in fact true: the kind of realism first popularized by Masefield was one of the major facets of the pre-war revolt against the dead hand of poetic tradition.

## FUTURISM

The most spectacular Continental revolutionary movement to strike England with something like a major impact at the beginning of the second decade was Futurism. Originally a revolt confined almost entirely to pictorial art, Futurism began around 1908 when a small band of Milanese painters—Marinetti, Buzzi, Palazzeschi—with that splendid Latin penchant for artistic coteries, creeds, and fiery *pronunciamentos*, declared themselves henceforward free from the chains of artistic Academism. The movement quickly caught on in both Italy and France, and its implications for poetry were soon recognized by some of its founders, principally Marinetti. On 20th February 1909 Marinetti published the first Futurist 'Manifesto' in *Le Figaro*, a document which launched Futurism not only as an artistic but also as a poetic movement.[8] It was followed by a spate of manifestoes during 1909 and 1910, most of them addressed to the artist—though one was addressed to musicians and another was concerned with motion pictures—and in 1910 the tenets of the movement were summed up by Marinetti's *Le Futurism*.[9] In 1912 Italian Futurist verse was collected in an anthology which, according to Harold Monro, had sold thirty-five thousand copies by late 1913.[10]

There could scarcely be a more cogent example than Futurism of the desire for the violent, the self-assertive, and the primitive, which was beginning to engulf Continental art and from art to spill over into poetry. 'We will sing the love of danger, and the habit of energy and fearlessness,' wrote Marinetti in the manisfesto of 1909.

> The foundations of our poetry shall be courage, audacity, and revolt.
> We announce that the splendour of earth has become enriched by a new beauty, the beauty of Speed. . . .
> All beauty is based on strife. There can be no masterpiece otherwise than aggressive in character. Poetry must be a violent assault against unknown forces to overwhelm them into obedience to man.
> We will sing the great multitudes furious with work, pleasure, or revolt; the many-coloured and polyphonic assaults of revolution in modern capitals; . . . stations, those ravenous swallowers of fire-breathing serpents; factories, hung by their cords of smoke to the clouds.[11]

Futurism lauded war, it praised violence for its own sake; taking a page from Henley's book, it idealized the machine, especially the automobile; it stood for speed, love of danger, noise, and the unrestrained ego.

If there was any organized rationale at all in Futurism, it argued fundamentally from the premise that twentieth-century sensibility had been completely changed by scientific discovery and its step-child, invention. In his 'New Futurist Manifesto' of 11th May 1913 Marinetti claimed that modern communication and machinery had brought about a change in man's psyche which, were he courageous or wise enough to admit it, must also cause a complete and violent change in his art. Explaining what he meant by 'The Futurist Consciousness', Marinetti claimed that twentieth-century life had effected at least fifteen specific results, chief among them: acceleration of living, speed; horror of the old, the familiar, the known; abhorrence of the quiet life, love of action and danger; destruction of 'the feeling of *the beyond*'; 'multiplication and inexhaustibility of human desires and ambitions'; equality of the sexes; 'depreciation of love (sentimentalism and luxury) produced by greater erotic facility and liberty of women'; a new sense of fusion of men and machines; 'nausea of the curved line . . . love of the straight line and of the terminal'.*

Upon such a tenuous foundation Marinetti erected the framework of the Futurist poetic. Twentieth-century poetry, he claimed, if it would accurately reflect the realities of twentieth-century life, must embody several Futurist precepts:

WORDS AT LIBERTY  Lyricism has nothing whatever to do with syntax; it is simply 'the exceptional faculty of intoxicating and being intoxicated with life'. The poet must communicate by using 'essential' words only, 'and these absolutely *at liberty*'.

WIRELESS IMAGINATION  By which Marinetti meant 'entire freedom of images and analogies expressed by disjointed words and without the connecting wires of syntax. . . . Poetry must be an uninterrupted sequence of new images'.

SEMAPHORIC ADJECTIVATION  Qualifying adjectives must be cut to the bone in Futurist verse. They should be considered only as 'semaphores' serving 'to regulate the speed and pace of the race of analogies'.

VERB IN THE INFINITIVE  Finite verb forms must be avoided at all costs because they tend to make units of meaning (i.e. sentences). The infinitive form is far preferable, indeed indispensable, because it negates 'in itself the existence of a sentence, and

* Trans. Arundel del Re, *PD*, I (1913), 319–21. The 'New Futurist Manifesto' of 11th May 1913, as translated and printed in *PD*, is one of the most significant single documents in the history of Futurism, for it contains not only the Futurist 'metaphysic' but also the Futurist poetic which was based upon it.

prevents the style from stopping or sitting down at a determined spot'.

ONOMATOPOEIA AND MATHEMATICAL SIGNS  Modern verse must have 'a most rapid, brutal, and immediate lyricism . . . a telegraphic lyricism'. To this end it must have the courage to introduce 'onomatopoeic chords, in order to render all the sounds and even the most cacophonous noises of modern life'. And it must make copious use of mathematical and musical symbols 'to regulate the speed of the style'.

TYPOGRAPHICAL REVOLUTION  The typographical harmony of the normal printed page of verse must be rigorously avoided. Typography must rather show 'the flux and reflux, the jerks and the bursts of style' represented on the page. Therefore the Futurist poet may 'if necessary' make use of three or four colours of ink and twenty kinds of type on a single page.

FREE AND EXPRESSIVE ORTHOGRAPHY  Words must continually be made and unmade *ad libitum*; they must be formed, reformed, and deformed in the process of every poem. No syntax is allowable by any stretch of permissiveness. We must have 'words at liberty'.[12]

Perhaps the most charitable course at this late date is thus to allow the Futurist poetic to speak for itself. Though it undeniably opened the door to all sorts of further experiments with verse forms, few English poets appear to have taken it very seriously as a guide for writing verse, if for no other reason than the English poet's fundamental distrust of Latin extremism. 'If Futurism had triumphed here,' Frank Swinnerton declared, 'it would have done so because the nation had lost its head.'[13] Indeed, it is difficult to imagine that even the most ardent poetic revolutionary in London in 1913 could have considered a poem like Marinetti's 'Bataille' as much more than mildly amusing.

BATAILLE / POIDS + ODEUR

Midi ¾ flûtes glappissement
embrasement toumtoumb alarme Gargaresch
craquement crépitation marche Cliquetis
sacs fusils sabots clous canons crinières
roues caissons juifs beignets pains-à-huile
cantilènes échoppes bouffées chatoiement
chassie puanteur cannelle

fadeurs flux reflux poivre rixe vermine
tourbillon orangers-en-fleur filigrane
misère dés échecs cartes jasmin + muscade
+ rose arabesque mosaique charogne
hérissement + savates mitrailleuses =
galets + ressac + grenouilles Cliquetis
sacs fusil canons ferraille atmosphère =
plombs + lave + 300 puanteurs + 50 parfums
pavé matelas détritus crottin charognes
flic-flac entassement chameaux bourricots
tohubohu cloaque.[14]

The major impact of Futurism upon London came not from the
Futurist poetic but in the person of its incredible founder and
publicist Filippo Marinetti. Marinetti lectured frequently in London from 1912 through 1914. A man of considerable wealth, he
was 'a flamboyant person', as Douglas Goldring recalled, 'adorned
with diamond rings, gold chains, and hundreds of flashing white
teeth'. His public performances were perhaps more spectacular
than edifying: during one recitation in 1914 he was accompanied
by the intermittent booming of a large drum off-stage, and he
sometimes exemplified Futurist tenets by imitating the sound of
machine-guns from the platform. But he spoke everywhere and to
all kinds of artists and poets, at the Lyceum Club and in Bechstein
Hall, to T. E. Hulme's Poets' Club, in the Dore Galleries, and in
the meeting-room of Harold Monro's Poetry Bookshop.[15] Not
everyone was impressed. Richard Aldington recorded in December 1913: 'M. Marinetti has been reading his new poems to London. London is vaguely alarmed and wondering whether it ought
to laugh or not.'[16] Perhaps Edward Marsh had attended the same
reading as Aldington; at any rate he wrote a lively account of one
to Rupert Brooke, absent in the South Seas, on 14th December
1913.

Did anyone give you an account of Marinetti's visit? I only attended one of his manifestations—a lecture at the Poetry Bookshop,
in a kind of loft which looked as if it was meant to keep apples in,
and one ought to get into it by a ladder through a trap-door. It was
illuminated by a single night-light, which I thought at first must be
a Futurist tenet; but it turned out to be only a fatuity of Monro's.
Marinetti began his lecture by asking how he could possibly talk in
a penumbra about Futurism, the chief characteristic of which was

Light, Light, Light? He did very well all the same. He is beyond doubt an extraordinary man, full of force and fire, with a surprising gift of turgid lucidity, a full and roaring and foaming flood of indubitable half-truths.

He gave us two of the 'poems' on the Bulgarian War. The appeal to the sensations was great—to the emotions, nothing. As a piece of art, I thought it was about on the level of a very good farmyard-imitation—a supreme music-hall turn. I could not feel that it detracted in any respect from the position of *Paradise Lost* or the *Grecian Urn*. He has a marvellous sensorium, and a marvellous gift for transmitting its reports—but what he writes is not literature, only an aide-mémoire for a mimic.[17]

Wyndham Lewis expressed his antagonism more actively. To one of Marinetti's lectures at the Dore Galleries in 1914 'Lewis took "a determined band of miscellaneous anti-Futurists", including Gaudier-Brzeska, Edward Wadsworth, and T. E. Hulme (all big men). They heckled Marinetti. Gaudier "put down a tremendous barrage in French, while the rest maintained a confused uproar".'[18]

But Marinetti was quite capable of giving as good as he got. In May 1914 Harold Monro remarked in a letter to Marsh: 'We had tremendous fun with Marinetti the other evening. He came around [to the Poetry Bookshop] and declaimed to Yeats and made the room shake.'* This was not the first time Yeats had been required to endure Marinetti's declamations. Sturge Moore, Pound, and Aldington had taken Marinetti to Yeats's flat in the Woburn Buildings upon an earlier occasion. As Aldington recalled the episode, Yeats read some of his poems and then politely asked Marinetti to reciprocate. 'Whereupon Marinetti sprang up and in a stentorian Milanese voice began bawling:

> 'Automobile,
> Ivre d'espace,
> Qui piétine d'angoisse,' *etc.*,

until Yeats had to ask him to stop because neighbours were knocking in protest on the floor, ceiling, and party walls.'[19]

Though Futurism did much to enliven the English literary and artistic scene in 1912 and 1913, by 1914 it was being replaced by other, more up-to-the-minute '-isms'. Among other reasons for

* Harold Monro to Edward Marsh, 12th May 1914, *MLC*. Almost without exception the many unpublished letters which I have used in this study have been found in the Marsh Letter Collection. See Acknowledgements and Bibliography for full explanations of the contents of this Collection.

the decline is the fact that the very word was being diluted by too loose and too frequent use. By 1914 'Futurist' had come to be applied in art circles not so much to Marinetti and his followers as indiscriminately to anyone trying to rebel against merely representational art. Moreover, by 1914 there were many artists—especially those in rival coteries like the Vorticists—who claimed that in the rush to modernity Futurism had long since been passed by; it was itself (to use their own phrase) *'passéiste'*.* Wyndham Lewis could write patronizingly in 1914 that Futurism, as bodied forth in a current exhibition of Futurist art, was only 'Impressionism up-to-date', with an admixture of 'Automobilism' and Nietzsche. It was 'romantic', the most damning of all epithets: 'a picturesque, superficial, and romantic rebellion of young Milanese painters against the Academism which surrounded them. . . . The Automobilist pictures were too "picturesque", melodramatic and spectacular', Lewis continued, 'besides being undigested and naturalistic to a fault. . . . Romance about science is a thing we have all been used to for many years, and we resent its being used as a sauce for a dish claiming to belong strictly to emancipated Futures'.[20]

In its more specifically poetic phase, too, several critics were quick to point out that Futurism was not so new as it pretended to be. Henley had anticipated by some years the Futurist effusions on the automobile and on the beauty of speed, and Kipling had long since remarked upon the romance of the modern machine. Even so sympathetic a critic as Harold Monro felt impelled to point out to the Futurists that the poetry which they believed so new was 'no more than frenzied Whitmanism, adulterated by an excessive, if diverting, admixture of meridional eloquence'.[21] Wyndham Lewis observed that in their praise of the machine the Futurists had also been anticipated by H. G. Wells.[22] And J. C. Squire pointed out that Futurist poetry bore traces of Impressionism, the very movement which the Futurists professed so cordially to detest. 'To me, at least,' wrote Squire, 'the Futurist verse of Signor Marinetti reads like slightly more disjected Whitman or Henley with a flavouring of French impressionism.'[23]

* The word itself, a favourite among the *avant-garde*, perhaps shows in a small way the influence of Futurism, at least upon the critical vocabulary of the English. It was a French—and therefore more familiar—rendering of the Italian *passatisti*, lovers of the past, who were the chief whippingboys of the early Futurist manifestoes (Wagner, *Wyndham Lewis*, p. 131).

But the rock on which Futurism finally foundered was the war. With its single-minded emphasis on energy as a goal of art, its love of the brutal, its open desire for and praise of war, Futurism could not weather the universal revulsion at the very real world of trench warfare in the mud of Flanders. 'What Futurist, either in the trenches or at home, honestly desires war to continue?' asked John Cournos, art critic of the *Egoist*, in January 1917. 'What Vorticist? They advocated violence, but violence has now become too common; devastation and anarchy sweep Europe.' And so the Russian Futurist Mayakovsky could claim with justification in early 1917: 'Futurism has died as a particular group, but it has poured itself out in everyone in a flood. Today all are Futurists.'[24]

## VORTICISM

An even more pyrotechnic phase of the pre-war revolt in the plastic and pictorial arts which had implications for poetry was Vorticism. In a sense both an outgrowth from and a rebellion against Futurism, Vorticism was not a Continental import, but a home-grown revolution. It was launched as a formal 'movement' by the second of Marinetti's lectures at the Dore Galleries on 5th May 1914, the one to which went 'a small band of miscellaneous anti-Futurists'—Hulme, Wadsworth, Gaudier-Brzeska—led by Wyndham Lewis to heckle Marinetti. Their success against so formidable an opponent apparently led the small band to consider formalizing their views, and so with the addition of several others to the group—among them Ezra Pound (who invented the word 'Vorticism')* and Richard Aldington—Vorticism began its brief but lively career.†

* *Letters of Ezra Pound*, ed. Paige, p. 122. It is difficult to overestimate the influence of Pound on the pre-war poetic scene. He was ubiquitous. His name and influence were recorded in the pages of most of the *avant-garde* little magazines as well as in the affairs of such a Centrist organization as the Poetry Bookshop or a journal like *PD*. Among all the pre-war poets, as Arundel del Re wrote, Pound was unique, 'the only one who without affectation lived up to the romantic tradition of the poet in looks, dress, and behaviour and, though his many enemies have accused him of it, without any intention of advertising himself. A true poetic genius and a born leader, there has been no really new and vital movement in English poetry since 1910, upon which he has not exercised a clearly marked influence either directly or indirectly, for his personality is probably the most remarkable (that of Robert Bridges excepted) that has appeared in English poetry during the present century' ('Georgian Reminiscences', *SEL*, XII [1932], 329).

† Geoffrey Wagner, *Wyndham Lewis*, pp. 130, 143–4. For a full account of the part played by Pound and Wyndham Lewis in guiding the fortunes of Vorticism, see Charles Norman, *Ezra Pound*, pp. 146–62; John Gould Fletcher, *Life Is My Song*, pp. 136–7; and Douglas Goldring, *South Lodge* (London, 1943), pp. 65–70.

Little more than a month later, in June 1914, Vorticism became vocal with the publication of that most amazing of all pre-war little magazines, *Blast*, which ran for only two numbers, the second and final one appearing in July 1915. Edited by Wyndham Lewis and published by John Lane at the Bodley Head, *Blast* was obviously out to shock both in content and format. The first number had a puce-coloured paper cover, the word 'BLAST' being written in huge block capitals diagonally across it. Inside appeared the inevitable manifesto printed in inch-high capitals, poems by Pound, Vorticist drawings, 'Vortices and Notes' by Lewis, stories by Rebecca West and Ford Madox Hueffer, and short pieces entitled 'Vortex' by Pound and Gaudier-Brzeska. Harrying the Philistines was certainly no new aim in British letters from the mid-nineteenth century on, but *Blast* did the job extraordinarily well.

Among other distinctions which fell to the journal, it was in *Blast* that Eliot's four 'Preludes' and the 'Rhapsody of a Windy Night' first saw print;[25] and Pound's small *tour de force* 'Ancient Music' first appeared there. Pound no doubt took some pride in the fact that three lines of one of his more scurrilous short poems in the first number had to be inked out by a censor.* And in the second number appeared a small poem of Pound's which must surely be the only published satiric poem about Rupert Brooke.[26] Both in truculence and in volume, however, the second number showed a considerable falling off from the first. Though its literary quality was higher, it took a doomed, if forthright, stand towards its task during wartime: 'This puce-coloured cockle-shell', Lewis wrote, 'will . . . try to brave the waves of blood, for the serious mission it has on the other side of the World-War.'[27] And though Lewis confidently looked forward to two more issues in 1915, even going so far as to list the contents of the next projected number, *Blast*, like most of the little magazines which so enlivened pre-war literary London, became a casualty of the war.

As one traces its tenets through the pages of *Blast*, Vorticism appears to have had several strings to its bow. In a bristling

---

* 'Fratres Minores', *Blast*, I (1914), 48. The curious will discover that the years have not dealt kindly with the censor's heavy ink. In the copies of *Blast* that I have seen it is possible precisely to decipher the censored lines with the aid of a strong light applied at a judicious angle. *Sic semper tyrannus!* The reward, however, is not entirely commensurate with the effort required. The poem may be read with less effort in *Personae: The Collected Shorter Poems of Ezra Pound* (London, 1952), p. 127.

statement of aims at the beginning of the first number, Lewis set forth the major principles upon which the journal would stand and upon which subsequent articles and contributors only rang the changes. 'Long live the great art vortex sprung up in the centre of this town!', he began.

> We stand for the Reality of the Present—not for the sentimental Future or the sacripant Past.
> We want to leave Nature and Men alone.
> We do not want to make people wear Futurist Patches, or fuss men to take to pink and sky-blue trousers.
> We are not their wives or tailors. . . .
> We believe in no perfectibility except our own. . . .
> We do not want to change the appearance of the world, because we are not Naturalists, Impressionists or Futurists (the latest form of Impressionism), and do not depend on the appearance of the world for our art.
> WE ONLY WANT THE WORLD TO LIVE, and to feel its crude energy flowing through us. . . .
> We want to make in England not a popular art, not a revival of lost folk art, or a romantic fostering of such unactual conditions, but to make individuals, wherever found.
> We will convert the King if possible.
> A VORTICIST KING! WHY NOT?
> DO YOU THINK LLOYD GEORGE HAS THE VORTEX IN HIM?
> MAY WE HOPE FOR ART FROM LADY MOND? . . .
> AUTOMOBILISM (Marinetteism) bores us. We don't want to go about making a hullo-bulloo about motor cars, anymore than about knives and forks, elephants or gas-pipes.
> Elephants are VERY BIG. Motor cars go quickly.
> Wilde gushed twenty years ago about the beauty of machinery. Gissing, in his romantic delight with modern lodging houses was futurist in this sense.
> The futurist is a sensational and sentimental mixture of the aesthete of 1890 and the realist of 1870. . . .
> We want those simple and great people found everywhere.
> Blast presents an art of Individuals.*

Vorticism was an artistic coterie to end artistic coteries. It set itself against any other school except Vorticism; it was equally disgusted by realism and aestheticism. Explicit in Lewis's mani-

* *Blast*, I (1914), 7–8. According to one of Pound's biographers, it was Wyndham Lewis, not Pound, who contributed most of the anti-Futurist jibes in *Blast* (Charles Norman, *Ezra Pound*, pp. 148–9).

*Courtesy of the photographer, Alvin Langdon Coburn*

John Masefield, January 1913

# Long Live the Vortex!

Long live the great art vortex sprung up in the centre of this town!

We stand for the Reality of the Present—not for the sentimental Future, or the sacripant Past.

We want to leave Nature and Men alone.

We do not want to make people wear Futurist Patches, or fuss men to take to pink and sky-blue trousers.

We are not their wives or tailors.

The only way Humanity can help artists is to remain independent and work unconsciously.

WE NEED THE UNCONSCIOUSNESS OF HUMANITY—their stupidity, animalism and dreams.

We believe in no perfectibility except our own.

Intrinsic beauty is in the Interpreter and Seer, not in the object or content.

We do not want to change the appearance of the world, because we are not Naturalists, Impressionists or Futurists (the latest form of Impressionism), and do not depend on the appearance of the world for our art.

WE ONLY WANT THE WORLD TO LIVE, and to feel it's crude energy flowing through us.

It may be said that great artists in England are always revolutionary, just as in France any really fine artist had a strong traditional vein.

Blast sets out to be an avenue for all those vivid and violent ideas that could reach the Public in no other way.

Blast will be popular, essentially. It will not appeal to any particular class, but to the fundamental and popular instincts in every class and description of people, TO THE INDIVIDUAL. The moment a man feels or realizes himself as an artist, he ceases to belong to any milieu or time. Blast is created for this timeless, fundamental Artist that exists in everybody.

The Man in the Street and the Gentlemen are equally ignored.

Popular art does not mean the art of the poor people, as it is usually supposed to. It means the art of the individuals.

Education (art education and general education) tends to destroy the creative instinct. Therefore it is in times when education has been non-existant that art chiefly flourished.

But it is nothing to do with "the People."

It is a mere accident that that is the most favourable time for the individual to appear.

To make the rich of the community shed their education skin, to destroy politeness, standardization and academic, that is civilized, vision, is the task we have set ourselves.

We want to make in England not a popular art, not a revival of lost folk art, or a romantic fostering of such unactual conditions, but to make individuals, wherever found.

We will convert the King if possible.

A VORTICIST KING! WHY NOT?

DO YOU THINK LLOYD GEORGE HAS THE VORTEX IN HIM?

MAY WE HOPE FOR ART FROM LADY MOND?

We are against the glorification of "the People," as we are against snobbery. It is not necessary to be an outcast bohemian, to be unkempt or poor, any more than it is necessary to be rich or handsome, to be an artist. Art is nothing to do with the cost you wear. A top-hat can well hold the Sixtine. A cheap cap could hide the image of Kephren.

AUTOMOBILISM (Marinetteism) bores us. We don't want to go about making a hullo-bulloo about motor cars, anymore than about knives and forks, elephants or gas-pipes.

Elephants are VERY BIG. Motor cars go quickly.

Wilde gushed twenty years ago about the beauty of machinery. Gissing, in his romantic delight with modern lodging houses was futurist in this sense.

The futurist is a sensational and sentimental mixture of the aesthete of 1890 and the realist of 1870.

The "Poor" are detestable animals! They are only picturesque and amusing for the sentimentalist or the romantic! The "Rich" are bores without a single exception, *on tout que riches!*

We want those simple and great people found everywhere.

Blast presents an art of Individuals.

---

EVERY CONCEPT, EVERY EMOTION PRESENTS ITSELF TO THE VIVID CONSCIOUSNESS IN SOME PRIMARY FORM. IT BELONGS TO THE ART OF THIS FORM. IF SOUND, TO MUSIC; IF FORMED WORDS, TO LITERATURE; THE IMAGE, TO POETRY; FORM, TO DESIGN; COLOUR IN POSITION, TO PAINTING; FORM OR DESIGN IN THREE PLANES, to SCULPTURE; MOVEMENT TO THE DANCE OR TO THE RHYTHM OF MUSIC OR OF VERSES.

Elaboration, expression of second intensities, of dispersedness belong to the secondary sort of artist. Dispersed arts HAD a vortex.

Impressionism, Futurism, which is only an accelerated sort of impressionism, DENY the vortex. They are the CORPSES of VORTICES. POPULAR BELIEFS, movements, etc., are the CORPSES of VORTICES. Marinetti is a corpse.

## THE MAN.

The vorticist relies not upon similarity or analogy, not upon likeness or mimcry.

In painting he does not rely upon the likeness to a beloved grandmother or to a caressable mistress.

VORTICISM is art before it has spread itself into a state of flacidity, of elaboration, of secondary applications.

## ANCESTRY.

"All arts approach the conditions of music."—*Pater.*

"An Image is that which presents an intellectual and emotional complex in an instant of time."—*Found.*

"You are interested in a certain painting because it is an arrangement of lines and colours."—*Whistler.*

Picasso, Kandinski, father and mother, classicism and romanticism of the movement.

## POETRY.

The vorticist will use only the primary media of his art.

The primary pigment of poetry is the IMAGE.

The vorticist will not allow the primary expression of any concept or emotion to drag itself out into mimicry.

In painting Kandinski, Picasso.

In poetry this by, "H. D."

Whirl up sea ——
Whirl your pointed pines,
Splash your great pines
On our rocks,
Hurl your green over us,
Cover us with your pools of fir.

154

---

## WOMEN BEFORE A SHOP.

The gew-gaws of false amber and false turquoise attract them.
"Like to like nature." These agglutinous yellows!

## L'ART.

Green arsenic smeared on an egg-white cloth,
Crushed strawberries! Come let us feast our eyes.

## THE NEW CAKE OF SOAP.

Lo, how it gleams and glistens in the sun
Like the cheek of a Chesterton.

## MEDITATIO.

When I carefully consider the curious habits of dogs,
I am compelled to admit
That man is the superior animal.

When I consider the curious habits of man,
I confess, my friend, I am puzzled.

---

(*above*) The first Vorticist manifesto, written by Wyndham Lewis and Ezra Pound, as it appeared in *Blast*, 1914

(*below, left*) A portion of Ezra Pound's definition of Vorticism as it appeared in *Blast*, 1914

(*below, right*) Several of Ezra Pound's Imagist poems as they were printed in *Blast*, 1914 festo was also Vorticism's intense hostility towards Futurism. Though its credo shared several fundamental points with that of the Futurists, Vorticism took a violent and forthright antipathy towards its predecessor. Futurism had become a dead issue in England by 1914, Lewis claimed, because it was too 'romantic' and 'sentimental'—sentimental about the future, to be sure, but no less sentimental than such outdated artistic movements as Impressionism, which Futurism claimed to supplant.[28] Vorticism set its face as resolutely against Impressionism as against Futurism. It had nothing but scorn for the 'lean belated Impressionists at present attempting to eke out a little life in these islands. . . . Our vortex is fed up with your dispersals, reasonable chicken-men', wrote Lewis.[29]

Behind the antipathy towards both Futurism and Impressionism, however, one detects a deeper hatred. Almost all the denunciations and manifestoes in *Blast* were directed towards what it was pleased to call 'sentimentalism', be it sentimentalism about the past or the future.

> Our Vortex is not afraid of the Past: it has forgotten its existence.
> Our Vortex regards the Future as as sentimental as the Past.
> The Future is distant, like the Past, and therefor sentimental. . . .
> Everything absent, remote, requiring projection in the veiled weakness of the mind is sentimental.[30]

In its emphasis on the anti-sentimental, the hard and dry, Vorticism attempted to do in art much the same thing that Imagism was contemporaneously attempting to do for poetry. Indeed, 'according to Pound', wrote John Gould Fletcher, the Vorticist principles 'were only an extension of the old principle of Imagism, developed to embrace all the arts. The basis for poetry . . . was not an abstract idea, but a concrete image; this emerged from a radiant node, a cluster of energy from which and into which and through which ideas and associations were constantly moving: therefore it could only be called a VORTEX'.[31]

Finally, Vorticism was aggressively, self-consciously English. Unlike Futurism, an import from alien, Latin shores, Vorticism took pains to distinguish itself as a native movement. It was thoroughly bored, Lewis declared, with 'that feeble Europeanism, abasement of the miserable "intellectual" before anything coming from Paris, cosmopolitan sentimentality, which prevails in so many quarters'. After all, because England 'practically invented this civilization that Signor Marinetti has come to preach to us about', Lewis protested, there should be nothing particularly intoxicating about modern machines to an Englishman.

> The modern world is due almost entirely to Anglo-Saxon genius, —its appearance and its spirit. . . .
> In dress, manners, mechanical inventions, LIFE, that is, ENGLAND, has influenced Europe in the same way that France has in Art.
> But busy with this LIFE-EFFORT, she has been the last to become conscious of the Art that is an organism of this new Order and Will of Man. . . .
> Once this consciousness towards the new possibilities of expression in present life has come, however, it will be more the legitimate property of Englishmen than of any other people in Europe.
> It should also, as it is by origin theirs, inspire them more forcibly and directly.
> They are the inventors of this bareness and hardness, and should be the greatest enemies of Romance.[32]

One runs a risk, perhaps, in taking *Blast* too seriously, with its long lists in three-quarter-inch capitals of random persons, events, and institutions to be 'blasted' or 'blessed'. Under the heading 'Blast' occur such items as English weather, 'Humour (English variety)', all things Victorian, the Bishop of London (and 'all his posterity'), Galsworthy, Dean Inge, Croce, Bergson, 'Beecham (Pills, Opera, Thomas)', A. C. Benson, the British Academy, William Archer, and the 'Clan Meynell'. Under the heading 'Bless' one finds 'cold, magnanimous, delicate, gauche, fanciful, stupid Englishmen', the Hairdresser, English humour (Swift and Shakespeare), French 'vitality, skepticism, pornography and females', the Pope, 'Barker (John and Granville)', the Salvation Army, Charlotte Corday, Castor Oil, James Joyce, Lloyd George, Chaliapin, and the Commercial Process Company.[33] One cannot take too seriously either some of Pound's poetic sorties in *Blast*, full of the new insolence, attacking all manner of persons and institutions which he saw as restricting the freedom of the artist. He hit out at the conservative reviewers:

> Let us deride the smugness of 'The Times':
> GUFFAW!
> So much the gagged reviewers,

66

It will pay them when the worms are wriggling
    in their vitals;
These were they who objected to newness,
HERE are their TOMB-STONES.
    They supported the gag and the ring:
A little black BOX contains them.
    SO shall you be also,
You slut-bellied obstructionist,
    You sworn foe to free speech and good letters,
You fungus, you continuous gangrene.[34]

And he lashed his literary contemporaries in general:

You say that I take a good deal upon myself;
That I strut in the robes of assumption.

In a few years no one will remember the 'buffo',
No one will remember the trivial parts of me,
The comic detail will not be present.
As for you, you will lie in the earth,
And it is doubtful if even your manure will
    be rich enough
To keep grass
Over your grave.[35]

The close relationship of Vorticism to Imagism is apparent in some of Pound's contributions to *Blast*. Several of his semi-Imagist efforts were printed in the first number:

L'ART
Green arsenic smeared on an egg-white cloth,
Crushed strawberries! Come let us feast our eyes.

WOMEN BEFORE A SHOP
The gee-gaws of false amber and false turquoise attract them.
'Like to like nature.' These agglutinous yellows![36]

But the relationship is more clearly seen in Pound's explanation of the meaning of Vorticism for poetry. Like the Vorticist painter, the Vorticist poet, too, 'will use only the primary media of his art', said Pound.

The primary pigment of poetry is the IMAGE.
The Vorticist will not allow the primary expression of any concept or emotion to drag itself out into mimicry.
In painting Kandinski, Picasso.
In poetry this by, 'H. D.'

67

> Whirl up sea—
> Whirl up you pointed pines,
> Splash your great pines
> On our rocks,
> Hurl your green over us,
> Cover us with your pools of fir.[37]

By July 1915, when the second number appeared, *Blast* had a slightly less belligerent tone. Surprisingly, *Blast* II even had a faintly patriotic odour about it. Active service in the trenches had begun to expel the youthful arrogance from at least one of the Vorticists. Gaudier-Brzeska wrote his last 'Vortex' from the trenches in France, a sympathetic, human document, warm with humility, bright with new insight, the more tragic because its gifted author was so shortly to be killed in action.

> I have been fighting for two months and I can now gauge the intensity of Life.
> Human Masses teem and move, are destroyed and crop up again.
> Horses are worn out in three weeks, die by the roadside.
> Dogs wander, are destroyed, and others come along.
> With all the destruction that works around us, nothing is changed, even superficially. *Life is the same strength*, the same moving agent that permits the small individual to assert himself. . . .
> This war is a great remedy.
> In the individual it kills arrogance, self-esteem, pride.[38]

Just as surely as Futurism, Vorticism too was a casualty of the war. It was a too self-conscious creed of ersatz violence which collapsed of anaemia when faced with the genuine, brutal violence of modern warfare on the Western Front.

## IMAGISM

Perhaps the most influential group of rebels in the pre-war poetic renaissance was that oddly assorted coterie to which one may apply the roughly descriptive term Imagist. This is not the place to trace the history of the Imagist movement, to deal with the controversial personalities which it attracted, or to enter the labyrinth of personal animosities and tempestuous civil insurrections which arose within its camp. That task has been done.* Here

---

* Glenn Hughes's *Imagism and the Imagists* (Stanford, Calif., 1931), though unsatisfactory in many respects, was long the standard work on Imagism. The subject

68

the Imagists must be considered primarily historically—that is, as
only one of several parties to the pre-war poetic revolt—and their
similarities to other pre-war Leftist coteries pointed out. Special
attention must therefore be given to two periodicals, the *New
Freewoman* and the *Egoist*, around which the Imagists rallied and
in which they assiduously whetted their knives for their enemies
and greeted their friends with partisan huzzahs.

The *New Freewoman*, a feminist paper edited by Dora Marsden
and financed by Harriet Shaw Weaver, appeared for the first time
on 15th June 1913. Because Miss Marsden and Miss Weaver engaged Ezra Pound for 'the task of finding literary contributors',
it became apparent almost from the beginning that the *New Freewoman* would become a repository for poems of the Imagist
school.[39] Aldington's work appeared early in the life of the journal,
along with verse by 'H.D.', Amy Lowell, F. S. Flint, Skipworth
Cannell, and William Carlos Williams. Early numbers also contained critical articles on modern poetry by Rebecca West and
Ford Madox Hueffer as well as frequent reviews of contemporary
verse by Pound.

With a slight change in format, the *New Freewoman* became the
*Egoist* with the number of 1st January 1914. Like its short-lived
predecessor, the *Egoist* was published fortnightly, until 1st January 1915, when it became a monthly for the duration of the war.
Never a journal to hide its light, the *Egoist* advertised itself as the
'only fortnightly in England that an intelligent man can read for
three months running'.[40] Miss Marsden edited the journal until
1915, the assistant editors being Richard Aldington and Leonard
Compton-Rickett. When it became a monthly the editorship was
taken over by Miss Weaver. When Aldington entered military
service around the middle of 1917, T. S. Eliot inherited Aldington's position as Assistant Editor.[41] By 1919 the Egoist Press had
been established, and the *Egoist* staff had become increasingly
interested in book publishing and less so in editing a magazine.
The last number of the journal appeared in December 1919. Its
leading contributors, Eliot, Pound, and Aldington, were shortly
to turn their efforts to the more famous and influential *Criterion*.

The *Egoist* succeeded in putting itself in the *avant-garde* of

was reopened with great profit by Stanley K. Coffman in his *Imagism: A Chapter for
the History of Modern Poetry* (1951), which, in spite of its modest sub-title, comes near
being definitive.

literary revolt from the beginning. A partial roster of those who contributed either verse or critical articles on poetry to the journal in 1914 amply suggests its penchant for the new: Aldington, Pound, Wyndham Lewis, F. S. Flint, Robert Frost, 'H.D.', John Gould Fletcher, Amy Lowell, and William Carlos Williams. One of its proudest accomplishments was the serial publication of Joyce's *Portrait of the Artist as a Young Man* in 1914–15 after it had been universally rejected by other publishers. Pound and Aldington alternated as book reviewers early in the life of the *Egoist* and, as one might expect, succeeded admirably in keeping things warm in their corner. Perhaps it was in the correspondence columns, however, that the hottest controversies raged. The *Egoist* had without doubt the most lively letters-to-the-editor columns in London. The editorial staff and friends of the paper were not above manufacturing letters under *noms de plume* to stir up a lagging controversy or start a new one. T. S. Eliot did so on several occasions,[42] and one discovers several amusingly fictitious names inscribed to letters in 1914 which bear unmistakable traces of the deft hand of Ezra Pound.

What did the prominent Imagists who contributed to the *New Freewoman* and the *Egoist* stand for?* By and large they took their position somewhere near the middle of the Left, in which status they both agreed and disagreed with their Leftist compeers. They agreed with all the pre-war rebels that the new twentieth-century consciousness demanded a new poetry, that old subjects, and particularly old techniques, were *passéiste*. Along with the Futurists, the Imagists 'proclaimed the need of the modern poet for a free form of verse. Both condemned rhetoric. Both . . . asserted the importance of complete freedom of play of images and analogies'. The Imagists were attracted to 'Futurism's vigour and energy, its hatred of the stylized, sentimental, and academic, and its concentration on its own times'.[43] On one crucial point, however, the Imagists took definite issue with Futurism: Marinetti's Futurist poems, Aldington argued, were not only too rhetorical and bombastic but also too formless and abstract. 'There is a vast dis-

---

* It is difficult to speak of 'the Imagists' as a cohesive or unified coterie, for they were neither. Aldington's brand of Imagism differed slightly from Pound's, and both differed from Hulme's or Flint's. Pound, moreover, was read out of the party in 1914 when yet another brand, 'Amygism', was introduced. And so one must almost always identify the particular Imagist one is using as an example. See Stanley K. Coffman, *Imagism*, p. 7.

organised energy in these poems,' he wrote, 'and good journalistic observation. Their great drawback to some of us is their utterly unrestrained rhetoric, their use of abstractions, their vagueness. . . . M. Marinetti's poems are born in confusion and may perish in it.'[44] It was in his emphasis upon the necessity for form in poetry, upon 'bringing content under careful, efficient control instead of allowing it to overflow onto the page', that the Imagist clearly parted company with the Futurist.[45]

In their opposition to representational art, again, the Imagists joined forces with both Futurists and Vorticists. The major question facing young artists in 1914, Aldington declared, was simply, 'Shall we, or shall we not have "parochialism in art"—or to put it in different words: should artists confine themselves entirely to modern life and to the modern world for their detail as well as for the "spirit" of their works?' The school of 'the dust-bin and the back yard' is gaining strength. 'If one does not deal in the latest type of aeroplane or the latest refinement in factories, then one is outside the pale.' Too much modern art insists on modernity not only of spirit, but also of detail. And Aldington advanced three reasons why realistic art was in his eyes bad art: first, realistic detail is uninteresting *per se* and quickly becomes 'tedious and out-of-date'; secondly, he claimed 'the right for every artist to use any subject he damn well pleases so long as he uses it well'; and thirdly, he found the realist 'a very bad artist—as a rule. To drag smells of petrol, refrigerators, ocean greyhounds, President Wilson and analine dyes into a work of art will not compensate for lack of talent and of technique'.[46] Against the dust-bin school the Imagist, in the person of Aldington in this case, broke out two banners: the banner of artistic individualism, a kind of latter-day art-for-the-artist's sake; and, though the devices upon it are somewhat dimmer, the banner of art as private experience, with all that such an aesthetic implies of the aloof, scholarly, sceptical disregard for the plain reader.

Finally, the Imagists shared with all the parties of the pre-war revolt, Left and Centre, a strong antipathy to all things Victorian. Along with all their compeers, they took arms, for instance, against 'cosmic' poetry. 'Mistrust any poet using the word *cosmic*,' Pound advised Harriet Monroe.[47] The adjective was never precisely defined, though it seems to have been coined in an attempt to describe that segment of nineteenth-century verse which was didactic in conception or in which the poet's aim seemed to be more to convey general ideas or absolutes than to objectify an emotion or describe an object in the existential world. By loose extension the word came simply to connote 'Victorian' or—an even more odious epithet—'Tennysonian'. In a withering burst of youthful scorn, Rebecca West, while praising the Imagists for bringing austerity back to English verse, managed to condemn the contributors to *Georgian Poetry* I as mere belated Victorians:

> Poetry should be burned to the bone by austere fires and washed white with rains of affliction: the poet should love nakedness and the thought of the skeleton under the flesh. But because the public will not pay for poetry it has become the occupation of learned persons, given to soft living among veiled things and unaccustomed to being sacked for talking too much. That is why from the beautiful stark bride of Blake it has become the idle hussy hung with ornaments kept by Lord Tennyson, handed on to Stephen Phillips and now supported at Devonshire Street by the Georgian school.*

In no coterie perhaps did anti-Victorian feeling take quite the extreme proportions that it did among the Imagists; and in no school was the specific anti-Victorian tone which one usually associates with the twenties so evident. In their bland offhand dismissal of all Victorian poetry as utterly unworthy of serious consideration in the twentieth century, in the tone of supercilious condescension which they adopted towards the nineteenth century, in the very language they used for their purposes, the Imagists were a decade in advance of their time. Perhaps Richard Aldington expressed it best:

> However often gentlemen from Highgate and the adjacent suburbs may write and protest it is nevertheless true that the majority of the poetry of the last century had nothing to do with life and very little to do with poetry. There was a plague of prettiness and a plague of pomposity and several other minor diseases—such as over-much suavity, the cult of decorated adjectives. And except for Browning and a little of Swinburne there was no energy which was not bombast, no rendering of life without an Anglican moral, no aesthetic without aesthetic cant.[48]

The Imagists were seldom reluctant to argue their aesthetic in

* *New Freewoman*, I, no. 5 (15th Aug. 1913), 86. The reference to Devonshire Street is a gratuitous slap at Harold Monro, whose Poetry Bookshop (situated on Devonshire Street) came to be associated in the general mind with the contributors to *GP* I.

public print or to trumpet their new verse. One entire issue of the *Egoist*, that of 1st May 1915, was devoted exclusively to spreading the gospel. Ferris Greenslet wrote on 'The Poetry of John Gould Fletcher'; John Gould Fletcher on 'The Poetry of Amy Lowell' (Miss Lowell, by this time intent upon her own special variety of Imagism, was not represented); F. S. Flint on 'The Poetry of H.D.'; and Richard Aldington on 'The Poetry of F. S. Flint'. The admiration was universally mutual and the praise on all sides fulsome. The only discordant note was struck by Harold Monro, who mildly bearded the lions in their own den, telling them in essence that their poetic was neither so new nor so startling as they believed. The Imagists dwelt too exclusively on their own uniqueness, he wrote; 'they would probably benefit in their own production by recognizing themselves more clearly as one of the latest groups in the forward march of English poetry—not the only one'.[49]

In spite of their shortcomings, the Imagists were no doubt the most significant pre-war Leftist coterie. The Futurists and Vorticists were sometimes more shocking than constructive, more symptomatic of the pandemic discontent among pre-war poets than influential. Though Ezra Pound coined the word 'Imagist' and served as chief publicist for the movement, it was the theories supplied by T. E. Hulme which gave the early Imagist experiments their 'authority and direction'.[50] Both men served their common purpose well; together they called the tune for one of the most lively phases of the pre-war poetic renaissance. With Hulme as metaphysician and Pound as impressario, the Imagists 'did a lot of useful pioneering work. They dealt a blow at the post-Victorian magazine poets. . . . They livened things up a lot. They made free verse popular. . . . And they tried to attain an exacting if narrow standard of style in poetry'.[51] Indirectly they did more. The Imagists, above all other pre-war coteries, put into the hands of the poets of the twenties the technical charts and compasses by which to find their poetic way across the hard dry sands of the Wasteland.

## 'RHYTHM'

A final phase of the poetic revolt at the turn of the decade centred around the figures of Middleton Murry and Katherine Mansfield and the fiery though precious periodical *Rhythm* and its short-lived successor *Blue Review*. One of the earliest of the *avant-garde* little magazines, *Rhythm* commenced publication in the summer of 1911, continued through four quarterly issues, and with the issue of June 1912 became a monthly. It ceased publication with its fourteenth number in March 1913. The *Blue Review*, its successor, ran for only three issues, beginning in May and ending in July 1913. *Rhythm* was edited by Murry alone, *Blue Review* by Murry with Katherine Mansfield as Associate Editor.[52]

Never coterie journals in the narrow sense of the word, neither *Rhythm* nor *Blue Review* adhered to any literary school to which a definite name can be given. Murry steered a decidedly independent course through the channels and shoals of literary revolt, and the pages of his journals were open to contributors of diverse literary persuasions: Max Beerbohm, D. H. Lawrence, Hugh Walpole, Frank Swinnerton, Rupert Brooke, Wilfrid Gibson, and W. L. George. Their very eclecticism, however, along with the youthful intensity of their two editors, invests *Rhythm* and the *Blue Review* with their charm and, for purposes of literary history, their importance. Even a short analysis of these two journals may tend to make them seem more influential than they actually were in their contemporary milieu, but it serves a useful historical purpose because it both augments and reinforces one's conclusions about the nature of the literary renaissance at the turn of the decade. Augments, because these two remarkable journals embody a few phases of the revolt which were either neglected or glossed over by other periodicals; reinforces, because in *Rhythm* and the *Blue Review* one obtains more forthright and often more extreme statements of certain tenets of the revolt than were discernible in some of the more narrowly conceived coterie journals like *Blast* or the *Egoist*.

One of the major features of the pre-war renaissance, for instance, to which attention has already been called, was the primitiveness, or brutality, of the new art. One sees this quality most readily of course in Futurism, and in intention at least it was a feature of the new Masefieldian realism; but *Rhythm* became quite explicit on the subject. In its attempts to be strenuously modern, to revolt as completely as possible against the spineless aestheticism of the nineties, *Rhythm*, said Murry in his first number, will stand on these premises: 'To treat what is being done to-day as something vital in the progress of art, which cannot fix its eye on yesterday and live; to see that the present is pregnant for the future, rather than a revolt against the past; in creation to give expression to an art that seeks out the strong things of life; in criticism to seek out the strong things of that art.' Aestheticism has had its day; art must now become 'brutal'; it must be 'an art that strikes deeper . . . that passes outside the bounds of a narrow aestheticism . . . to a humaner and a broader field'. Modern art must by definition be aggressive: 'To leave protest for progress, and to find art in the strong things of life, is the meaning of *Rhythm*.'[53] Many of the 'strong things of life' seem a bit tame to one who turns the pages of *Rhythm* today, but a few of them were evidently too strong for British tastes at the turn of the decade. In 1912 Murry was forced to announce to his readers with regret that his printers had 'strongly advised' him not to publish a certain story by W. L. George because it was allegedly salacious. Murry reluctantly accepted the advice, though not without a good deal of editorial bombast deploring 'that the state of public opinion in England should be such that it is impossible to obtain any degree of free expression for a serious work of art'.[54]

Another of the aspects of the pre-war literary renaissance most strikingly evident in the pages of *Rhythm* and the *Blue Review* was implicit, if not explicit, in every literary movement and little magazine of the era: an overwhelming, self-conscious concern with 'Art'. Though the abstraction 'Art' meant different things to different coteries during the period, most of the rebels, whether Left or Centre, agreed that the status of 'Art' in modern society was a matter of primary concern. One may take the position, along with Ford Madox Hueffer, for instance, that in the pre-war years a new aesthetic was consciously and deliberately being constructed for the first time since the nineties;[55] or with a more modern concern for the specific, one may pursue the countless arguments about Art through the little magazines of the time to a somewhat more cynical conclusion. But is it not more than a little ironic that the artistic rebel of 1912, who detested above all things *fin-de-siècle* aestheticism, should have failed to see in his excessive concern with 'Art' as an abstraction his own close kinship to the period he was rebelling against? In 1912, as in 1890, the air was full of hazy talk about the aims of Art, talk which had meaning more or less according to the connotations one attributed to the word itself. Murry's grandiloquent editorials on Art in *Rhythm* were justifiably attacked on the grounds of vagueness.[56] It is perhaps some defence to point out that almost every other little magazine of the time was open to similar charges. At least from the misty, often fatuous talk about Art in the pages of *Rhythm* several tenets of the pre-war aesthetic are underscored.

First, the new art must be private. Advocated in *Rhythm* more explicitly than in any other periodical of the time is the theory that art is a private experience to be created and enjoyed only by the gifted few. Twentieth-century art is not and cannot be democratic, wrote Murry and Miss Mansfield jointly, for the spiritual qualities it demands for both creation and appreciation are not to be found in democratic society. It demands 'intuition'; and 'intuition is a purely aristocratic quality'. It demands 'freedom'; and what is freedom in the artist but a 'consciousness of superiority'? And it demands 'individuality'.

> Individuality in the work of art is the creation of reality by freedom. It is the triumphant weapon of aristocracy. It is that daring and splendid thinking which the mob hates because it cannot understand and by which it is finally subdued. Only by realizing the unity and strength of the individual in the work of art is the mob brought to the knowledge of its own infinite weakness, and it loathes and is terrified by it.[57]

It is well to be reminded that such forthright claims for the natural superiority of the artist-aristocrat were being written in 1911. The cult of private art and the creed of the superior artist can by no means be considered either the hallmark of the eighteen-eighties or the exclusive discovery of the nineteen-twenties.

Such a concept of the Artist as Hero led naturally and almost imperceptibly to a pose of martyrdom on the part of the superior artist enmeshed in his own poor clay as well as in a world of clods and Bumbles. *Rhythm* shows that Murry did not escape the pose of unappreciated genius. 'The men who try to do something new for the most part starve,' he cried.[58] He was willing—even eager, one sometimes feels—to be branded an artistic snob for the future glory of Art.

A second tenet of the pre-war aesthetic affirmed in the pages of *Rhythm* is that modern art must be both amoral and anti-humanistic. Again one may observe that there is little new and nothing unique in such a creed. Imagism in particular drew its aesthetic

76

from the anti-humanistic creed of T. E. Hulme; and one would think that the principle of the amorality of art had been sufficiently established, at least among artists, during the late nineteenth century that by 1911 twentieth-century rebels were merely beating a dead horse. But in its zeal to protect Art from the unspeakable Philistines, *Rhythm* took to the battlefield as if anew. Art is against both conventional morality and 'morbid humanitarianism', Murry cried. 'Art is beyond creeds, for it is the creed itself. It comes to birth in irreligion and is nurtured in amorality. Religion and morality alike mean for the western world that this life fades away into the colourless intensity of the world to come.' Again one detects echoes from the nineties. Unlike the art of the *fin de siècle*, however, the new modern art must be violently, fiercely of this world worldly. It is 'movement, ferocity, tearing at what lies beneath. It takes nothing for granted; and thrusts mercilessly, pitilessly'.[59]

It follows, too, that *Rhythm* should share with most of the other little magazines of the Left another tenet of the modern aesthetic: the abhorrence of merely representational, or realistic, art. Representational realism has brought English art to the position of being 'a trade instead of an art', Murry and Miss Mansfield declared in a joint editorial. It can be rescued only by a new 'seriousness' on the part of artist and public alike. Precisely what the new quality of 'seriousness' is one cannot clearly say, for like most of their joint manifestoes, this one, too, is nebulous and prolix. It is clear enough, however, that they set themselves uncompromisingly against realistic art, which they vaguely equated with 'democratic' art, and that 'seriousness' cannot be a quality of democratic society. 'The life of democracy depends upon the absence of enthusiasm and true seriousness. For these two qualities . . . are the hallmark of aristocracy, the essentials of the leader. . . . True seriousness is a thing alive and spontaneous, liberating the artist for his art, and consciously expanding into ever wider rhythms.'[60]

One final quality which emerges from the pages of *Rhythm* and *Blue Review*, as from most of the little magazines of 1910–14, is the unmistakable feeling that something was in the air at the turn of the decade. By 1912 some of the young Georgian rebels were almost too aware of their own rebelliousness. The feeling for newness, indeed the glorification of newness for its own sake, was implicit in most that Murry and Miss Mansfield wrote in *Rhythm*

77

and *Blue Review*. At its worst it led to extravagant overstatement and a cocksureness of judgment that now seem preposterous. It is perhaps skirting the edge of unkindness to recall now that in reviewing the *Hill of Vision*, Murry claimed unequivocally:

> James Stephens is the greatest poet of our day. With this book he has stepped at once into the company of those whom we consider the greatest poets the world has ever known . . . Sappho, Catullus, Shakespeare, Coleridge, Heine, Villon, and Verlaine. . . . For 'The Lonely God' is a supreme and ultimate poem. With the clearest consciousness that we must stand or fall as critics by this judgment, we give it as our deliberate opinion that this poem, for splendid imagination, for true passion, for all the music and majesty of which the English speech is capable in a master's hands, must rank immediately as one of the supreme achievements of English poetry.[61]

And in an adulatory, emotional article of 1912 Murry claimed for Frank Harris the title of 'the greatest artist alive in England'. Specifically, Harris was 'the greatest writer of short stories that England ever possessed'. Even more: he was 'the greatest creative critic whom the world has known . . . he has seen where his greatest predecessors in criticism, Coleridge and Goethe, have had but a half-vision'![62]

In spite of occasional lapses into over-enthusiasm, however, *Rhythm* and *Blue Review* breathed the genuine spirit of newness. In them, more clearly than in the pages of any other little magazines of the time, one observes the new Georgian age in the process of achieving self-consciousness. It was in *Rhythm* in 1911 that Holbrook Jackson penned one of the earliest and most cogent pleas for a general 'revolt in attitude', a new, 'primitive' outlook, towards art.[63] In *Rhythm*, too, appeared D. H. Lawrence's eloquent paean to the 'Georgian Renaissance', the momentous 'sense of joy . . . the exultation in the vast freedom, the illimitable wealth that we have suddenly got'.[64] In 1912, several months before Edward Marsh's declaration of a new dawn for poetry in the preface to *Georgian Poetry* 1, Laurence Binyon had used the pages of *Rhythm* to proclaim the final demise of the Victorian poetic tradition and the birth of the new Georgian age.[65] And a year later, in 1913, Frank Swinnerton found ample evidence in both creative and critical literature that British letters had embarked upon a period of 'new and sanguine vitality'. In criticism, as in poetry, consciousness of the new was achieved in large part by rejection of the old, especially the Victorian. For the first time, Georgian critics, 'at the beginning of a new era', Swinnerton smugly declared, can now 'examine the corpses of ancient energies by the light of distinct, unprejudiced intelligence'. Criticism of Victorian men of letters, he found, was itself no longer Victorian.

> It is a clear sign of the death of the Victorian spirit that so many of our younger critics should now be saying the final word about its various exemplars. . . . All sorts of monographs upon the Victorian writers, artists, and notabilities are appearing; and it is noticeable that, for the most part, they reveal a resolve that this new Georgian Age should really begin clear of all muddled notions of its amorphous predecessors.[66]

Obviously, by 1913 the new Georgian age had achieved an abundance of self-consciousness. It was a vigorous, confident, rebellious age, full of youthful buoyancy and optimism. It was also a smug age. But surely, in their brief morning, unaware, happily, of the cataclysm which would shortly sweep their familiar world from under them, the young Georgians may be allowed their moment of smugness and swagger.

# 3

# Harold Monro

With the possible exception of Edward Marsh and Ezra Pound, who in their very different ways organized and directed opposite phases of the poetic renaissance, no figure looms more influential in pre-war poetic circles than Harold Monro. Zealously dedicated to removing poetry from the study of the aesthete or the scholar— 'we desire to see a public created that may read verse as it now reads its newspapers', he wrote in one of his more sanguine moods[1]—Monro put himself in a unique position to accomplish his crusade. He was editor successively of *Poetry Review* and *Poetry and Drama*, publisher of the works of many modern poets as well as the five volumes of *Georgian Poetry*, and owner of the Poetry Bookshop. An evaluation of the full extent of his influence will have to await publication of the history of his unique venture, the Poetry Bookshop.* But it is neither anticipating the conclusions of such a study nor overstating the facts at hand to observe that from 1911 until about 1916 or 1917 the influence of Harold Monro was a dominant one in almost every phase of the poetic renaissance.

To what can one attribute this influence? To Monro's position, certainly, as editor, publisher, and dean of the Poetry Bookshop

* Such a history is being undertaken by his wife, Alida Klementaski Monro. An editor of poetry in her own right, Mrs. Monro has an intimate personal knowledge of the major literary figures and movements of the period gained by working alongside her husband in the Poetry Bookshop from 1912 until his death in 1932. Moreover, she has in her possession unique and exhaustive records of the Bookshop's activities. In an interview in June 1955, Mrs. Monro gave me a great deal of information about her husband's activities during the pre-war period and allowed me to examine some of the records in her possession. I have not presumed to make use of any of the documents she showed me, but I acknowledge that some of the factual material for this chapter is drawn from our conversation.

circle. But perhaps more important, to the enthusiasm generated
by an overwhelming ideal: Monro lived to make poetry popular.
To that end he devoted his energies, his zeal, and a not inconsider-
able private purse.

Monro came down from Cambridge in 1901 a fervent Fabian
Socialist. Though he had gone to the University interested in
nothing more serious than horse racing, while there, he had seen
Shelley plain and had become 'a gloomily serious young man'
who intended to read for the bar and devote himself to the
Socialist cause.[2] Marriage in 1903 and birth of a son in 1904 forced
him to relinquish his plans for the bar, and after several unsuccessful years as a land agent in Ireland, Monro returned to England
and to Haslemere, where he devoted himself to being a practising
Socialist and vegetarian. Along with a Fabian friend, the craftsman
Romney Green, he founded the Samurai Press around 1906. 'For
a time,' wrote F. S. Flint, one of his subsequent close friends,
Monro 'felt at home' at Haslemere because 'there was a bleak side
of him which he translated into a romantic idealism, one of the
worst forms of self-deception, and the friendships he formed at
Haslemere fostered this weakness.'[3] But only for a short time.
After publishing such eminently unmarketable volumes as John
Drinkwater's *Lyrical and Other Poems* (1908), the Samurai Press
foundered; and Monro, disillusioned by the failure of his Fabian
enterprise and disappointed as well in other, more personal matters, went abroad to live. Settling finally in Florence, he joined a
colony of expatriate English writers which included, among
others, Gordon Craig, Helen Bayley, 'Vernon Lee' (Violet Paget),
and old Edward Carpenter.*

Monro was not a happy exile, for he was not—and was never
destined to be—a genuinely happy man. In Italy as in England, he
was torn between the extremes of his own nature. All his life 'he
was haunted, the wild Celt in him at odds with the thrifty heir of

* In Florence, fortunately, he also met the young Arundel del Ré, whom he was
to take back to England with him and install as sub-editor of *PR* and, for a time,
*PD*. To del Ré we owe much of our information about Monro's activities from 1911
to 1914. His three-part study already referred to above ('Georgian Reminiscences',
*SEL*, XII, 322–31, 460–71; and XIV, 27–42) is one of the two major sources of
information about Monro, the other being F. S. Flint's biographical preface to
Monro's collected poems. Although del Ré is a good reporter, he is not an unbiased
witness. His little-known study is a mine of information, but when he turns from facts
to conclusions he sometimes loses objectivity. Monro's influence on English poetry,
especially during the pre-war period, has too long and too frequently been underestimated, but del Ré seems a bit too completely sealed of the tribe of Monro.

a line of cautious physicians. He was a living contradiction in terms. . . . It is hardly possible to state one of his characteristics without immediately being reminded that in him too was its opposite'.[4] During his stay in Florence he fell under the spell of Edward Carpenter, but though he undoubtedly shared many of the older man's views on guild craftsmanship and the virtues of the rural life, Monro's Lowland Scots sense of practicality never permitted him to get out on to some of the more extreme fringes of the Socialist movement. Even as a Fabian, Monro managed to stay, characteristically, in the centre.

Nevertheless, there is perhaps no more apt example than Harold Monro of that typical pre-war marriage between the spirit of political liberalism and the zeal for poetic renaissance. By 1910, from out of his creed of Fabian social and political liberalism he had begun to fashion some abiding convictions on the place of poetry and the task of the poet in the new age. He had come to believe that 'it was the duty of the modern poet to give poetical expression to the ideas and feelings of the new age that, he believed, was dawning; an age in which man must finally cast off worn-out beliefs and meaningless traditions and begin to live more joyously and rationally because better acquainted with the laws of nature and of his own being'. Monro was never either exclusively an editor, publisher, shopkeeper, or poet. He was also deeply concerned with social, economic, and political problems of the new century. Poetry for Monro was not a fine art, esoteric, remote from everyday life, but rather 'an integral part of life itself', and he believed firmly 'that cultivation of the mind along broad lines is a necessary condition for the writing as well as for the proper understanding and criticism of poetry'.[5] In these respects Monro was thoroughly typical of that group of young poets who graduated from the Universities and reached their majority during the Edwardian decade, 'that brief morning, unsuspicious of war, when youth was developing the programme by which it meant to reform the world . . . a time oppressed by the gigantic shadows of the Victorians, but not yet come into its own daylight, [when] everyone feared to play the under-butler to Tennyson, and rushed in horror from sentimentality into realism, from aestheticism into self-realization and the cheerful robustness which seemed to be implied in the doctrine of the superman'.[6]

Both his personal convictions and outward events conspired to make it inevitable that Monro should return to England. Urged on by his good friend Maurice Hewlett (who offered Monro his own considerable assistance and prestige in whatever literary venture he should undertake), Monro returned to London in the fall of 1911 to embark upon his crusade to make poetry popular. The period of apprenticeship, of half-hearted, tentative trials and failures was drawing to a close. 'Hitherto, Shelley, vegetarianism, romantic idealism, a vague socialism, and his own fundamental incapacity to submit to discipline had rendered him ineffective both as a man and as a poet. He was to learn about men by the experience of them which money dealings give, and about poetry by the lash of other poets' tongues.'[7]

Precisely what Monro meant by the 'popularization' of poetry is difficult to say. It is even more difficult to point out which elements of the 'public' he wished to influence or appeal to. Monro himself was more often than not vague on both points. The central tenet of his faith, however, was that, given a proper chance, good poetry would sooner or later be taken to heart by the reading public. 'No one who has had any experience in the matter', he urged, 'imagines that the public taste in poetry, however perverted, is instinctively bad.'[8] It has merely been misguided by dilettanti, aesthetes 'in velvet coats and baggy trousers', who try to trick the public with their shoddy verse and then grow angry when the public resents being tricked. 'Our opinion', Monro cried, 'is that the poets and professors, instead of abusing the public for its deficiency of appreciation, should, with occasional humbleness, remember rather to deplore their own inability to provide the public with the poetry it desires.'[9]

But in his attack on public taste Monro was wise enough not to attempt to take the fortress by frontal assault. In the beginning at least, he attacked from the flank. He would never 'flaunt' his purposes before the reading public, he promised. He disavowed any intention of a 'conscious popularization of poetry' or of attempting to force the views of any coterie upon readers. His own creed was disarmingly simple: he believed only, he wrote, in the 'persistent cultivation and discussion [of poetry], and in its interpretation through the art of speaking verse'. His purpose, therefore, as he explained it at the beginning of his publishing career, was not to print large quantities of new verse or to 'discover' new poets—though he did both—but to change and educate public

taste. He would 'aim not so much at producing poetry', he concluded, 'as at stimulating the desire for it. We shall strive to create
an atmosphere. We shall attempt to coordinate the bases of
thought from which poetry at last emerges'.[10]

Monro became editor of *Poetry Review* in the fall of 1911. Earlier
in the year Galloway Kyle, Secretary of the Poetry Society, had
asked him to take over the editorship of the *Poetical Gazette*, official
organ of the Society, but Monro had refused, suggesting instead
that he found an independent periodical of his own into which the
*Gazette* could be incorporated. His offer was accepted, and a relationship was begun which was to turn out pleasantly for neither
the Society nor Monro. The first number of *Poetry Review* was
published in January 1912. Monro continued as editor until December of the same year, when his connection with the journal was
terminated by a curt announcement by the Director of the Poetry
Society: 'Mr. Harold Monro, having decided to enlarge the scope
of his periodical by issuing it quarterly under the title *Poetry and
Drama*, the *Journal of the Poetry Society*, beginning with the next
number, January, will be issued under the Editorship of Mr.
Stephen Phillips.'[11]

Behind the announcement lay several months of tempestuous
disagreement between Monro and the Society, at the centre of
which was Monro's well-founded conviction that the Society desired primarily to puff the poetasters and conduct a well-mannered,
safe, and uncontroversial repository for the work of amateur
poetesses from Brighton, irrelevant lists of the Society's sponsors,
and notices of Society meetings from the provinces. Monro saw
the aims of his new journal in quite another light. He tried to make
*Poetry Review*, among other things, a journal of modern verse, 'the
representative organ chiefly of the younger generation of poets',
as he wrote. This course he promptly discovered to be distasteful,
if not to the Poetry Society as a whole, certainly to its Director.
Moreover, Monro 'refused to compromise to advertisers, supporters, famous people, or friends', and he 'insisted on bad verse
being called bad verse as often as the occasion required'. To make
matters worse, in his impatience to get on with the job in the fall
of 1911 Monro had, as he claimed, 'practically sold [himself] to the
Society'. He had consented to support the new journal for one
year from his own financial resources; to give the profits, if any,
to the Society after deducting only interest on the capital he had

invested; to incorporate the *Gazette* within its pages; to submit to decisions of a committee appointed by the Society to formulate both financial and editorial policies; and to respect any censure which might be passed by the Council of the Society.

The wonder is not that *Poetry Review* had its occasional weaknesses, but that any magazine at all was published. Opposed at every turn, hampered by the terms of his own precipitous agreement, Monro concluded by September 1912, that 'the future of the *Review* depended entirely upon the degree to which it could be kept clear of the influence of the Poetry Society'. After a culminating disagreement over making the journal a quarterly instead of a monthly, Monro withdrew from *Poetry Review* to found an entirely new journal.[12]

In the preface to his first number Monro clearly stated the position of *Poetry Review*. It would be neither conservative nor *avant-garde*, neither Right nor Left. *Poetry Review* would state the case for the Centre. Monro agreed with the Left at more than one point, however. Faint echoes of Futurist tone, and even phrasing, can be discerned in his strictures against the modern 'poetry of despair':

> Today the community must disguise rather than express its emotions; the best poetry of the time is the poetry of despair, a cry of the lost: the expression of our joy has fallen into the hands of literary tinkers and pedlars, or it is muffled in the roar of cities.
>
> Time is ripe for the forging of a weapon of criticism and for an emphatic enunciation of literary standards. Poetry should be, once more, seriously and reverently discussed in its relation to life, and the same tests and criteria be applied to it as to the other arts.[13]

Like most of the Leftists, too, Monro was convinced that the new poetry must be a strong, vigorous expression of the artist's personality, not spineless copying from the mouldy volumes of the past. 'Poetry is the finer essence of thought, the vivid expression of personality; it is never the mere product of literary skill and craftsmanship. Therefore we believe in personality before we believe in books, in life rather than in letters. We admire sincerity more than originality.'[14] But unlike the Leftists, Monro was not given to rant. *Poetry Review* was notably lacking in manifestoes, scurrility, or partisanship. 'We do not believe in destructiveness,' he wrote; 'nor do we propose to waste our energy in deploring what is, and thundering what might be. We shall try to avoid platitudes and windy denunciations: our attitude is that of the smiling philosopher. We shall discuss, not rant and quibble: we are earnest, but not too grave. Above all we hope we shall never be dull.'[15]

The general tone of *Poetry Review* corresponded closely to its stated aims. Its pages were open equally to all schools; Henry Newbolt and Maurice Hewlett were contributors as well as Ezra Pound and Filippo Marinetti. And though it was sympathetic to modernism, it insisted at the same time on retention of a good measure of poetic convention. Victor Plarr, for instance, commented on the necessity for conservatism in the midst of a radical age. The modern poet, he argued, was too much addicted to ' "new scholarship", new rhythms, and divers other futurist vagaries'. That experiment was necessary went without saying: 'man's time-worn feet have always needed a new pair of shoes'. But, he warned the Leftists, 'the shoes, after all, must be made on the old lasts if they are to be shoes at all'.[16] John Drinkwater, arguing the problem of 'Tradition and Technique', was equally equivocal. Let us be modern by all means, he seemed to say—but not too modern. Pattern in verse may 'be allowed to become irregular, but it must never be allowed to disappear altogether'.[17] Such criticism was eminently safe and unprovocative, stretching a tentative foot ever so slightly first to one side then to the other of the critical fence it straddled.

Monro's own contributions to *Poetry Review*, while also keeping a foot gingerly on each side of the fence, leaned more unmistakably to the Left. Attacked by the *New Age* for 'puffing the poetaster', Monro replied with a characteristic attack on extremism: 'we suffer from no illusions. Most of the best modern work is interesting rather as experiment than as achievement'. But, he added, it is far healthier that English poetry should be rife with experimental and, consequently, bad verse than that it should merely copy the stylized, derivative versifers of the past decade.[18] In his views on poetic technique Monro often showed himself to be well to the left of Centre. In his rejection of the forms of the past as models for the present and in his insistence upon a new poetic diction he made common cause with both Futurists and Imagists:

Poetry, like Society, has its laws, dogmas, conventions—and its rebels. Reform was never, perhaps, so expedient as now. Moreover, on all sides we find experimenters breaking the old rules. A new diction is demanded, and a return to life. We love the great poetry of the past for ever; but the life of to-day claims a manner of to-day, and the modern poet will be free, at all hazards, from the conventions of his predecessors. . . . We love the poets of the past and the older methods of poetry, and so of our reverence we ask the modern world no longer to imitate and repeat them.[19]

And on the question of poetic rhythms one sees portents even in 1912 of Monro's subsequent conversion to the cause of *vers libre*. Rhythms have become too regularized, he argued; modern poetry must turn to more fluid rhythms, those implicit in the subject, or as he called them (borrowing Ezra Pound's phrase), 'primary rhythms'.[20]

As a reviewer Monro also betrayed his Leftist leanings. He found Emilia Stuart Lorimer's poems worthy of publication in *Poetry Review* precisely because they were difficult and because they expressed the artist's personality. Her poetry, he said, is 'not literature for the indolent or superficial reader. . . . It is difficult because it is close and robust'. It is obscure; 'its mystery is not on the surface; it is never transparent, obvious, or too facile. Its manner is not forced; its archaisms are not affected . . . it is the raw and inevitable product of personality, or nothing'.[21] The reviewers of the *Egoist* or of *Rhythm* could scarcely have chosen any more 'modern' aspects of Miss Lorimer's poetry to praise than did Monro.

In spite of Monro's critical acuity, *Poetry Review* could not escape the pandemic disease of the little magazines: too much discussion of Art with a capital 'A' and Poetry with a capital 'P'. Much as he may have pledged his journal to avoid windy generalities, Monro nevertheless allowed such a heady definition as this one (by Darrell Figgis) to creep into its pages:

> For poetry is something before it comes into a form of words; it is Life being true to itself and defying the clock-face of Time in a perfection of eternal Being; it is an ecstasy and rapture that catches man away from the sordidness and ugliness of barter and exchange to a perfect realization of himself and his divinity; and it is therefore the secret of power and splendour, couching itself in rites and rhythms as power and splendour must always do.[22]

*Poetry Review* also had more than its share of uncritical reviews. In attempting to keep to the Centre, the journal frequently watered down its critical tenets until they had no tang at all. The nadir was reached with the fifth number (May 1912), which was devoted entirely to women poets. One of the reviewers—a lady of kind heart but dubious critical acumen—wrote, 'the rule should be: Appreciate all you can; be as catholic as possible. Destructive criticism impoverishes the world, and depreciation is only permissible in so far as it may be necessary to distinguish between the bract and the flower lest the honey be lost, or to warn off the imitator'.[23] The entire fifth number was in much the same vein. Each reviewer bowed reverently in the direction of his subject; each tried valiantly to find something kind to say about each poetess; each alluded to one or two faults which had been critical commonplaces since the first review of the subject's first book; and each chose as praiseworthy either the kinds of passages which were usually chosen on such occasions or passages which were patently sentimental or inept.*

Yet upon occasion Monro himself, as well as some of his contributors, could be delightfully trenchant. On 21st May 1912 an American poetess, Miss Beatrice Irwin, saw fit to give a public recital of her poems in Crosby Hall, Chelsea Embankment, in an attempt to demonstrate the principle of 'Geometric Harmony' in verse. One gathers that the lady considerably enlivened the recital by accompanying her readings with divers Chinese gongs of awesome size and formidable timbre. Monro gave her short shrift: 'If Miss Irwin's poetry has any merit, she herself is its worst enemy. . . . Poetry . . . had very little to do with Miss Irwin's performance.'[24] Arundel del Re dismissed Ezra Pound's *Sonnets and Ballate of Guido Cavalcanti* with the charge that, among other deficiencies, Pound's command of the Italian language was inadequate to the task he had attempted.[25] Edward Marsh reviewed Gordon Bottomley's *Chambers of Imagery (Second Series)* in a far more caustic manner than was customary in *Poetry Review*. Taking off the gloves, he attacked Bottomley's poetry for its 'turbid, obscure, not to say meaningless' language; its grossly irregular stanzaic structure; and a 'clumsy, prosaic, commonplace or redundant' word too frequently and obviously inserted 'for the sole purpose of rhyming'.[26] Now and then amid the ambivalent reviews of Monro's journal one finds a healthy drop of acid.

By the end of 1912 *Poetry Review* had made a start towards

---

* To his credit, Monro was not blind to the deficiencies of his journal and subsequently admitted that his fifth number was the nadir of *PR*.

achieving the aim Monro had set down for it in the first number. In spite of its deficiencies, it did stand for some 'literary standards', as Monro had claimed it would. Though it was obviously experimental, its circulation had almost constantly increased throughout the first year. And though Monro himself recognized that its success was limited, his experience during the probationary year hardened his enthusiasm into an unshakeable conviction that given the opportunity and some critical direction, the intelligent reading public would respond to good modern poetry in increasing numbers.[27] Moreover, *Poetry Review* had sponsored one of Monro's most cherished projects (and one which was subsequently to grow to sizeable proportions in the Poetry Bookshop), public readings of and lectures about poetry. Monro himself delivered the first of a series of lectures on poetry on 15th May 1912. At least two others were held in June and July 1912, the second being given by Darrell Figgis on 'The Sanction of Poetry', and the third by T. E. Hulme (advertised as 'the well-known lecturer on Bergson'), speaking on 'The New Philosophy of Art as Illustrated in Poetry'.[28] But the major contribution of *Poetry Review* to the poetic renaissance lay inside its own pages. As its sub-editor pointed out, the journal did at least judge poetry on its own merits: 'However tentative and even crude the critical attitude . . . may have sometimes been, it did consistently uphold the Crocean principle (at that time little recognised) that poetry is to be judged as poetry and not according to standards and prejudices that . . . have nothing to do with poetry.'[29]

The successor to *Poetry Review* was *Poetry and Drama*, the first issue of which appeared in March 1913. It was published quarterly until December 1914, when it announced suspension of publication for one year, a casualty of the war. It was destined never to reappear, being replaced after the war by yet another of Monro's journals, the *Chapbook*. In format *Poetry and Drama* closely resembled its predecessor, but it was rather markedly expanded over *Poetry Review* in both size and content. It contained far more new poetry and more and better critical articles. Monro exercised a freer and more direct hand in its critical policies, establishing an editorial section in which he frequently held forth at length on all matters poetic. In spite of the considerable sums of his own capital which Monro put into the magazine, *Poetry and Drama* ran into financial heavy weather, a fate common to every one of the little magazines of the period. In May 1914, Monro admitted privately that his journal was perilously near insolvency, and it might have foundered had not several supporters, among them Maurice Hewlett, banded together to save it.[30]

Out from under the hobbling agreement with the Poetry Society, and freed from incessant squabbles, Monro could for the first time freely indulge his own critical principles and tastes. He set out to make his new journal, in the first place, a more representative organ than *Poetry Review* had been. A glance at the book reviewers as well as the volumes chosen for extended review in the initial number of *Poetry and Drama* suggests not only its general excellence but also its catholicity: Henry Newbolt reviewed *Georgian Poetry* 1; Rupert Brooke, Gibson's *Fires*; F. S. Flint, Pound's *Ripostes*; Arundel del Re, Rabindranath Tagore's *Gitanjali*; Monro himself, Goldring's *Streets*; Bonamy Dobree, Middleton's *Poems: Second Series*; and Edward Storer, Mary Mills Patrick's *Sappho and the Island of Lesbos*. In the same number appeared an announcement of a thirty-pound prize awarded Rupert Brooke for 'Grantchester' as the best poem published in *Poetry Review* in 1912. The committee of judges which made the decision, and from which Brooke's poem received a 'decided majority', was as varied a body as one could wish for: Henry Newbolt, Ernest Rhys, Edward Thomas, Victor Plarr, Edward Marsh, T. E. Hulme, and Harold Monro.[31]

In *Poetry and Drama*, too, Monro pursued his aim of popularizing poetry, but with a slightly different method; now, instead of attempting only to create the proper environment for the florescence of poetry, Monro printed much more of the poetry itself. In view of the tentative and experimental tone of *Poetry Review*, in its pages Monro could, perhaps with some justification, disavow all intentions of '*conscious* popularization of poetry'.[32] In *Poetry and Drama* no such disclaimer could possibly appear. Among the more spectacular schemes broached in *Poetry and Drama* in 1913 was one which appeared very 'conscious' indeed: the publication of broadsides and chapbooks. The removal of poetry from the street to the study, Monro argued, was after all a phenomenon of the recent past. The trend could be reversed. 'No one', as he said, could believe that the public's taste in poetry was 'instinctively bad'; it was only 'perverted'. And he wanted to test his faith in the public's discrimination by printing and selling broadsides and chapbooks which would be 'accessible, portable, unconfusing, and above all, inexpensive'. The Lowland Scots side of his nature, however, soon led to second thoughts. The time was perhaps not yet entirely ripe for such a venture, he reluctantly admitted. Perhaps the commuter to East Croydon might still prefer the *Evening Standard* even to Masefield.[33] Monro had the opportunity—but only after the war—of putting his theories to the test in his *Chapbook*, a pocket-size monthly which, however, was not entirely what its title implied, and which came at a time (in 1919) when the poetic revival had lost much of its momentum.

He broached an even more visionary scheme privately to several of his friends in late 1912. 'We've something tremendous on the carpet,' he wrote John Drinkwater. 'Roughly the project is to read poetry in villages without formality, payment, pose, condescension, propaganda, or parson. You just give it to them like Eastern story-tellers, who gather people together at street corners. . . . It does not sound very much like this, but you should hear me explain it.'[34] The scheme came to nothing because it understandably failed to arouse any marked enthusiasm among Monro's friends and supporters and because it was too giddy even for Monro in a more reflective moment.

*Poetry and Drama* also demonstrates an intensification of Monro's swing towards modernism. He was by no means as yet sealed of the tribe of Ezra, but he had many good words to say for Imagism in general and Pound in particular because they gave short shrift to the poetasters. While characteristically warning his readers against taking Imagism and its practitioners too seriously, at the same time he professed nothing but admiration for 'their conviction and courage' in outfacing the British Bumbles.[35] The third issue of his new journal Monro devoted almost completely to the Futurist movement, especially as it affected English poetry. The concern with this alien and strange movement, he was aware, shocked many of the readers of *Poetry and Drama*, but his reasons for it must have been an even greater shock to those who had failed to remark the difference in tone between *Poetry and Drama* and *Poetry Review*. We are interested in this movement, Monro said bluntly, because 'we claim ourselves, also, to be futurists'! The distinction between his use of the lower-case letter *vis-à-vis* the blatantly capital 'F' habitually used by the Futurists undoubtedly escaped many readers. Monro sounded suspiciously like a genuine

Futurist as he indited a 'manifesto' of his own, setting forth his futurist first principles: 'I. To forget God, Heaven, Hell, Personal Immortality, and to remember always the earth. II. To lift the eyes from a sentimental contemplation of the past, and, though dwelling in the present, nevertheless, always to *live*, in the future of the earth.' Lest one might suspect that his futurism was not modern enough, or that it bore the slightest trace of odious nineteenth-century Positivism, Monro was quick to reassure the suspicious and the dubious: he was not 'hypothesising progress'. The very 'thought of perfectitude is odious to us: we reject it utterly'. Man must look to the future, cease his regretful, sentimental contemplation of the past and 'turn round and walk face forward, in love of the future'.[36]

Monro's flirtation with Futurism was not an entirely selfless *affaire de cœur*. One suspects that he was not above making what use he could of the shock value of Futurist doctrine and verse in order to forward his own cause of popularizing poetry. He himself testified that much of his admiration for the Futurists came about because he saw in them the living embodiments of his guiding principle that poetry could be popular. Impressed by the startling fact that the Italian Futurists had sold over 35,000 copies of their *Book of the Futurist Poets*, Monro concluded that the Italian Futurist movement at least 'propagated its doctrines actually and successfully in verse'. Their poetry, produced in an admirable 'spirit of fun and recklessness . . . automatically' thereby gains 'something of its popular appeal'.[37] It was the patent success of the Italian Futurist movement that Monro admired—and envied—not necessarily either its poetic ends or means.

By the end of 1913 Monro had grown noticeably cooler to Futurism. He felt impelled to warn his countrymen against a too slavish imitation of Futurist models, and he had begun to question the value of Futurist verse as anything beyond mere self-advertisement. By December 1913 he could write, 'We admire [Marinetti's] extraordinary inventiveness; we were enthralled by his declamation; but we do not believe that his present compositions achieve anything more than an advanced form of verbal photography.' Second thoughts assailed him, too, on the relevance of Futurism to the English poetic renaissance. English literature, he asserted, showed little of the kind of 'sentimental eroticism' of Italian literature against which the Futurists had successfully taken arms in 1909. More important, the poetic revival had endowed England by 1913 with a poetic middle class, so to speak. The Marxist analogy is not far-fetched: by 1913 a large buffer group of young poets stood between and blunted the shocks of the struggle for eminence between the aristocratic Right and the proletarian Left which had rent Italian artistic and poetic circles in 1909. These were the Centrists, the important group of young poets who, said Monro, were 'content neither to draw their inspiration from the past nor to suffer its forms to pass unmodified to their needs'. Italy solved its artistic problems according to its own temperament; England must work out its poetic resurrection according to the English temperament.[38]

Concurrently with the publication of *Poetry and Drama* Harold Monro embarked upon the venture which was to become his most famous and in many ways most valuable contribution to the poetic revival, the Poetry Bookshop. One would like to say that the founding of the Bookshop was the result of years of planning, Monro's conscious and deliberate response to the demands of the burgeoning poetic renaissance, a dream realized. Actually, the beginning of the Poetry Bookshop was a good deal less dramatic; indeed, it was almost fortuitous. In October and November 1912, when Monro was making every effort to get his newly founded *Poetry Review* out from under the influence of the Poetry Society, he thought it expedient to transfer the *Review's* offices from 93 Chancery Street to a place farther removed from the Society's immediate scrutiny. A magnificently proportioned eighteenth-century house at 35 Devonshire Street, off Theobald's Road in Bloomsbury, captured his fancy and suited his purse. In an area of decayed grandeur, the house contained an empty shop on its first floor. Monro's enthusiasm and imagination turned the apparent defect into a virtue, for seeing the shop he was struck with the idea of making the entire house into the centre of what he called 'an informal guild' for poets. In the shop he would sell volumes of poetry; in several of the second-floor rooms he would edit his journal and set himself up as a publisher of poetry as well; a large garret room would be used for his cherished project of public poetry readings; and several smaller rooms would be rented to indigent poets. Such was the off-hand, almost accidental, genesis of one of the most famous poetic landmarks of twentieth-century London.[39]

If the conception of the Poetry Bookshop was unpremeditated, the birth was well and deliberately advertised. Monro first published the happy news abroad in the November issue of *Poetry Review*. Announcing that on 1st January 1913 there would be opened at 35 Devonshire Street 'a Bookshop for the sale of poetry, and of all books, pamphlets and periodicals connected directly or indirectly with poetry', he disavowed any desire to compete with recognized book-sellers, claiming that his shop would deal in volumes which they would consider unmarketable or uneconomical to handle. In other ways, too, the Poetry Bookshop was designed to be a bookshop with a difference. Monro candidly recognized the obvious advantages of publishing a critical journal in conjunction with a bookstore: in the periodical 'we shall recommend to the public what to read'; and 'in the Bookshop we shall sell them what we have recommended'. Monro's motives, however, were not purely financial. The Bookshop never made a profit. To the contrary, during its first ten years it cost Monro between seven and eight thousand pounds out of his own pocket.[40] His motives were rather more selfless. The poetry-reading public, he explained, though sizeable, was scattered and unorganized. He proposed 'to draw this public together and bring it into touch, through the Bookshop, with poetry as a living art, and as represented in the work of living poets'.[41]

Monro also intended the Poetry Bookshop to function as an avenue for popularizing the work of the new, young poets of whatever school who were clamouring to be heard. In the pre-war years, not only *Georgian Poetry* and the poetry of James Elroy Flecker and Ralph Hodgson, but also F. S. Flint's *Cadences*, Richard Aldington's *Images*, and Ezra Pound's anthology *Des Imagistes* were published under the Poetry Bookshop imprint. Owing to a curious (and temporary) blind spot in his poetic judgment, however, Monro muffed his chance to publish a work which might eventually have made the Bookshop imprint more widely known than that of any other publisher of poetry in London. Conrad Aiken records that when he met T. S. Eliot in July 1914, Eliot 'rather shyly' showed him the manuscript of 'The Love Song of J. Alfred Prufrock'. Impressed, Aiken offered to help place it with a publisher. He sought out Harold Monro, but, as Aiken writes, Monro 'called it "absolutely inane" and practically threw it back at me, saying, "I can't be bothered with this".' Not daunted, Aiken returned the manuscript to Monro for a second reading but was again rebuffed, and so he turned to Ezra Pound, who of course saw to it that the poem was published in Harriet Monroe's *Poetry*.*

In his statement of aims Monro made it clear that the Poetry Bookshop would stand with the Centre. Although it would fight for the principle that new poetic forms were necessary to meet new exigencies, Monro wrote, 'formlessness is only permissible where it is absolutely necessary'. The Bookshop would abhor 'formalism, pose, affection, inflation, and all kinds of false traditionalism'; it would be sworn enemy to 'the monotonous jingling of the rhymed quatrain', to 'flat, heavy, blank verse', to 'everlasting repetition of worn-out phrases, symbols, and images', in a word, to '*cliché* in all its tedious and detestable forms'. Above all it would stand for artistic freedom, for the right of the artist to write on what subjects he chooses as he chooses. But again, in the name of the Bookshop, Monro warned the innovators: 'Liberty in our time is too prone to become license, the desire merely to startle the public is on the rapid ascendant. Perhaps the public needs startling; yet, if so, let it be by beauty, not mere novelty; may the surprise excite wonder, not fizzle out in satisfied curiosity.'[42] The tone is familiar: let us by all means be modern—but not too modern.

The Poetry Bookshop opened its doors in December 1912. The first public reading of poetry in its famous garret room took place in January 1913, when Rupert Brooke read from his *Poems*.† The locale of the Bookshop lent it a touch of Bohemia from the start. Devonshire Street was, to put it bluntly, in the slums, a fact scarcely mitigated by Monro's attempt to court respectability by advertising the Bookshop as being 'only five minutes' walk from the British Museum' (which was indeed the truth, if not the whole

---

* Charles Norman, *Ezra Pound*, pp. 165–6. A year later, however, Monro had apparently changed his views on 'Prufrock'. On 25th Sept. 1915, Ezra Pound wrote Harriet Monroe: 'Monro discovered "Prufrock" on his unaided own and asked me about the author when I saw him last night. . . . He was very glad to hear that T. S. E. was in the forefront of our [*Catholic*] *Anthology*' (*The Letters of Ezra Pound*, ed. Paige, p. 108).

† Though the point is perhaps not crucial, some confusion has been occasioned by the fact that although the Bookshop subsequently advertised itself as having opened in January 1913, evidence exists that it was in operation in December 1912. The difficulty is resolved by distinguishing between the formal opening—which did in fact take place in January—and the actual opening of the doors of the shop for the purpose of selling books, which occurred in December. My data are taken from my interview with Mrs. Monro and were corroborated by Mr. Hassall, who cited as his authority Sir Edward Marsh's diary.

truth). Sir Osbert Sitwell, an *habitué*, described the establishment as 'a medium-sized house of Rowlandsonian aspect—with a pediment bearing in its centre, with an elliptical frame, an appropriate date—in Devonshire Street: a narrow street running out of Theobald's Road, rather dark, but given over to screaming children, lusty small boys armed with catapults, and to leaping flights of eighteenth-century cats'.[43] The suspicion soon grew to a certainty that in an equally Rowlandsonian house across the street from the Bookshop several ladies of pleasure plied their trade in a distinctly Hogarthian manner. Of more menace to would-be customers and congregating poets, however, were the hordes of urchins armed not only with catapults but with sharp tongues. One of their chief delights was to follow Rupert Brooke up the street to the Bookshop taunting him with shrill cries of 'Buffalo Bill!', an epithet which Brooke earned by his affectation of long hair.[44]

In the upstairs rooms several poets took up residence, availing themselves of Monro's offer to rent rooms 'at a moderate rate to those in sympathy with our aims, who are temporarily in London, and care to avail themselves of our hospitality'.[45] Among the poets who lived in Devonshire Street in 1913 and 1914 were Wilfrid Gibson, Wilfred Owen, and T. E. Hulme. Robert Frost took rooms for himself and his whole family for some weeks in 1913. It was a memorable experience for the self-exiled American poet just beginning to come into his own in a foreign land. Frost wrote home in March 1913: 'The fellow that runs [the Bookshop] and edits the quarterly I speak of is a poet and all about him are the poets my friends and enemies. Gibson had a room there for a year before he married the proprietor's secretary. Epstein, the futurist sculptor . . . whose work is such a stumbling block to the staid and Victorianly but who in spite of all is reckoned one of the greatest living geniuses, will be across the hall from us. It will be something that Lesley and the children will be sure to remember.'[46] Accommodations above the Bookshop varied considerably according to availability of rooms and the size of the prospective guest's purse. Gaudier-Brzeska, who did not always report facts entirely accurately, commented on a visit to Devonshire Street:

> I went with Marsh to see Gibson. . . . All the poets have joined together to hire a big house near the British Museum, where they live and work, and have underneath it a shop where they sell poetry by the pound—and talk to the intellectuals. Some of them have huge,

(*right*) Harold Monro
hanging the sign of the
Poetry Bookshop after it
moved to new premises
at 38 Great Russell Street
in October 1926

(*below*) Harold Monro at
his desk in the Poetry
Bookshop, 1926

*Courtesy of Mrs. Harold
Monro*

John Drinkwater, *c.* 1910

vast rooms, while those like Gibson have only a tiny hole. He is boxed in a room, over the door of which is written, 'In case of fire access to the roof through this room'.[47]

One of the chief attractions of the Poetry Bookshop was its utterly informal atmosphere. 'Here,' said Monro in truth, 'we have simply a few people gathered together, and, since the English climate is bad, a house—otherwise a field or a beach might have done.' Summing up the accomplishments of the first year of the Bookshop's existence, Monro astutely recognized his major asset, and he predicted that his Bookshop could become a permanent part of the literary scene only if it did 'not depart from its present happy vagabond way of existence and seek to become an *institution*'.[48] Wisely, Monro never allowed the Bookshop to take on the aura of an 'official' society for the propagation of poetry. His experience in 1912 had warned him well of the limitations inherent in such societies. The 'happy vagabond way of existence' was well exemplified by the public readings of poetry. Bound into every copy of *Poetry and Drama* was a detachable card admitting the bearer to one of the readings, held bi-weekly on Tuesdays and Thursdays at six p.m. Admissions to single readings could also be acquired by placing in a box in the Poetry Bookshop—threepence. The readings, or 'poetry squashes', as they came to be called, were held in a poorly lighted attic room which Edward Marsh described as 'a kind of loft which looked as if it was meant to keep apples in, and one ought to get into it by a ladder through a trap-door'.[49] How many members of the general public they attracted is nowhere recorded; one suspects not many. But the readings were well attended by all sorts of poets, and although many a vociferous argument raged in Monro's reading room, many useful friendships were also begun. It was at a reading in January 1913, for instance, that Robert Frost struck up an acquaintance with F. S. Flint, the first professional English poet Frost had met; and through Flint he was quickly introduced to Ezra Pound.[50] The poetry squashes were often considerably enlivened by outbursts from unexpected quarters. Incongruously, the formidable Amy Lowell came to hear Rupert Brooke read his poems. Sitting towards the back of the room and being unable to hear Brooke, whose voice had small carrying power, she rose imperiously and shouted at the young poet, 'Speak up! Speak up!'[51]

Monro was almost fanatically certain that the best means of

getting poetry out of the study and into the public consciousness was by sensitive oral interpretation. So important a role did his public readings assume, in fact, that he came to refer to the volumes of poetry for sale in the Bookshop as merely 'printed scores for the convenience of refreshing the memory in hours of study or indolence'. Poetry could not be allowed to become, he asserted, merely 'pure literature'; rather, 'it is the supreme form of verbal expression, and, as such, is of no signification in the dusty shelves of libraries, of no specific value until brought out into the active ways of life'.[52]

Another feature which the pre-war poets found attractive in the Poetry Bookshop was its catholicity. Any organization which attracted to its meeting-rooms poets of such divergent persuasions as Filippo Marinetti and W. H. Davies, Ezra Pound and Lascelles Abercrombie, F. S. Flint and John Drinkwater, T. E. Hulme and Robert Frost, was certainly not narrowly secular. In his basic poetic sympathies Monro himself was obviously not, in 1913–14, coterie-minded. He managed to get along with Futurists, Vorticists, Imagists, verslibrists, and, later, with even the more or less intractably modern poets who clustered around the Sitwells' *Wheels*. Sir Osbert Sitwell's testimony must be allowed to sum up that of many others, for its essence is repeated again and again by poets, both lesser and greater, contemporaneously and in retrospect.

> The Poetry Bookshop constituted, under the most considerate and, indeed, inspired of hosts, Harold Monro, a great meeting-place: for not only was he a friend of all the poets of his generation, but new work always attracted, though it may sometimes have irritated, him. He was indulgent to all poets. He liked new ideas even when they did not match his own, and in the large comfortable, panelled rooms above the shop, he would often of an evening bring together whole schools of poets of the most diverse faith, opinions, and temperaments. . . . Sometimes there would be a battle, but always one heard the literary news and was told of small incidents which, though the world's foundations have been shaken since those days, continue even now to come back to the mind. . . .
>
> Whatever outbreaks had taken place, one left Harold Monro's parties enlivened, and grateful to him: for he was an excellent host.*

* Sir Osbert Sitwell, *Laughter in the Next Room*, p. 34. In this particular passage Sir Osbert is speaking of the Bookshop immediately after the war, but it was if anything even more cosmopolitan in the pre-war years.

It is too much to expect, however, that either Monro or his methods would have been universally popular. His personality, forthright and precipitate, raised the hackles of a few of his fellow-poets. Others were by no means so enthusiastic about public reading as Monro. Though they felt compelled from self-interest to read their verse whenever they were requested, several began to look upon their appearances as more of a chore than an opportunity. Such an attitude is apparent in several letters which Lascelles Abercrombie wrote Edward Marsh in late 1913 and 1914. In one Abercrombie pleaded with Marsh to come to his (Abercrombie's) reading at the Bookshop on 29th May. 'Monro has asked me to supper afterwards,' he added; 'I couldn't but accept—tho' with a certain reluctance. . . . However, I get on very well with Monro.' In another he referred to his forthcoming reading as 'a dreary affair', and in several of them he made it quite clear that he did not want to stay at the Bookshop any longer than absolutely necessary to finish what he called his 'stunt'.[53]

Monro's editorial judgments also irked some of the would-be contributors to his journals. In his determination to avoid being taken in by flattery, he no doubt wounded some feelings. When the young John Gould Fletcher, fresh from America, went to the Poetry Bookshop to try to interest Monro in his work, he testified that he encountered only 'Monro's iron gruffness and lack of cordiality'. Rebuffed, he sent Monro 'a laudatory sonnet, entitled "The Bookshop in the Slum",' hoping, as Fletcher confessed, 'through overmuch flattery' to enkindle Monro's interest in his verse. Monro was unimpressed: Fletcher received in reply only 'a vaguely noncommittal note that was even more deadly than a flat refusal'.[54]

The comments which accompanied Monro's rejection slips were not always non-committal; they were more likely to be blunt to the point of rudeness. Though he was determined to keep the standards of *Poetry Review* and *Poetry and Drama* on the highest level, his judgments were both highly personal and, sometimes, arbitrary. James Stephens was among those poets who received a rejection slip apparently accompanied by a rather too graceless comment from Monro. He wrote Edward Marsh from Paris:

> By the way, isn't Harold Monro a friend of yours? My heavy curse on him. He has just returned me the best poem I've ever written with the statement that it isn't up to his standard. . . .

99

> I sometimes am afflicted with the idea that poetry is all damn rot (except when it's been written by me). Look at Monro! Imagine that chap turning me down and I hitting him with masterpieces. Do kill him. Kill him bloodily and painfully.... Do agonizing things to him. Read him his own poetry as long as you can stand it and then choke him with his own book. Make him eat his words.[55]

Obviously Stephens's comments were jocular, but the pique at Monro none the less showed through his Irish good humour.

In spite of certain obvious shortcomings, by 1913 Harold Monro had made himself a figure to be reckoned with on the London literary scene. The precise source of his power is difficult to define. Certainly he could be expected to have wielded some influence by virtue of being editor of *Poetry and Drama*, for a good review or a poem or two published in that journal was a considerable feather in the cap of any poet, especially a young one. But if his influence lay in anything tangible, it lay primarily in the Poetry Bookshop. The Bookshop was all things to all people. To the poetry-reading public it was a unique bookstore where one could receive friendly advice and, if required, direction; and where upon occasion one could rub elbows with the great and the near-great and hear them read their own verse. To the young poet with a manuscript it was a publishing house, the only one in London which specialized in publishing the work of new poets. To the more mature poet of whatever coterie it was a meeting-place where he could gather with his peers and be assured of conversation which ranged from the austerely intellectual to the merely gossipy. But above all, for Harold Monro it afforded the means of keeping his finger constantly upon the pulse of the poetic renaissance. No flutter, however slight, could escape him.

# 4

## Edward Marsh

As editor of *Georgian Poetry* from 1912 to 1922 Edward Marsh gained the kind of fame to be compared in the history of English poetry perhaps to that of Tottel.* Moreover, as an influential anthologizer and as the recognized doyen of a circle which included most of the famous names of early twentieth-century British poetry, Marsh organized and gave direction to one of the most important phases of the poetic renaissance. It was largely owing to Marsh's zeal for popularizing new poets, his extraordinary talents for organizing, and his literary tastes that for better or worse there came into being a new poetic coterie during the second decade. Marsh came upon the scene, of course, at precisely the right moment. By late 1912 the poetic renaissance was in full swing, but it was disorganized and sporadic. Marsh set out to organize a public reception for the new poetry. He succeeded beyond the wildest hopes of any of the poets who participated in

* Edward Marsh was later (1937) to become Sir Edward Marsh, K.C.V.O., C.B., C.M.G. Richly deserved though it was, the title strikes the ear as just a bit incongruous, for the first thing one discovers in reading the literature of the period is that among friends, enemies, and mere acquaintances alike he was referred to almost without exception as Eddie Marsh. Somehow the very euphony of the syllables seems to fit the man. Not that one is therefore tempted to use such a familiar appellation in a literary history. But when one writes from inside the point of view of Sir Edward's close friends, as I must frequently do, and especially when one deals, as I must in this and subsequent chapters, with a large body of correspondence written to him by contemporary poets, the 'Sir Edward' comes hard, not to say unnaturally. One therefore readily understands how the familiar and ubiquitous 'Eddie' has been —unfortunately, as I believe—acquiesced in by several scholars who have preceded me in writing of the Georgian period but to whom Sir Edward was as much a stranger as he was to me. At the risk of a tone, then, which must strike one as just a shade too formal to do entire justice to the man, I have shunned the familiar 'Eddie' in any circumstances except, of course, direct quotation. No race of men should be more zealous to preserve British proprieties than American Anglophiles.

his first venture. But he also succeeded, though unwittingly and perhaps unwillingly, in founding a poetic school as well.

At first glance there would seem to be no more unlikely figure than Edward Marsh to stand forth as champion of the new poetry. He was born in 1872, the son of an eminent surgeon and Professor of Surgery at Cambridge who before he died had become Master of Downing. His upbringing was in the best tradition of the Victorian upper middle class. He was a day boy at Westminster and went from there to Trinity College, Cambridge, where he took a Classical Tripos. Studying under the great A. W. Verrall, who, as he was later to record, had an immeasurable effect on shaping his literary tastes, Marsh learned the Classics to perfection. He was aided in his studies, as throughout his life, by an incredible memory for verse by means of which he could recite almost the whole of *Paradise Lost* or recall, years after having read the text, the precise syntax of the most obscure Latin poet.

From Cambridge Marsh entered the Civil Service. He had become a First Class Clerk in the Colonial Office at the end of 1905, when, at the urging of several of Marsh's titled friends, Winston Churchill made Marsh his private secretary. It was in this position, indeed, that Marsh was to spend his most fruitful and important years in the Civil Service. When Churchill went to the Board of Trade in 1908, and then to the Admiralty in 1911, Marsh accompanied him, playing Ruth, as he phrased it, to Churchill's Naomi. In 1912 Edward Marsh, if he was known at all outside a very select circle, was known as Winston Churchill's private secretary, an efficient, knowledgeable, and self-effacing Civil Servant who moved in the most rarified strata of titled and upper-class England.

To those who knew Marsh more intimately his appearance as editor of an anthology and champion of the new verse seemed neither so sudden nor so out of character as it must have seemed to the less well informed. Marsh's tastes had always been literary; he had grown up surrounded by good books and was in all seasons of life an omnivorous reader. His inclinations and ability had led him to cultivate from among the literary figures of the time a wide circle of friends which included both his contemporaries and the authors of the older generation. The list of his literary friends and acquaintances before and during the first decade of the century is impressive: Edmund Gosse, Henry James, Robert Bridges, Sidney Colvin, E. M. Forster, Bernard Shaw, James Barrie, Maurice

Baring, Walter de la Mare, John Galsworthy, John Masefield, and Bertrand Russell.

The interest in modern verse which was eventually to lead to the editorship of *Georgian Poetry* came upon Marsh slowly and was the result of a series of events which occurred largely in 1911 and 1912. He unconsciously prepared himself for his conversion from ancient to modern poetry by first allowing himself to be converted from classic to modern art. An inveterate and perceptive collector of pictures throughout his life, Marsh possessed at his death one of the finest selective private collections in England. Until 1911 he had confined himself largely to eighteenth- and early nineteenth-century water colours and to one courageous purchase of the entire Richard Horne collection of drawings by such masters as Rowlandson, Constable, Gainsborough, and Blake.[1] 'It was inevitable,' however, as Brinsley Ford wrote, 'that sooner or later so warm-hearted a humanist should turn from the work of the dead to that of the living, and we know that the "conversion" took place about 1911 when he bought Duncan Grant's *Parrot Tulips*. From then onwards he collected only the works of young painters.'[2] In spite of the predilection for his contemporaries after 1911, Marsh was still capable of such catholicity of artistic taste that, as John Rothenstein remarked, he often 'provoked his friends to wonder whether there was any work of art which he *didn't* like'.[3] It was always an open question among his friends which of two motives more strongly impelled Marsh to collect contemporary works: whether he bought many of them because, like the true collector, he felt his desire for the possession of beauty aroused, or whether he purchased them in order to encourage a climate for good art. Marsh himself confessed to both motives. He was at once a patron of artists and a man of discerning tastes, who, by frequent judicious purchases from young and striving artists, became, as a colleague in the Contemporary Art Society called him, 'the greatest friend that our painters and poets have found in the twentieth century'.[4]

From an interest in modern art it was only a short step to an interest in modern poetry. Marsh himself recorded the fortuitous event. Tiring of a life which he felt was being too single-mindedly devoted to social pleasures, he was searching in 1911, as he said, for 'some other object for my spare time'.[5] Most opportunely he chanced to meet Francis Meynell and soon had become not only a good friend of the young poet but also a welcome guest in the circle which included his mother, Alice Meynell. In 1911 both the Meynells, mother and son, had become greatly interested in contemporary verse. Until then, Marsh had scarcely dipped into that field, preferring his poetry, as he said, 'vintage'; but Francis Meynell 'poured the new wine into my old bottle, and I drank deep'. Through the ministrations of the Meynells he was brought to an awareness of the new age dawning. 'The country seemed to be pullulating with new poets,' he wrote later, 'but there were two "events" of that year [1911] which to my mind put it past a doubt that a golden age was beginning. One was Masefield's *Everlasting Mercy*, which I read in such a turmoil of excitement that I have never dared read it again, for fear of not recapturing the rapture. The other was Rupert Brooke's *Poems*.'[6]

Marsh's enthusiasm for Brooke's volume and his new-found poetic convictions made inevitable further and headier draughts of the new wine. In February 1912, through the good offices of Francis Meynell, Harold Monro offered Marsh an opportunity to proclaim his ardour from the pages of *Poetry Review*: 'Meynell tells me that you are enthusiastic about Rupert Brooke's poems, and that . . . you are willing to write a review of them for the April issue of this paper,' Monro wrote. Brooke's *Poems* had been selected as 'the Book of the Month', Monro explained, and therefore the 'article on it should be rather in the nature of an appreciation than of a criticism'.[7] Marsh acceded with alacrity, and his review of Rupert Brooke, which was published in April, became his introduction not only to Monro but to many other young poets who were contributors to *Poetry Review* and whose work tended to place them in the Centre party of the contemporary poetic scene. During 1912 Marsh further cemented his friendship with Harold Monro which, though it lacked the warmth and intimacy of his relationships with several other poets, was long and fruitful.

In addition to wide learning and consuming zeal, Marsh had other attributes which well qualified him to take a leading hand as patron of the new poetry. As private secretary to one of the most widely discussed figures in the land, Edward Marsh found few important doors closed to him. He was not slow to use his influence in many quarters on behalf of his poets. Nor did he fail to take some pride, one suspects, in his wide acquaintanceship among

London literary, artistic, and political lions. By means of it, at any rate, he was able to dazzle the eyes of some of the less cosmopolitan poets who habitually used his rooms in Gray's Inn as their head-quarters during occasional visits to London. Returning to rural Gloucestershire after such a visit, Lascelles Abercrombie expressed to his host the mixture of awe and gratitude which many poets felt after a few heady evenings with Marsh in London: 'It is quite impossible for me to thank you for the perfectly glorious time you gave me. The time of my life, nothing less. I seem to have been in the visions of God, on a Miltonic mount of speculation, viewing the whole of modern life in an amazing succession of dazzling instants, from Henry James to Austin Harrison, from lovely ladies to Cubists. I never had anything like it before. Henceforth you stand for London to me.'[8] Indeed, for this particular visit Marsh had outdone himself. Writing to Rupert Brooke, who was more accustomed than Abercrombie to rubbing elbows with the mighty, he ill concealed his pride as he outlined for Brooke's approval a truly impressive round of activities:

March 22nd, 1914

I had a delightful visit last Saturday to Wednesday from Lascelles Abercrombie. I tried to show him as many aspects of London as could be got into the time, here is the programme, do you think it was good? Sat. Denis Browne and Clive Carey to tea, then *Midsummer Night's Dream* with a visit to Lillah [McCarthy] between the acts. Sunday, W. H. Davies and Michael [Sadleir] to breakfast—luncheon with the Dunsanys—a beauty-party at tea here, Cathleen [Nesbitt], Diana [Manners], Katharine [Horner] and Ruby Peto, all looking their very best (Lascelles almost speechless with admiration, he didn't know there *were* such people!), dinner with Gosse and Henry James who was *magnificent*, with adjournment to Cathleen's rooms (to meet Sarah Allgood and Marie O'Neill, but they didn't turn up). Monday the Ihlee show at Carfax, which is very good, Ralph Hodgson and Basil Dean to luncheon, the Palace in the evening to see Nijinsky, but alas he was suddenly ill so we only had Wilkie Bard, then Café Royal with Mark Gertler and Jack Squire and a distant view of Epstein. Tuesday I was no good, as it was the Naval Estimates. I got L. into the House to hear Winston's speech which was rather dull and tech-nical, and L. had to go before the end part, which was better, to read the *End of the World* at the Bookshop, and we only met at T. E. Hulme's after 11—and L. had to go next morning.[9]

Small wonder Brooke could reply, in the face of such a muster roll of personages and events, 'even the best of the best people in Ryton—nay, Dymock itself—must have seemed a little tame after that'.[10] And many another poet fared almost as well as Abercrombie when he visited Gray's Inn. One should not suggest, however, that Marsh's activities on behalf of his poets were undertaken solely for the purpose of impressing them with the London scene. He was assiduous in cultivating what he considered proper and useful contacts for the poets he befriended. In reading the correspondence Marsh left behind, one is struck by the large numbers of letters from poets of all kinds thanking him for a valuable introduction to another poet, a critic, an editor, or a publisher.

In addition to the prestige which came from unquestioned position, Marsh possessed what one may call a collector's instinct. He collected his circle of poets, one feels, in much the same manner and for much the same motives that he collected the modern paintings which were beginning to cover his walls. There is little doubt that Edward Marsh was the kind of person who enjoyed playing the benefactor. He was always ready to befriend unheralded or impecunious poets. Several of strenuously independent mind were notably averse to being taken under anyone's wing, including Marsh's, and misunderstandings ensued. But by and large the young poets were happy to receive the Marsh benefactions, for nothing beyond friendship was requested or required in return.

Moreover, Edward Marsh had money. And he was generous to an extreme. He was never by his own reckoning a wealthy man, but as most of the poets he admitted to his circle discovered, sizeable financial aid could be counted on from Marsh at need. It would be entirely futile even to attempt to list the numbers of poets who received loans or gifts of money from Edward Marsh when they were financially hard pressed. Frequently the loans were repaid; more frequently, one suspects, they were not. Marsh found indirect ways of aiding his poets, too, such as paying generously for his board and room whenever he visited their homes for any extended period. Working through his friend Edmund Gosse, he was the instigator of action which eventually resulted in grants from government funds to both Lascelles Abercrombie and Gordon Bottomley; and he made Abercrombie the additional beneficiary of a twenty-five pound gift deposited anonymously to the poet's account.[11] Thoroughly characteristic, too, was his early assistance to Wilfrid Gibson. He paid a pound per week to Middleton Murry, who in turn hired Gibson, at Marsh's suggestion, to act as sub-editor of *Rhythm* and paid him the pound for his services.[12] It was typical of Marsh's arrangements in such delicate matters that Gibson did not discover the truth until Murry published his autobiography in 1935.[13] Indeed, as Murry admitted, *Rhythm* itself 'owed its very existence to Marsh's generosity', a generosity which included, among other things, a loan of a hundred pounds.*

Even though he possessed many attributes which admirably qualified him as the Georgian impresario, Edward Marsh was not the perfect anthologist. In the first place, in spite of his enthusiastic advocacy of modern verse, in spite of the wide range of his poetic tastes, Marsh's heart remained sufficiently with his 'vintage' poets that he was unable to tolerate much of the work being done by the more experimental poets of the age. His antipathy towards Marinetti has been remarked; his antipathy towards Pound and his school was no less severe.† One should not conclude, on the other hand, as too many critics have done, that Marsh's tastes were entirely hidebound. In many ways they were like those of Harold Monro, and he no doubt felt most comfortable, poetically speaking, among the group of Centrist poets who tended to gravitate towards Monro's Poetry Bookshop. Like them, like Monro, Marsh was willing, even eager, to be thought modern—but not too modern.

Secondly, Marsh's approach to poetry was essentially that of the

---

* John Middleton Murry, *Between Two Worlds*, pp. 237–8. Like several others, Murry sometimes felt himself too greatly indebted to Marsh for his own peace of mind. Even after it had become apparent in 1914 that repayment of approximately eighty pounds of the hundred-pound loan would be long delayed, if not impossible, Marsh sent Murry a gift of five pounds. Murry was moved to express his gratitude and to ask a question of Marsh which must also have occurred to other less forthright recipients of the Marsh largesse: 'I don't know why you do these things, Eddie. Is it to heap coals of fire? I'm sure it isn't—but it hit me all of a heap. My normal state of mind towards you is one of fright because of all that money. . . . You see that the real trouble is that no one has ever treated me as you have. It's outside my experience, and it makes me nervous and afraid' (undated letter, but *c.* mid-1914, *MLC*). See also Murry's detailed account of his early friendship with Marsh in Hassall, *Edward Marsh*, pp. 215–20. For an account of Marsh's part in salvaging *Rhythm* from threatened bankruptcy, see F. A. Lea, *The Life of John Middleton Murry*, p. 34.

† Edward Marsh, *A Number of People*, pp. 276, 328. The antipathy may best be observed not so much in what he says of Pound as in the curious fact that he can write a 410-page memoir, much of it devoted to literary London of the second and third decades of this century, and contrive to mention the ubiquitous Pound (unfavourably) in only two places.

cultivated amateur. He sometimes allowed a natural, momentary enthusiasm to prevail over his normally discriminating tastes. In a lifetime full of friendships with hundreds of creative artists, Edward Marsh remained more often than not the outsider, the entranced onlooker. Not himself an artist, he was seldom able to overcome the amateur's natural wonderment before the process of artistic creation. 'He could not mix with creative artists,' as Alan Pryce-Jones observed, without a certain 'headiness . . . over-coming his natural caution. The poets and painters were like brilliant creatures in an aquarium; himself was always on the outer side of the tank, looking eagerly in. And so, like all spectators, he was affected by the charm of the spectacle.'[14] Marsh's poetic standards were also those of the amateur. 'He believed that they were the standards of a large educated public, and in this he was right. His outlook . . . was characteristically English. Theorizing about art was foreign; announcing aesthetic and critical doctrines was foreign. His approach to artistic problems was pragmatic and amateur. If his formula for an anthology worked, it was good.'[15]

In his memoirs Marsh made abundantly clear the poetic tastes by which he was guided in selecting poems for *Georgian Poetry*. A good poem, he claimed, should have at least one, preferably two, and ideally all three, of the following attributes: intelligibility, music, and raciness. And he added a fourth quality, though not as a *sine qua non*: 'I was happier with it if it was written on some formal principle which I could discern, and from which it departed, if at all, only for the sake of some special effect, and not because the lazy or too impetuous writer had found observance difficult or irksome.' His first quality, intelligibility, he admitted, 'is a relative term', but not intended to 'exclude the poetry of suggestion'. He meant by it, rather, the opposite of obscurity, which was Marsh's poetic *bête noire*. 'I hold strongly', he argued, 'that poetry is communication, and that it is the poet's duty, to the best of his ability, to let the reader know what he is driving at.' The second criterion, music, is, as he said, a 'still more precarious' poetic yardstick, 'for the ear changes with the generations'. And so he contented himself with affirming generally 'that poetry which renounces the singing quality plucks its own wings'. In the third quality, raciness, Marsh showed his limited modernity perhaps to best advantage. 'My third adjective, "racy",' he conceded, 'is perhaps too slapdash,' but by it he excluded from Parnassus with one sweep the watery verse of the Watsons and the Phillipses and the languid poetry of the nineties. For by that quality 'I mean to imply', he wrote, that poetry must have 'intensity of thought or feeling, and to rule out the vapidity which is too often to be found, alas, in verse that is written with due regard to sense, sound, and "correctness".'[16] As for form, Marsh was again with the Centre party. His creed was based upon a maxim drilled into his head as a schoolboy: 'nine-tenths of the Tradition might be rubbish, but the remaining tenth was priceless, and no one who tried to dispense with it could achieve anything at all'.[17]

Although Marsh's advocacy of his principles grew more strenuous during the second decade as the tide of formlessness increasingly swept away the landmarks of traditional verse, his insistence not only upon form but upon near-perfection of form landed him in revealing arguments with several poets as early as 1912. His first brush occurred with no less intrepid a champion than Sturge Moore. The specific point at issue was the inclusion of Robert Trevelyan's 'Dirge' in *Georgian Poetry* I. Against Moore's strongly phrased recommendation, Marsh had decided that the 'Dirge' could not be included in the anthology because it violated his canon of discernible formal pattern. Among other deficiencies, Marsh alleged, it had too many unrhymed lines. His decision resulted in one of the most outspokenly critical letters Edward Marsh was ever to receive.

> I protest strongly [Moore wrote] about Trevy's Dirge. There will be very few things in your book so genuinely poetry. . . . As to your criticism about formally perfect. It is the very type of the criticism which I abominate; that is, it refers to a mechanical criterion as ultimate. There is no reason or common sense in any such reference.
>
> There is an unrhymed line in most of the divisions of Lycidas, and they do not occur in the same relative position.
>
> Its not being what you call formally perfect is really in its favour, and means that the writer's mind was more dominated by real taste, than by mechanical pedantry when he wrote it. . . .
>
> It is certainly far finer than anything of Bottomley's, and I think as fine as the best of Bridges. It has grandeur. . . . It is very possible that it will be near upon the best thing in the book.
>
> In fact I don't suppose I shall ever really forgive you if you leave it out.[18]

To such pressure Marsh could only bow, especially since he was determined to include in his first volume, for diplomatic if not poetic reasons, the work of a few older men like Moore and Chesterton. The next letter found Moore magnanimous in victory but still ruffled over critics who would judge poetry as if it were an exercise in metrics.

> My dear Marsh,
>     How fine of you! Few nowadays have the generosity to allow themselves to be conquered. You deserve to win next time and I will try to remember to let you. A perfect form may be beautiful but we know so many impeccable ones that are not. A broken vase may be more beautiful than a new one uncracked, so may a broken form. . . . Success conforms to no standard. . . . Mere conformity is never a virtue. . . .
>
> Yours sincerely,<br>T. S. MOORE
>
> I think we should not look on poets as little boys who have not done their exercise.[19]

Thus in spite of its formal deficiencies, Trevelyan's 'Dirge' appeared in *Georgian Poetry*. The result was quite different in several subsequent cases when some of the younger or more expendable poets attempted to argue Marsh's poetic canons with him.

A year later Marsh became embroiled in an even more revealing controversy over form, this time with D. H. Lawrence. The friendly argument began when Marsh returned some verses Lawrence had sent him for criticism objecting, among other things, to their being cast in *vers libre*. He undertook to lecture Lawrence on the virtues of regular metre and underscored his arguments by scanning, in conventional stress fashion, one of Lawrence's favourite poems, Dowson's 'Cynara'. Marsh not only goaded the poet into a cogent defence of *vers libre* but also invited an attack upon all scansion. 'I rather suspect you of being a young Philistine with the poetry of youth on you,' Lawrence replied.

> But I *am* being a David that throws stones. . . .
>     I only *know* that the verse you quote against me is right, and you are wrong. And I am a poor, maligned, misunderstood, patronized and misread poet, and soon I shall burst into tears. . . .
>     I think I came a *real* cropper in my belief in metre over Shelley. I tried all roads to scan him, but I could never *read* him as he could be scanned. And I thought what bit of Latin scansion I did was a *horrible*

fake: I never believed for an instant in the Sapphic form—and Horace is already a bit of mellow varsity man who never quite forgot Oxford.

But the greater part of Lawrence's assault was more personal. He attacked Marsh's own prosodic canons as not only outmoded but insensitive as well:

You *are* wrong. It makes me open my eyes. I think I read my poetry more by length than by stress—as a matter of movements in space than footsteps hitting the earth. . . . I think more of a bird with broad wings flying and lapsing through the air, than anything, when I think of metre. . . . It all depends on the *pause*—the natural pause, the natural *lingering* of the voice according to the feeling—it is the hidden *emotional* pattern that makes poetry, not the obvious form. . . . It is the lapse of the feeling, something as indefinite as expression in the voice carrying emotion. It doesn't depend on the ear, particularly, but on the sensitive soul. And the ear gets a habit, and becomes master, when the ebbing and lifting motion should be master, and the ear the transmitter. If your ear has got stiff and a bit mechanical, *don't* blame my poetry. That's why you like *Golden Journey to Samarkand*—it fits your habituated ear, and your feeling crouches subservient and a bit pathetic. 'It satisfies my ear' you say. Well, I don't write for your ear. This is the constant war, I reckon, between new expression and the habituated, mechanical transmitters and receivers of the human constitution. . . .

You are wrong, I think, about the two rhymes—why need you notice they are rhymes? You are a bit of a policeman in poetry. I *never* put them in because they are rhymes. . . .

D.H.L.

Your letter was jolly good to me really—I always thank God when a man will say straight out to me what he has to say. But it's rare when one will. I call it affectionately not anything else.[20]

Marsh was not soon to forget Lawrence's 'policeman in poetry' charge, for it was to become the essence of attacks upon his taste by poets of the Left for many years to come.

The argument continued through 1913, but by the very nature of the contestants it could have had no decisive outcome. The old and the new, the formalist and the verslibrist, were at loggerheads. It should be noted, however, that Lawrence was represented in four of the five volumes of *Georgian Poetry*, and though strongly disapproving of Lawrence's poetic technique in general, Marsh had sufficiently catholic tastes to reprint two of Lawrence's masterpieces, 'Snake' and 'Snapdragon'. An amusing footnote to the controversy is formed by a poem which Lawrence sent his adversary for Christmas 1913. A singularly obscure poem, but marked by utter regularity of metre and flawless rhyme scheme, it was dedicated, tongue in cheek, 'To Eddie Marsh, with much affection, this poem for a Christmas card, which, albeit a trifle lugubrious, *pray God may go daintily to his ear.*'

### GRIEF

> The darkness steals the forms of all the queens,
> But oh, the palms of his two black hands are red!
> It is death I fear so much, it is not the dead,
> Not this grey book, but the torn and bloody scenes.
>
> The lamps are white like snowdrops in the grass,
> The town is like a church-yard, all so still
> And dark now night is here,—nor will
> Another torn red sunset come to pass.
>
> And so I sit and turn the book of grey,
> Feeling the darkness like a blind man reading,
> All fearful lest I find some new word bleeding—
> —Nay, take my painted missal book away.
>                         David Herbert
>                         Son of Arthur John Lawrence
>                         wrote this poem:
>                         December 16—1913

Requiescat in pace[21]

Though Edward Marsh was in many ways admirably qualified for the editorial mantle he was about to assume, then, he possessed at least one serious shortcoming. In an age 'pullulating' with new poetry, much of it frankly experimental and some of it downright bizarre, Marsh was barred by his essentially formal approach to verse from understanding the significance of a good deal of the new work going on around him. Marsh was naturally fitted by training and temperament to popularize the poetry of the Centre, a feat which he performed superlatively well, but one could not expect that his anthologies would become entirely representative of all phases of the poetry of the age.

The idea for the anthology that was to become *Georgian Poetry* originated, strictly speaking, not with Marsh but (as will become evident in the next chapter) with Rupert Brooke. The story of the

Edward Marsh, September 1912

Rupert Brooke, 1913

close friendship between these two remarkable men has been largely told by Marsh himself and by his biographer, and some of the significant correspondence between them has long been printed.* Anything beyond a cursory recounting of a few aspects of their relationship is now superfluous. The friendship with Brooke was for Edward Marsh the high spot in a life full of many and varied friends. Indeed, the events in Marsh's life can almost be dated pre- and post-Rupert, for Brooke's death in the Aegean in 1915 was a blow from which Marsh never entirely recovered. As he confessed in a letter to Brooke's mother on the evening that news of the poet's death reached England, 'Most things in my life depended on him for a great part of their interest and worth. It is your glory to be his mother—and mine to be his friend—the loss to the future cannot be guessed.'[22] Brooke remained for Marsh throughout his life the embodiment of all a young man and poet should be. Twenty-three years after Brooke's death Marsh could still write of him: 'My friendship with Rupert Brooke was certainly one of the most memorable things in my life. In his combination of gifts, of body, character, mind and spirit, he was nearer completeness and perfection than anyone I have known; intellect and goodness, humour and sympathy, beauty of person and kindness of heart, distinction of taste and "the common touch", ambition and modesty, he had them all; and there is no telling what he might have done if he had lived.'[23]

Marsh first met Brooke at Cambridge in 1906 and by 1909 had become a sufficiently intimate friend of both the poet and the Brooke family that he was spending many of his summer weekends with them. In the beginning, Marsh scrupulously avoided asking to read any of Brooke's poems because he was fearful of being disillusioned; as Marsh wrote, 'I liked him so much that I should have hated not to like his work.'[24] The publication of

* See Edward Marsh, *A Number of People*, Ch. 12, and E. M.'s *Memoir*, a long, tragic, and sensitively written account of the friendship, which forms the preface to Brooke's *Collected Poems* (1918). At the time my book first went to print in America (April 1964), the fullest and most objective account of the Brooke-Marsh friendship was to be found in the late Christopher Hassall's *Edward Marsh*, Chs. 9–13. Subsequently, however, Hassall's *Rupert Brooke: A Biography* was published both in England and the United States (London, Faber and Faber Ltd.; New York, Harcourt, Brace; 1964). Although the book affords no new—in the sense of startlingly new—insights into the friendship between Brooke and Marsh, it does contain many additional details gathered from several sources which were unavailable to Hassall when he wrote his biography of Marsh. It is, moreover, nearly a model literary biography. On the Brooke-Marsh friendship see especially Chs. 8–13.

Brooke's *Poems* in 1911 not only thoroughly allayed that fear but also convinced him that young Brooke was a potentially first-rate poet. Indeed, Marsh's enthusiasm for modern poetry and his desire to stand forth as its champion may well have sprung as much from the fact that Rupert Brooke was writing modern verse as from all the other influences together. From 1911 on, Marsh took Brooke under his tutelage. He judiciously introduced both the man and his poetry to the proper people, he entertained him sumptuously during his visits to London, and he took care especially that Brooke should meet on easy, informal terms the growing circle which was forming around Marsh and which included such poets as Gibson, Monro, and Abercrombie. In short, he set out to act as literary mentor to the young poet.[25]

It required considerable tact and deftness on Marsh's part, and perhaps not a little courage, to champion Brooke's poetry in 1911 and 1912, for among his contemporaries Brooke was far from being a universally popular poet. In its own place and time the early verse of Rupert Brooke was capable of shocking many readers. Even Ezra Pound, who seemed to judge a fellow-poet's worth in large part by the degree to which he was capable of shocking Bumbledom, conceded that Brooke was 'the best of all that Georgian group'.[26] Brooke's youthful arrogance irked even many of those who were in his poetic camp, and his overfrank realism stung some of the more conservative critics to a sharp attack on the brash young interloper who would storm Parnassus. One of his close contemporaries summed up from first-hand observation Brooke's poetic reputation in 1912:

> Everybody was talking about 'Channel Passage' and 'Menelaus and Helen': the younger people admired him for daring to write a sonnet about seasickness and to describe so cynically and realistically the old age of Helen and Menelaus, but, on the whole, even those who admired him were inclined to be shocked, many were indeed frankly annoyed at his bad taste and at the way in which, with arrogant undergraduate bravado, for so they considered it, he deliberately set out to flout long-cherished poetic conventions.[27]

Although Brooke valued Marsh's criticism and respected his tastes, on several poetic matters the two men amicably but thoroughly disagreed. Chief among these was Brooke's tendency towards realism. Publicly, to be sure, Marsh defended Brooke's verse from attacks made on the grounds of its excessive realism.

But in private he was far more frank with the young poet. He heartily agreed when Brooke's publisher, Frank Sidgwick of the firm of Sidgwick and Jackson, suggested that two sonnets be eliminated from the manuscript of the *Poems*. Brooke won the day over both his formidable opponents by invoking the characteristic argument of the Centrist poet: poetic sincerity and truth to life are more important to poetry than conventional morality. To remove these poems, he argued, 'would be to over-balance the book still more in the direction of unimportant prettiness. There's plenty of that sort of wash in the other pages for the readers who like it. They needn't read the parts which are new and serious'.[28] A satisfactory compromise was reached when Brooke agreed to change the title of one sonnet from 'Lust' to 'Libido' and the other from 'The Sea-Sick Lover' to 'Channel Passage'.

In public print Marsh made the best of the bargain. In reviewing Brooke's *Poems* for *Poetry Review*, he praised the poet's passion and liveliness in verse, his youth and exuberance; but he charily sidestepped the issue of the over-frank realism with the comment that though he himself was 'a somewhat doubtful apologist' for Brooke's realism, and though it was most certainly 'an aspect of Mr. Brooke's achievement which many readers will find distasteful', at least a liberal-minded reader would admit that Brooke's 'coarseness' was 'less sardonic' and 'more exuberant and rollicking' than Swift's.[29] One wonders how many prospective purchasers of the *Poems* in 1912 were likely to be reassured by such a comparison. In a letter to Brooke enclosing a copy of his review, Marsh warned the young poet more pointedly. When he had shown the *Poems* to Edmund Gosse and Austin Dobson, Marsh wrote, he had 'steered them clear of the ugly poems', but to his surprise they had taken exception to 'Dead Men's Love', a poem which he had always 'thought quite safe'. The elder poets had interpreted it as 'an out-pouring of youth's contempt on the love-affairs of persons past a certain age—and seem to think that you cast aspersions on their own powers!'[30] In another letter a few months earlier Marsh had elaborated upon his objections to Brooke's realism. In his printed review of the *Poems* he voiced only a mild demurrer to several of the poems 'on the old-fashioned score of taste', but in the letter, though he praised Brooke for having 'brought back into English poetry the rapturous beautiful grotesque of the 17th century', he protested both 'Channel Passage' and 'the "smell" line in *Libido*'. The former he found only mildly offensive: 'Channel Passage', he conceded, 'is so clever and amusing that in spite of a prejudice in favour of poetry I can read at meals I can't wish it away'. He found the line from 'Libido' a more serious breach of good taste. Turning the matter off first into a sly joke, Marsh wrote: 'For one thing, it will prevent my giving away at least twenty copies of the book as Christmas presents to women.' But then he added more earnestly: 'even for my own sake I think there are some things too disgusting to write about, especially in one's own language. I wonder you didn't call *Dining-room Tea* "pump-shipping in the drawing-room" and write "the p" instead of "the tea" hung in the air in amber stream. Surely the idea of the poem would have fitted quite as well'.[31] Again, as in the argument with Sidgwick, Brooke was stung to an earnest if good-natured defence of the line of grounds of the necessity for poetic sincerity.[32] He was too considerate of his friend's feelings, one suspects, to throw in Marsh's face the obvious implication that an Englishman might more safely write of disgusting subjects in a language other than English. Presumably, erotic poetry was not to be condemned because it was erotic but because it was understandable to too many people. The critical standards which Marsh disclosed in this exchange of letters, indeed, do not bear very close scrutiny.

In fairness to Marsh it must be added that too much can be made of his objections to realistic verse. Raciness, after all—'in tensity of thought and feeling'—was one of his four criteria for good poetry. One must recall, too, his admiration for *The Everlasting Mercy*, a poem which, in 1911, represented realism *par excellence*. And one can never be entirely certain whether Marsh's disagreement with Brooke over the *Poems* was motivated more by the dispassionate canons of poetic taste or by loyal friendship. Above all other considerations he wanted Brooke's *Poems* to succeed with the public, and his astute reading of English poetic tolerance in 1911 told him that several poems in the volume placed it in some danger of slipping just a bit beyond the pale. The way to public acceptance, then, seemed to lie in attempting to convince Brooke of the undesirability of publishing some of the more offensive verses, or, at the least, in cautioning him not to repeat the error in subsequent volumes. Moreover, if Marsh's taste was beginning to have its effect on Brooke in the years immediately following the war, perhaps his friendship with Brooke was effecting some broadening of Marsh's taste as well. Surely by 1915, when *Georgian Poetry* II was published, the new poetic realism was not so distasteful to him as it had been in 1911–12. Over the strong objections of several poets, including D. H. Lawrence, Marsh gave the places of honour in *Georgian Poetry* II to Abercrombie's 'End of the World' and Bottomley's 'King Lear's Wife', two poetic dramas which caused a critical flurry at the time by reason of their alleged brutality and coarseness.

Because of the intimate friendship of Brooke and Marsh, and because of the considerable sway which Brooke exerted over his mentor, Brooke was perhaps the most significant single influence which led *Georgian Poetry* almost from the start to exploit one major phase of the poetic renaissance, the new realism. But his influence on the anthology was to be more immediate and direct. The very idea which led to the publication of *Georgian Poetry* was in the beginning Rupert Brooke's.

# 5

# Poetry in the Market-place

Because his first volume of verse had achieved only mediocre success, Rupert Brooke, like most other young poets in 1912, had long been musing over the British public's unwarranted neglect of modern poetry. As Marsh himself told the story, an amusing idea for wooing the public came to Brooke on the evening of 19th September 1912, as he sat undressing on his bed in Marsh's spare room at Gray's Inn. He would startle British readers into taking some notice, good or bad, of modern poetry by an audacious scheme; he himself would write a volume of verse and publish it, under convincing *noms de plume*.[1] He anticipated using all possible experimental and revolutionary forms in order more effectively to play the gadfly. Had the idea been allowed to bear fruit, perhaps the result would have anticipated some of the more blatant efforts of the Leftist poets in subsequent months; for in his aim simultaneously to advertise the new poetry and to bait the public Brooke stole a march on both the Futurists and Vorticists. But his idea was to result in a literary movement more enduring than either Futurism or Vorticism, for once having heard Brooke's plan, Edward Marsh took it over, remoulded it nearer to his heart's desire, and edited the first volume of *Georgian Poetry*.

Although Marsh was instantly enthusiastic, in the ensuing discussion of the scheme that evening he managed to persuade Brooke to two fundamental modifications. In the first place, 'it occurred to me', wrote Marsh, 'that as we both believed there were at least twelve flesh-and-blood poets whose work, if properly thrust under the public's nose, had a good chance of producing the effect he desired, it would be simpler to use the material which was ready to hand'.[2] An anthology, not a one-man *tour de force*, was in the making. Secondly, Marsh succeeded in dissuading Brooke from his initial conception of the book as a volume of experimental verse. Experiments, Marsh argued, 'were best confined to the poet's rough notebook; such an anthology must present only fully evolved and finished work if it was to win over an apathetic public'.[3]

Marsh and Brooke talked on into the small hours of the morning, and with each new idea their enthusiasm grew as they became increasingly aware of the exciting potentialities of the scheme they had so fortuitously hit upon. They readily agreed on several particulars. Upon Brooke's suggestion, Marsh consented to edit the anthology, but only on the condition that he not be required publicly to identify himself as editor because 'the Private Secretary at the Admiralty openly shepherding a group of poets might strike the uninitiated as a trifle absurd and so damage the cause'. Harold Monro would be approached to publish the book, though Marsh agreed to use his personal funds to guarantee Monro against possible financial loss. When Marsh off-handedly suggested using the adjective 'Georgian' in the title of the book, Brooke at first demurred; 'it sounded too staid', he thought, 'for a volume designed as the herald of a revolutionary dawn'. But when Marsh pointed out that far from being 'too staid', the word contained multiple connotations of newness and vigour and that 'the new reign was itself as new and hopeful as the renaissance in poetry', Brooke consented to the use of 'Georgian' in the title.[4]

If the new book was to appear in time for the Christmas market, speed was of the essence, and so the next day, 20th September, Marsh gathered together for a luncheon at Gray's Inn Wilfrid Gibson, John Drinkwater, Harold Monro, Arundel del Re, and Brooke.\* If Brooke had not been entirely won over to the anthology pattern by Marsh's arguments of the night before, the assemblage at luncheon succeeded in persuading him to 'the more dignified aim of attempting to elevate instead of merely trying to startle'.[5] All the young men present were quickly caught up in the contagion of Brooke's and Marsh's enthusiasm. Brooke insisted,

---

\* In addition, Lascelles Abercrombie may have attended the meeting. Relying on memory, authorities differ. Drinkwater is the only authority I can find for claiming that Abercrombie was present (see *Discovery*, p. 228). On the other hand, Drinkwater apparently forgets the presence of Arundel del Re, who, by his own testimony, can be claimed to have been there.

wrote Drinkwater, 'that England must be bombarded with the claims of the new poets'; and to that end he was willing to use his influence on potential purchasers of the book 'as brazenly as a commercial traveller'. Before the group left Gray's Inn late that afternoon, they had not only become zealous partisans of the anthology but had appointed Monro publisher, drawn up a list of poets who were to be asked for selections, and given to Edward Marsh 'sole discretionary powers . . . as editor'.[6] Though several persons at the luncheon shared Brooke's misgivings about the title, *Georgian Poetry*, no better suggestions were forthcoming, and so 'it was agreed to publish under that name before Christmas an edition of 500 at 3s 6d a copy'.[7]

The aim of *Georgian Poetry* I remained the aim originally enunciated by Rupert Brooke—'to strike a blow for young and eager poets who felt that in the solid publicity accorded to the novel and play their own art was treated as of too little account'[8]—but the means by which that aim was to be carried out were controlled by Edward Marsh alone. Not that he entirely rejected suggestions from others; as editor, he sometimes turned to Brooke, Monro, or Gibson for bits of advice, and he accepted some assistance, too, from T. E. Hulme, 'whose judgment', according to del Re, 'he greatly respected'.[9] There rapidly came to be small doubt, however, that matters of major editorial policy were to be the province of Edward Marsh and no one else. For several of the more inflexibly modern young poets, including Brooke, Marsh's strict exercise of his editorial prerogatives may have been more fortunate than they knew, for he was far more willing than they to trim his sails to the prevailing winds of public taste. Against the objections of several of them who wanted any but their own kind rigorously excluded, Marsh solicited contributions from several of the older, better-known poets of the age, such as A. E. Housman, G. K. Chesterton, and Sturge Moore. Housman declined Marsh's invitation, claiming, 'I do not really belong to your "new era", and none even of my few unpublished poems have been written within the last two years.' He suggested, however, that excerpts from Chesterton's *Ballad of the White Horse* might be included; therefore, 'out of deference to Housman, who was a friend of Marsh's father, Chesterton was approached and a section of his *Ballad* included in the book'.[10] How much the inclusion of the work of such un-Georgian poets of the Establishment as Chesterton and Sturge

Moore increased the sales of *Georgian Poetry* I is of course open to question. It seems reasonably certain, however, that Marsh's judicious mixture of a dram of the old with liberal portions of the new, though it may have slightly vitiated the headiness of the new wine, did much to increase its market value among those with untrained or traditional palates.

With rare exceptions—such as when he allowed Sturge Moore to win the argument over Trevelyan's 'Dirge'—Marsh made himself entirely responsible for the specific poems selected from the works of chosen poets. Even Brooke appears to have had no direct hand in helping Marsh select poems for *Georgian Poetry* I. One would suspect that second only to Brooke, Harold Monro might have been in the best position to exert considerable influence. As publisher of the anthology, as editor of a successful and influential periodical, as a moderately close friend to Marsh by the end of 1912, Monro had as wide a knowledge of modern poets and poetry as any young man in London. Moreover, even though he was insured by Marsh's word against sizeable loss, Monro carried the initial cost of publishing the anthology. Nevertheless, all the available correspondence between Monro and Marsh in late 1912 indicates that Marsh managed to keep the relationship between Monro and himself one strictly of editor and publisher. Marsh relied heavily on Monro's knowledge of printing, bookmaking, and binding; Monro handled printing bids, submitted specimens of paper to Marsh, and gave advice on how to submit manuscript poems to the printer. But that was all. There is no hint that in 1912 Monro was ever asked for advice on specific poems or poets for inclusion in the anthology.*

Marsh wasted no time in canvassing potential contributors to *Georgian Poetry* I. Only six days after the luncheon of 20th September, Sturge Moore had given Marsh permission to reprint the 'Sicilian Idyll'.[11] Within two weeks Masefield, Davies, Drinkwater, Bottomley, de la Mare, and Lawrence had either acknowledged Marsh's request or consented to inclusion of their work in the anthology.[12] As a general rule Marsh appears to have presented most of the poets with a *fait accompli*. Having decided which of their poems he considered worthy of inclusion, he then wrote for

---

* One must add in fairness that this was not always to be the case. Marsh sought Monro's advice in editing subsequent volumes to a larger extent than he did in the case of *GP* I.

permission to reprint those poems only. The poets did not always agree with his selections. Though he gave willing assent to the reprinting of all the titles Marsh had chosen, W. H. Davies also appended an unsolicited suggestion: he specifically desired his 'Kingfisher' included. 'It is a better poem than any you name,' he told Marsh.[13] Marsh agreed, and 'The Kingfisher' appeared in *Georgian Poetry* I. From Lawrence, Marsh requested permission to use only one poem, 'Snapdragon'. Lawrence readily consented, and added, 'If there is anything else I could at any time give you, some unpublished stuff, I shall be glad. I shall love to see the book. It will be quite profit enough in itself.'[14] Ezra Pound refused Marsh's request to reprint 'The Goodly Fere'. 'I'm sorry I can't let you have *that* poem,' Pound replied to Marsh's overture, 'as I'm just bringing it out in a volume of my own. Is there anything in the earlier books that you like? (not *The Goodly Fere* as it doesn't illustrate any *modern* tendency). Also I'd like to know more or less what gallery you propose to put me into.' None of Pound's earlier work suited Marsh's taste, and so Pound was unrepresented in the anthology.[15] Most poets, like Bottomley and Drinkwater, failed to make any counter-proposals, general or specific, contenting themselves only with expressing their pleasure at being selected for the anthology.[16]

With John Masefield, Marsh was willing to make a major strategic exception to his usual method of solicitation. The reason cannot be far to seek: Masefield was without doubt the most widely known poet Marsh was required to approach. By late 1912 he was riding the crest of a wave of popular acclaim for *The Everlasting Mercy* and the recently published *Widow in the Bye Street*. A 'modern' anthology—and a financially successful one—was unthinkable unless some of Masefield's work could be included among that of his less famous coevals. His current poetic eminence obviously demanded a less arbitrary approach than that made to other poets. In the beginning Marsh's prospects for success appeared none too bright. Masefield agreed to Marsh's suggestion of a meeting, but his reply was couched in terms which were anything but encouraging. 'As to the scheme, I would much like to talk it over with you,' he wrote Marsh, 'but I own that I am not very sanguine. Sir Ronald Ross had a scheme for a poetical monthly, "Musa Miscella", which pleased me more; but let us meet and talk over yours.'[17] The meeting was held, and Marsh apparently proved himself a superior salesman on this occasion, as on so many others. On 30th September Masefield not only gave permission for inclusion of his work in the anthology but also offered to hold back publication of his forthcoming *Biography* for 'a few months', meanwhile giving Marsh complete discretion to print in *Georgian Poetry* I any poems he chose from the unpublished volume. Now Marsh had secured possibly his most important contributor; the anthology could scarcely fail. Perhaps the result did not come about entirely because of salesmanship on Marsh's part or altruism on Masefield's. To be sure, out of deference to Masefield's eminence and in order to take the wind out of the sails of Sir Ronald Ross's rival plan, Marsh had astutely invited Ross to contribute a poem to *Georgian Poetry*; but as Masefield clearly saw, and probably Marsh as well, a *quid pro quo* had been arrived at.[18] By postponing publication of *Biography* for a 'few months', Masefield wrote Marsh, he would be able to capitalize on whatever popularity would accrue to his new verse by having it appear first in *Georgian Poetry*. And he added, 'I feel that your book may be a useful fillip, as there has been nothing like it for some years.'[19] Just how useful a 'fillip' *Georgian Poetry* was to be, not only to *Biography* but to others of his subsequent volumes as well, Masefield could not then have guessed. During the next two years, however, he was to express to Marsh on several occasions his congratulations on *Georgian Poetry* and to recant his initial misgivings about contributing to it.[20]

In addition to assuming sole responsibility for choosing poems and obtaining permission to reprint them, Marsh also assumed direction of an incredibly thorough pre-publication campaign to organize and insure a favourable reception for his anthology. Though he was aided by Rupert Brooke and, to a lesser extent, by others among his about-to-be-enshrined Georgians, Marsh was the generalissimo in charge of strategy. So skilful and thorough was his campaign that one is tempted to conclude that if there had not been a poetic renaissance before publication of *Georgian Poetry* I, it would have been necessary to invent one after. Had *Georgian Poetry* I turned out to be a mediocre anthology or worse, it would nevertheless have been assured of creating a considerable critical splash.

Marsh's most enthusiastic lieutenant in the campaign was Brooke. Feeling a strong sense of proprietorship, Brooke set out to push the volume by almost any means which came to hand. Few persons in London were better fitted both by position and temperament to succeed at such a task. Much as he disliked reading his poetry aloud, Brooke readily agreed to give public readings at the Poetry Bookshop if such a course were necessary to increase interest in the anthology.[21] His letters to Marsh in November and December 1912 were full of the subject. He was lying awake nights, he wrote Marsh from Germany, trying to think of novel ways to 'advertise'—the word is Brooke's own—*Georgian Poetry*. And he sent Marsh several pages of detailed instructions as to which journals and which reviewers should be approached to write critical notices in Germany, France, and Italy. If all his schemes were put into effect, he predicted to Marsh, 'You'll be able to found a hostel for poor Georgians on the proceeds' of the anthology.[22] Perhaps the most impressive result of Brooke's strategy was to be seen in the fact that, as John Drinkwater reported, 'the Prime Minister's car was waiting outside Bumpus's shop in Oxford Street at opening-time on the day of publication'.[23]

Drinkwater's testimony notwithstanding, it would not be surprising if that particular press-agent's *coup* had been the result of Marsh's rather than Brooke's strategy. If Marsh's campaign was less spectacularly conceived and more thorough than Brooke's, it was still by no means pedestrian or lacking in dash. He planned it to the last detail: which journals would be asked to publish reviews; which among his influential literary friends would be given pre-publication copies and requested to mention the book publicly, either orally or in writing; and even what tone would be suggested for each review.[24] Marsh was also careful to enlist the aid of his potentially most effective salesmen, the poets represented in the anthology itself. He adhered to an astute scheme of division of labour; each poet was asked to use his influence where that influence was likely to be most effectively felt. He asked John Drinkwater, for example, to see to it that the *Birmingham Post* reviewed the anthology as favourably as possible. Drinkwater gladly agreed, as expected, adding, 'I do a good deal of work for them, and can generally manage to direct their attention in the right way in matters of poetry.'[25] Wilfrid Gibson, who happened to be making an opportune lecture tour through several Scottish cities immediately after publication of the book, was equally ready to use his influence in the cause. During his lectures in Edinburgh and Glasgow, he wrote Marsh, he pushed *Georgian Poetry* 'in season and out of season'.[26]

Among the entire field of influential British publications in which his anthology might be reviewed, none was more important than the *Times*. A conspicuous and favourable review in that journal was of course essential. And so to Bruce Richmond, editor of the *Literary Supplement*, Marsh sent a review copy in late November 1912 and a letter suggesting a prominent review, if possible on the first page. Unfortunately the letter reached Richmond after he had gone on holiday, but Marsh's name was not without influence. Richmond replied from Italy:

> I wish I had known earlier about your volume. Before I left, a fortnight ago, I planned out the next five front pages—which takes it up to Christmas (and I imagine you want if possible to catch the 'Christmas present' market)—one of the five was to be Couch's Victorian Verse—and my immediate fear is that my colleague may propose to tack you on to him.
>
> I've written at once to try to prevent that—and hope that we shall be able to do it properly—either two cols. inside before Xmas, or a front page after. Good luck to the venture.*

Marsh used much the same kind of approach to professional free-lance reviewers not connected with established periodicals. Again he wasted no time. As early as the beginning of October, only a few days after the idea for the anthology had been broached, and before its final make-up could possibly have been determined, he wrote to potential reviewers outlining the concept of the book and apparently requesting favourable notices should the chance to review *Georgian Poetry* fall to them. In many cases his appeal seems to have been made more on a personal than a professional basis, not as the editor of *Georgian Poetry* writing to a potential reviewer, but as Edward Marsh writing to an old friend. With some of the

---

* Bruce Richmond to E. M., 5th Dec. 1912, *MLC*. An approach to the *TLS* was obviously necessary, but perhaps only Edward Marsh would have considered sending a copy of *GP* 1 to *Punch*. But send it he did, and to A. A. Milne. What he could have expected beyond the creation of good will is not clear. As Marsh must have known he would, Milne replied that he could not 'review (or have reviewed) your anthology—such works not getting much of a show in *Punch*'. But at least Marsh had aroused his friend's interest in the Georgians: 'I hope I am to have the felicity of meeting you shortly *chez* Thorpe,' Milne continued, 'when you can tell me who Rupert Brooke is who writes that jolly poem about Grantchester. . . . Countless labours—together with the natural shock of reading what the *Daily Mail* thinks of us all—has [*sic*] prevented me from (1) writing before and (2) reading the book sufficiently carefully to accuse you of any faults of commission or omission' (A. A. Milne to E. M., undated, but *c.* 10th Dec. 1912, *MLC*).

recipients his approach was successful, with others less so. Even though he had not been invited to contribute to the anthology, Alfred Noyes replied that although he was doing little reviewing at the time, he would be delighted to help in any way he could.[27] Maurice Hewlett was not quite so tractable. He had some reservations about the book and was hard put to discover among the kinds and conditions of poets and poetry projected for *Georgian Poetry* any motif around which to organize a review. He was for that reason reluctant to assent to Marsh's persuasions. Not daunted, Marsh continued the campaign, which ended with only a tentative victory. Hewlett wrote, 'We are talking about different things: *you* about the general excellences of poetry; *I* about what broad lines I could find in your collection to make a review about. To write a "notice" of a book of verses is one thing: I can stroke surfaces etc.—but a review a bigger thing. However, we'll see.'[28]

By tactics which shrewdly combined the right amounts of finesse and brashness, boldness and humility, art and salesmanship, Edward Marsh assured the success of *Georgian Poetry* I. Deliberate and well planned as his campaign was, however, he worked even better than he knew, for retrospectively one can see that it was not only the success of one volume of the anthology which was at stake. In spite of the best efforts of such dedicated men as Harold Monro, in spite of the fact that almost all the *cognoscenti* were convinced of an imminent burgeoning of poetic talent in late 1912, the general public still remained by and large either ignorant of or indifferent to the claims of the new generation. By his artful and pre-eminently successful direction of the reception of *Georgian Poetry* I, Marsh took the first significant step towards making modern poetry popular. And thereby he began the transformation of the Georgian revolt into the Georgian revival. As orders for *Georgian Poetry* I poured in to the offices of the Poetry Bookshop at a rate which surprised Marsh and even Monro, sceptical critics and well-wishers alike were forced to admit with pleased surprise that there existed an audience for poetry the extent and size of which had hitherto been underestimated, if not unsuspected, by all but the most optimistic. The sales of *Georgian Poetry* I were the first tangible evidence that the fact of a poetic renaissance had finally impressed itself upon the public consciousness and that there existed a sizeable public whose poetic tastes had not stopped with Tennyson or Dowson. One cannot but agree with Arundel del

Re's judgment: without Marsh's efforts in behalf of his anthology in late 1912, 'poetry would have scarcely been able either to regain its rightful *public* position among the arts, or to preserve it through the war crisis and afterwards'.[29]

The sales of *Georgian Poetry* went astonishingly well from the very first. According to a pre-publication agreement between Marsh and Monro, the profits from this volume—and from all successive volumes, too, as it turned out—were to be evenly split, half going to the Poetry Bookshop and half being divided among the contributors.[30] Marsh himself received no fee as editor. Monro kept all the accounts and at approximately six-month intervals transferred to Marsh's hands half of the profits. It was then Marsh's happy duty to divide that sum evenly among the contributors. Such an arrangement, informal as it was, had obvious advantages for Edward Marsh, for it kept him in touch with his poets in perhaps the pleasantest of ways, as dispenser of cheques. Only seven months after publication, *Georgian Poetry* had reached a sixth edition. By the end of 1913 the volume had gone into a ninth edition,[31] and by 1st May 1914 into a tenth (though Monro was forced to report at this time that the ninth edition had sold rather more slowly than the previous eight).[32] The number of editions is a slightly misleading way to reckon the popularity of *Georgian Poetry* I, however, for Monro was guilty of what he himself called 'bibliographical insincerity'. Referring unquestionably to *Georgian Poetry* II, and probably to the first volume as well, Monro wrote Marsh that it was 'a trade secret' that several editions were printed at once. Asking Marsh not to noise the fact around, Monro added: 'I am rather ashamed of doing it, but under present exceptional circumstances anyway, it seemed absolutely necessary.'* He suggested that in the future such 'bibliographical insincerity' be avoided by having inserted in *Georgian Poetry* I 'seventh thousand' and in *Georgian Poetry* II 'fourth thousand', as he said, 'these figures being nothing shameful anyway'.[33] This practice was approved by Marsh, and notation of edition numbers henceforward disappeared from *Georgian Poetry* I and II.

If *Georgian Poetry*, in Marsh's phrase, 'went up like a rocket', it was by no means so short-lived. By the end of 1919 the first

---

* The 'exceptional circumstances' were the acute paper shortage brought on by the war, a situation which Monro continually fretted over during negotiations preceding publication of *GP* II and to which he alluded several times in his correspondence with Marsh during this period.

volume had reached its thirteenth thousand (the second volume being in its twelfth thousand and the third in its eleventh).[34] Only in late 1921 did Monro report that for the first time *Georgian Poetry* I was showing a slight deficit, a state of affairs which could not have been very long-lived, for in the same letter he recorded an order just received from a rather unusual source. The Indian Army Education Office had written to inquire whether it was still possible to order one hundred copies each of all four volumes of the anthology.[35] By mid-1922 all four of the volumes published to that time were once again showing a good profit.[36]

Marsh estimated in 1939 that in the final reckoning *Georgian Poetry* I sold 15,000 copies. *Georgian Poetry* II, published in November 1915, was even more successful: it sold 19,000 copies.[37] During the short years in which these two volumes were published the new Georgian age emerged from its tentative springtime into a brief but fruitful summer. The very title of the anthology, plus the judiciously phrased preface to *Georgian Poetry* I, was enough to convince a reading public already well prepared for the fact that a poetic renaissance was at hand. Even subsequent critics who, like F. R. Leavis, saw in *Georgian Poetry* only a *réchauffé* of Victorian verse were forced to admit not only that the anthology was 'warmly supported by the public', but also that the first volume was a poetic turning point; only following its publication could it justifiably be claimed that 'in general acceptance, the age was a poetical one'.[38]

The contributors to *Georgian Poetry* I were to a man astonished and delighted at their financial return from the venture. None of them, with the exception of Brooke, had even remotely guessed at the size of the profits that would fall to them. Most of them, one suspects, shared in the beginning Masefield's initial pessimism. And so it was with a pleased and almost incredulous surprise that they wrote to thank their benefactor at Gray's Inn for the cheques that started coming their way, as if Edward Marsh had brought off a feat of magic—which indeed he had—in making money from poetry. As James Stephens remarked upon receiving a cheque, the anthology had broken not one but two records, 'first, in getting to a 6th edition, and, second, in paying its contributors'. 'The latter', he added, 'does seem like a forecast of an overdue millennium.'[39] John Drinkwater wrote: 'I congratulate you most warmly on the splendid success' of *Georgian Poetry* I; 'we are all your

*Photograph by Herbert Lambert*

Walter de la Mare, 1923

(*left*) D. H. Lawrence, *c.* 1920

(*below*) W. H. Davies, detail from a portrait by Sir William Rothenstein, *c.* 1927

grateful debtors. Your venture has put a good livery once again on patronage.'[40] W. H. Davies declared candidly that the volume had succeeded 'far beyond my reckoning'.[41] And D. H. Lawrence wrote from Italy: 'That Georgian Poetry book is a veritable Aladdin's lamp. I little thought my Snapdragon would go on blooming and seeding in this prolific fashion. So many thanks for the cheque for four pounds, and long life to G.P.'[42]

Even after the initial surprise had worn off, the sustained popularity of *Georgian Poetry* I was a source of recurrent astonishment to most of its contributors. As Marsh's semi-annual cheques continued to reach them, a few of the poets were moved to estimate the total of their receipts from this single volume. 'I should think by now', Walter de la Mare told Marsh in late 1916 or early 1917, that 'my small contribution to the 1st G.P. has brought almost as much . . . as "S[ongs] of C[hildhood]", "Poems", and "The Listeners" in volume form together.'* No small achievement indeed! Perhaps W. H. Davies most succinctly summed up the attitude of the contributors towards the editor of *Georgian Poetry* I. 'You have performed a wonder,' he confessed to Marsh—'made poetry pay!'[43]

One of the surest indices of the popularity of *Georgian Poetry* I was the alacrity with which other anthologists were willing to pay it the compliment of imitation. After the success of Edward Marsh's first volume the anthologizing idea quickly caught on, and the corporate publication of verse became the vogue. Ezra Pound's scheme for anthologizing some of the Imagist poets, for example—which resulted in *Des Imagistes*—'appears to have been a direct result of the successful launching' of *Georgian Poetry* I.[44] And during the war years probably a good many more poetry anthologies were rained down upon the heads of the British public than bombs from the Kaiser's zeppelins. Each coterie seemed compelled to anthologize the efforts of adherents; one thinks of such works as the Sitwells' *Wheels*, of the several collections of Imagist verse, and of the countless anthologies of war poetry, most of them intensely patriotic, unspeakably maudlin, and thor-

---

* Walter de la Mare to E. M., undated, *MLC*. Internal evidence dates this letter sometime shortly after publication of *GP* II (i.e. late 1915 or early 1916), for de la Mare added, 'I hear from Monro that the 2nd volume is doing even better' than the first. Unfortunately, in his letters to E. M., de la Mare, like the rest of the Georgians, estimated his gains from *GP* only in such general terms as these. It is therefore quite impossible to determine from *MLC* how much the anthology brought in to any one poet.

oughly fourth-rate. Even as early as six months after the publication of *Georgian Poetry* 1 the imitators were at work. By mid-1913 Marsh began receiving letters from many of his poets noting the fact that they had been approached by other anthologists apparently on the strength of their having been chosen for *Georgian Poetry*. The extent of the anthologizing boom can be estimated by a letter from James Stephens, who wrote Marsh in mid-1913: 'There seems to be a number of anthologies in preparation just now; whether your magical 6th edition is responsible for them or not I don't know, but I am contributing to three and have refused to contribute to ten.'[45]

Another amusing, if short-lived, result of the popularity of *Georgian Poetry* 1 was a marked increase in the popularity of the Poetry Bookshop. Doubtless owing to Edward Marsh's efforts and connections, *Georgian Poetry* quickly became the *dernier cri* among the rich and leisured of London society, who began in 1913 to look in on the Bookshop in increasing numbers. As Rupert Brooke reported to Marsh after a visit to the Bookshop, 'The most extraordinary people keep dropping in and spending immense sums.'[46] Though Monro could scarcely have objected to an increase in revenues, the new clientele must continually have ruffled the stubbornly maintained Bohemian atmosphere of his Bookshop. Nevertheless, once begun, the embarrassment of riches continued, and for a few months in 1913 'the grubby urchins who played hop-scotch in Devonshire Street saw more smart cars than they had ever seen before in their lives'.[47] But the novelty wore off, and the Poetry Bookshop soon reverted to its less affluent *habitués*, students from the University of London, readers from the British Museum, and enthusiastic but penurious clerks spending a lunch hour browsing among the poets.

It is unclear whether, when Edward Marsh published *Georgian Poetry* 1 in 1912, he considered the volume a one-time venture, or whether, even at that date, he envisioned it as only the first in a series of anthologies. In view of his immediate aim of popularizing the work of modern poets, perhaps the former assumption is the more likely. The immediate success of his first volume, however, clearly posed an opportunity which Marsh could not overlook. It is inconceivable that the idea for a second volume should not have occurred to Marsh himself, but even if it had not, the prompting of the contributors to volume 1 would have led him seriously to consider it. Sturge Moore, for instance, was in all probability doing no more than putting Marsh's own musings into words when he wrote Marsh in January 1914, wondering 'whether a collection like the G.P. might not be possible periodically'.[48] Obviously a second *Georgian Poetry* was not only a possibility but for Edward Marsh a happy duty.

In early February 1914, after a week-end visit with the Gibsons and Abercrombies in Gloucestershire, Marsh decided to publish *Georgian Poetry* II later in the year.[49] Plans were far enough advanced by May that Monro and Marsh could discuss the granting of American publishing rights for the forthcoming volume.[50] By the middle of July the task of selecting poets to be represented in the new volume was well under way, and Marsh was receiving suggestions, mildly solicited, from his poets about new faces for *Georgian Poetry* II. An American poet was at least momentarily considered for inclusion, as both Wilfrid Gibson and Lascelles Abercrombie attempted to convince Marsh in mid-July 1914 that the work of Robert Frost ought to be printed in *Georgian Poetry* II.* The campaign came to nothing, for Marsh excluded Frost on the grounds of his not being British.† Towards the end of July

---

* By mid-1914 Frost's relationships with many of the Georgian poets were close and cordial. He knew Harold Monro well, and he and his family lived near both the Gibson and Abercrombie families. Gibson and his new wife lived in the Old Nail House at Greenway, north of Dymock just over the Gloucestershire border in Herefordshire; Abercrombie and his family lived at The Gallows in Ryton, south-east of Dymock. Together the two poets had persuaded Frost to move and had acquired a cottage for him at Ledbury in Herefordshire, near both their houses. Several of Frost's poems of this period appeared in *New Numbers*, an imaginatively conceived though short-lived Georgian periodical published from The Gallows by Abercrombie, Gibson, and Rupert Brooke. During the spring and summer of 1914, Edward Thomas was a frequent visitor at both the Frosts' and the Abercrombies' cottages.
The poets' bucolic idyll was shattered in August, by the coming of the war, but for a few months in 1914 the Ryton, Dymock, poets lived in a near-perfect world. They tramped over the hills, talking or remaining silent, as the spirit moved; they discussed poetry over pints of country cider long into the night; amid the Gloucestershire spring they wrote their verse and read it to one another; and they edited a journal of poetry. Together they lived such a life of creative intensity, intellectual stimulation, and literary amity as would be difficult to duplicate in the history of twentieth-century literature. For a detailed, perceptive account of these months—and especially of Robert Frost's relations with the Ryton, Dymock, poets—see Elizabeth S. Sergeant, *Robert Frost: The Trial by Existence*, pp. 121–47. See also Mrs. Lascelles Abercrombie's recollections of the period in *The Listener*, 15th Nov. 1956, pp. 793–4.
† Wilfrid Gibson to E. M., 18th July 1914; Lascelles Abercrombie to E. M., 15th July [1914], *MLC*. Marsh made the decision to restrict his anthology to British poets only with *GP* II, in 1914. In 1912, when *GP* I was under consideration, it will be recalled that he had directly approached Ezra Pound for a contribution (see above, this chapter).

Marsh was also experiencing a difficulty unusual in the history of the early volumes of *Georgian Poetry*: two poets demurred at inclusion of their work in the forthcoming volume. For reasons unknown Ford Maddox Hueffer declined to permit his 'Heaven' to be reprinted in *Georgian Poetry* II;* and John Masefield entirely declined, in the beginning, Marsh's request for poems of the past two years. Masefield's reasons are clearer than Hueffer's. Much of his work of the period under review was shortly to be published in a new volume, and he refused to risk decreasing the potential sales of that volume by publishing any of the same poems simultaneously elsewhere. Moreover, he argued, his best works of the period were long poems, which he might wish 'at some future time to revise, cut or suppress. . . . I feel that a writer ought not to print long poems in anthologies, for this reason, that his doing so gives them from his control into other hands, where, in spite of the utmost good will on both sides, it may be impossible for him to correct or annul if the wish arise. I am very sorry to be disobliging to you, and to be out of such distinguished company, but with so small a body of work to choose from, and the other quite cogent reasons always in one's mind, I'm afraid I must stand aside'.[51] This absolute refusal did not stand long, for Marsh's persuasive powers soon softened Masefield to the point where he at least offered two of his 'antique lyrics' (as he called them) first published in 1911 and 1912, for the forthcoming anthology. But Marsh could not convince Masefield that there was no essential difference between publishing one's poems in volume form and in an anthology. Against Marsh's most urgent persuasions he remained firm.[52]

A little less than two weeks after the argument was settled on Masefield's terms, all such disputes became suddenly and entirely irrelevant. On 4th August 1914 England went to war. *Georgian Poetry* II was indefinitely postponed. The initial impact of the war was no less stunning upon the Georgian poets than upon the average British citizen. In the first weeks many of the poets gave way to a pessimism over the future of poetry which was shortly to prove unfounded. The Poetry Bookshop would immediately have to close its doors, Monro reported. 'Everything else' except

* Lascelles Abercrombie to E. M., 15th July [1914], *MLC*. His opinion having been requested by E. M., Abercrombie criticized an unnamed poem by Hueffer. On the margin of the letter in E. M.'s hand appears the notation, 'About *Heaven* by Ford Maddox Hueffer, wh. I wanted to put into *Georgian Poetry*. Hueffer refused.'

the war 'has sunk into silly insignificance', he wrote; ' "business" has absolutely stopped. From the day war was declared scarcely anyone has entered the shop'. Perhaps by next spring, he predicted, a second volume of *Georgian Poetry* could again be considered, but for the moment it was out of the question.[53] Lascelles Abercrombie, far removed from the Bohemian atmosphere of Devonshire Street in his rural haven in Ryton, Dymock, nonetheless felt much the same spirit as Monro. 'My occupation is gone, as completely as if it never were,' he wrote Marsh. 'God knows if anything will turn up. Meanwhile, I try to write poetry, which seems ridiculous fiddle-faddle these terrific times.'[54] W. H. Davies wrote more matter-of-factly: 'The arts are out of the question. . . . Of course you can't publish a second G.P. now,' he told Marsh.[55]

But there is no evidence that Marsh himself abandoned the idea of publishing his second volume. Rather he notified his poets merely that publication had been postponed. Marsh expressed nothing but the most cordial agreement with such of his contributors as Wilfrid Gibson, who argued that even if *Georgian Poetry* II were to turn out to be an unsuccessful venture it should eventually be published for two reasons: 'I think it essential to do all we can to keep our flag flying during this triumph of barbarism. And, at the least, the more reasonable diversions people have just now the better.'[56] And so the eventual appearance of *Georgian Poetry* II was virtually assured, though in the case of the second volume, at least, the biennial pattern of the series would have to be abandoned in favour of a triennial. If the postponement were to be too long, one of the contributors facetiously predicted to Marsh, 'I expect it'll have to come out as "Wilhelmian Poetry"!'[57]

After the first few months, despite all the early pessimism, the war perceptibly quickened the demand for poetry. The 'Business as Usual' signs which began appearing in windows of London tradesmen also apparently expressed the attitude of the poets. As the *Times Literary Supplement* reported in 1917, the pre-war 'frenzy for poetic composition' continued to 'sweep through the country without abatement' during the beginning war years, a fact which 'shows certainly that the love of letters in this country is not weakening, but was never more alive'. In 1915 that journal had received 265 volumes of 'original verse' for review (excluding anthologies, one presumes), but in 1916 that figure had leaped to 335.[58] The Poetry Bookshop failed to bear out Monro's gloomy predictions, for by mid-1915 it was serving more patrons than it had during its first year—though perhaps their cultural competence left something to be desired (e.g. the enthusiastic lady who inquired of Monro which poets would be 'incarcerated' in *Georgian Poetry* II. Monro added, not unkindly, 'She looked unhappy after she'd said it.').[59]

By mid-July 1915 Marsh had decided to publish his second volume the following November even though he had received only three months before the most grievous blow of his life: the death of Rupert Brooke in the Aegean. The book was in a very real sense Marsh's first memorial to his friend, the dedication being to both Brooke and Flecker, who had also died (though of natural causes) in early 1915. The Georgians were delighted at positive word from Marsh on the resumption of the series, not only because of possible personal gain from a new volume, but primarily because they agreed that the time was propitious to strike a second blow for the cause of modern poetry. 'Apart from my own personal interest,' wrote Gordon Bottomley, 'this does seem the one moment, while Rupert Brooke and Flecker seem still almost here, for a G.P. that would gather up the past and open out to the future, and I feel that if it is issued in the coming months it might have a drive and an urgency that would not be the same for a post-war publication.'[60] Even Monro, naturally more cautious and more familiar with publishing conditions than his editor, agreed that the volume ought to be published in November. In fact, one of the contributors to the volume, W. H. Davies, suggested that it was Monro who persuaded Marsh to bring it out at that time, though such an assumption appears unlikely.[61]

The pre-publication chores in the late summer of 1915 were comparatively light because most of the necessary decisions had been made the previous year, before the interruption of the war. By 5th September the volume was virtually ready to go to the printer; by mid-October the proofs were being turned out. Wartime vicissitudes seem to have intervened less than might have been expected. One finds Monro fuming at one point that sheets were held up because a compositor had been removed from his task as midwife to the muse to set up type for a front-page advertisement for the *Daily Mail*. Said Monro, 'they couldn't have made a more ugly excuse'.[62] But the volume appeared precisely on schedule in November 1915. The only visible Doubting Thomas among the contributors was James Stephens, who commented sourly to Marsh some four months after the volume had been published, 'I doubt if your second book will break records like the first—the times are out of joint.'[63] He proved an extremely poor prophet. *Georgian Poetry* II not only duplicated but surpassed the triumph of its predecessor. By the end of March 1916 the volume had sold almost 4,000 copies, and Monro had ordered a reprint of 3,000 in anticipation of even larger sales.[64] He was not disappointed. Both the semi-yearly accountings which he rendered Marsh and an astounding total sale of 19,000 copies reinforce the assertion that *Georgian Poetry* II, poetically superior to any of the other four volumes, was also the most popular. 'If there is ever a "quotation" for English poetry in the market-place again,' Gordon Bottomley wrote Marsh, 'I shall always hold that it has been your doing; but, beyond that, I and all your filial Georgians must always be grateful to you for your invention and happy daring that have found so many new-ways-in-one for our work to make its appeal.'[65]

# 6

## Georgian Summer

From the historical point of view *Georgian Poetry* I and II are both of a piece; their differences are largely differences in degree, their similarities inherent and fundamental. The poems in both volumes were essentially products of the pre-war temper, even though the second was not published until fifteen months after the outbreak of war. *Georgian Poetry* II of course had first been prepared for publication in November 1914, and the selection of poems and poets had been all but completed by August, when war had intervened.

There is no evidence to suggest that the book which finally appeared in November 1915 was in any essential respect very much different from the one Edward Marsh had planned fifteen months earlier. The twelve poets whose work was the strength and sinew of the first volume remained in the second: Abercrombie, Bottomley, Davies, Brooke, de la Mare, Drinkwater, Flecker, Gibson, Lawrence, Masefield, Monro, and Stephens. Five peripheral poets whose work had appeared in *Georgian Poetry* I were excluded from II. G. K. Chesterton, Sturge Moore, and Sir Ronald Ross, having served Marsh's purpose by lending a note of respectability and tradition to the chorus of new voices, were not to be found in *Georgian Poetry* II because, as Marsh explained, 'they belong in fact to an earlier poetic generation, and their inclusion must be allowed to have been an anachronism'. Edmund Beale Sargant and Robert Trevelyan were not represented in the second volume because, Marsh charitably observed, 'they have published nothing that comes within its scope'.[1] Only two new names appeared in *Georgian Poetry* II, Ralph Hodgson and Francis Ledwidge.

It seems reasonable to expect, moreover, that an anthology which purported to exhibit the best achievement of British poetry from 1913 through 1915 might have contained a fair sprinkling of war poems. But *Georgian Poetry* II ignored the war almost completely. Turning its pages, one sees almost no evidence that fifteen months of war had even slightly ruffled British poetic sensibilities. Among the fifty-two poems and two poetic dramas which appeared in *Georgian Poetry* II, only three poems dealt directly with the subject of war, Brooke's 'The Soldier', Drinkwater's 'Of Greatham', and Flecker's 'The Dying Patriot'.* By the calendar of *Georgian Poetry* II the time was still early 1914.

From the critical point of view *Georgian Poetry* I and II also appear remarkably similar. Though the pattern is far clearer in 1915 than in 1912, both volumes were cut from the same cloth. Taken separately, to be sure, *Georgian Poetry* I appears tentative, even random. There is certainly no evidence in it alone which would lead one to doubt Edward Marsh's disavowal of any intention in 1912 'of founding a school, or tracing a course for Poetry to follow'. Between the covers of *Georgian Poetry* I was poetry to satisfy a wide range of tastes: a fragment of Chesterton's *Ballad of the White Horse*; the first part of Sturge Moore's *Sicilian Idyll*, as 'traditional' a bit of verse as one could wish for; two of Flecker's symbolic poems in the Parnassian tradition; Abercrombie's 'Sale of St. Thomas' and Bottomley's 'End of the World', both excellent examples of the new realism; Lawrence's 'Snapdragon', an emotionally charged poem which blinds by a fine excess; Davies's finely chiselled nature lyrics; or de la Mare's 'The Listeners' and 'Arabia', haunting evocations of the far-away and the strange. In view of such diversity, one can readily believe that Marsh's 'sole and simple object', as he said, 'was to provide a means by which writers whose work seemed to me to be beautiful and neglected might find a hearing from the reading public—to get the light out from under the bushel'.[2]

With the benefit of hindsight, however, one comes to see that in spite of its apparent lack of direction, *Georgian Poetry* I had sufficient homogeneity to act at least as 'a symptom and a rallying point of the new tendencies' in pre-war verse.[3] But it is only from the vantage point of 1915, with *Georgian Poetry* II in hand, that one

---

* Gibson's 'The Going', a short poetic tribute and farewell to Rupert Brooke, might possibly be added to this category.

can recognize where these 'new tendencies' were leading, for in *Georgian Poetry* II, far from being altered, several of the themes which had been only tentatively suggested in the first volume were reinforced and made more clearly evident. Taken together, then, *Georgian Poetry* I and II afford some evidence for claiming the existence of a specifically 'Georgian' poetic.*

As many a critic has discovered, however, the word 'Georgian' is treacherous, for, among other difficulties, the term must be applied to an uncomfortably large number of very different poets. How can one meaningfully claim that the verse of both Walter de la Mare and John Masefield is 'Georgian'? Moreover, as the history of the first two volumes of *Georgian Poetry* suggests, in the beginning at least, Georgianism was not a poetic 'movement' at all. It 'started in reaction against nothing except a general neglect of modern poetry'; its beginnings 'were more or less casual and entirely untheoretical'.[4] There were no Georgian manifestoes; through 1915 the Georgian poets were 'a group rather than a movement'.[5] And so one is suspicious when a critic like Herbert Palmer draws up a list of fourteen specific canons by which he believes 'Georgian' poetry can be defined. Among other Georgian traits he lists: restraint of diction; avoidance of archaic diction like 'thee' and 'thou', 'o'er' and 'ta'en'; avoidance of the obscure, bizarre, or vernacular; avoidance of symbolism; avoidance of national or patriotic themes; rejection of 'all verbal cheapness and facility'; and emphasis on nature and country life.[6] Unfortunately, major exceptions can be pointed out to each of these canons; the definition of 'Georgian' is nowhere near so precise or so neat as Palmer would make it. As Edward Marsh wrote in rebuttal, in drawing up such a formidable list of canons Palmer 'pays my lucidity and my purposefulness a compliment which they do not deserve'.[7] If it is to be defined at all, the term 'Georgian' must be placed in a far less rigid—and even less literary—context than Palmer's, for from 1912 to 1915 it connotes not so much a poetic coterie as a state of mind held in common by poets of divergent aims and methods. As Arundel del Re remarked, Georgianism was

---

* Obviously, the term 'Georgian', as it is used here and will be used in subsequent chapters, has a more restricted meaning than heretofore (cf. Ch. 1). I am beginning to use the adjective not in its merely generic or temporal sense, but to describe specifically the work of those poets chosen for representation in *GP* I and II. Much of the present chapter is devoted to explaining what is implied, in this restricted sense of the word, by 'Georgian' poetry. One more distinction in terms yet remains to be made below. Cf. 'Neo-Georgian', Ch. 7.

'not created artificially by the deliberate acceptance of narrow technical articles of [poetic] belief'. The term 'Georgian' 'indicated an attitude more spiritual than intellectual'.[8]

What did it mean, then, to be 'Georgian' in 1912–15? It is not begging the question to answer simply, in the first place, it meant to be 'modern'. For *Georgian Poetry* I and II were clearly children of their age—just as clearly as *Blast*, the *Egoist*, or *Des Imagistes*. And they were 'new', in the same sense that feminism, moving pictures, and airplanes were 'new'.[9] Indeed, for a few brief years just before the war, 'the image of modern poetry in the minds of most educated readers was that presented by the Georgian movement'.[10] However fusty they may appear to a later generation, in their own place and time the first two volumes of *Georgian Poetry* were deemed fresh and exciting because they were thought to share many of the 'new tendencies' of the pre-war poetic renaissance. They shared, for example, that sense of spiritual buoyancy common to most of the poets of Left and Centre. The Georgians had abandoned, they thought, the effete scepticism of the poets of the nineties. They were possessed of positive, definite beliefs about life and art; they tried to see once again with their own eyes, feel with their own passions. And, as one of them wrote, 'any belief is better than none, and any passion is better than a languid devotion to absinthe'.[11]

'Good morning, Life—and all / Things glad and beautiful,' cried W. H. Davies. The characteristic tone of *Georgian Poetry* I, its cohesive force, wrote D. H. Lawrence, was 'a note of exultation in the vast freedom . . . we have suddenly got'. One sees it in poems so diverse as Abercrombie's 'Sale of St. Thomas', where 'the deadly sin is Prudence, that will not risk to avail itself of the new freedom'; and 'Dining-room Tea', where Brooke sees

> every glint
> Posture and jest and thought and tint
> Freed from the mask of transiency
> Triumphant in eternity,
> Immote, immortal;

and even in Masefield, who, though he 'seems nearest to the black dream behind us', can still 'trust the happy moments' and write

> when men count
> Those hours of life that were a bursting fount

> Sparkling the dusty heart with living springs,
> There seems a world, beyond our earthly things,
> Gated by golden moments.

Nor was the new 'exultation' to be confused with the joy which arises from desperation, the snatching at golden moments only because nothing gold can stay. 'There is no "carpe diem" touch,' Lawrence exclaimed. 'The joy is sure and fast. It is not the falling rose, but the rose for ever rising to bud and falling to fruit that gives us joy. We have faith in the vastness of life's wealth. We are always rich. . . . There is no winter that we fear.'[12]

Again, the Georgian poets shared with all the 'modern' pre-war poets the conviction of standing at the beginning of a poetic renaissance. While freely admitting that their age had no Wordsworth, no Tennyson, no one poetic luminary *sui generis*, still most Georgians, critics and poets alike, agreed in the main with one of their number who claimed that 'for mass of good work fit for the anthologies and produced by many hands I do not see any age since the Elizabethan which can compare with ours'.[13] In the eyes of many observers the mere appearance of *Georgian Poetry* I, to say nothing of Edward Marsh's astute preface, was evidence enough that something new and vital was stirring the poetic air in late 1912. And its immediate success convinced all but the most sceptical. To be sure, there were a few who, even after the demonstrable success of *Georgian Poetry* I, remained unconvinced. The poetic renaissance was in fact too well organized to seem entirely genuine or spontaneous, they argued; it smacked too much of a stunt; it was based on synthetically stirred-up enthusiasm.[14] There were also those who did not entirely share Edward Marsh's confidence in either the new age or the new verse, who pointed out that no quantity of 'good work fit for the anthologies', however new, could make up for a certain lack of quality. The new poetry, 'like everything else in the democratic age, seems to be more remarkable for extent and size than for distinction', wrote one of them.[15] But such Jeremiahs were the exception. Even when *Georgian Poetry* II was published, in November 1915, there was no evidence that the war had as yet caused many Georgian readers, critics, or poets to question the continuance of the poetic renaissance. To the contrary, Edward Marsh's second volume seemed in most quarters to afford fresh evidence of the vitality of the new poetry.[16] Confidence in a renaissance, a new surge of creative energy in poetry,

marks the spirit of the times into which both *Georgian Poetry* I and
II fell, as it marks the spirit of the volumes themselves.

To be 'Georgian' in 1912–15 meant also to share in the prevailing anti-Victorianism of the age. When Ezra Pound claimed in
1912 that 'modern' poetry must 'move against' Victorian 'poppycock'—that it must no longer 'try to seem forcible by rhetorical
din, and luxurious riot', must have 'fewer painted adjectives impeding the shock and stroke of it', and must be 'direct, free from
emotional slither'—he was speaking not only for the Leftist poets
but for most of the Georgians as well.[17] The Georgians, too,
resolved to liberate their poetry from what they considered the
two major nineteenth-century vices: Victorian lushness—the 'cult
of the decorated adjective', as Richard Aldington called it—and
*fin de siècle* enervation. This resolve was reflected in the tone, form,
and diction of much Georgian verse.

Contemporary critics accepted the anti-Victorian tone of Edward Marsh's first two volumes almost as a matter of course. One
of them even argued that *Georgian Poetry* II had bent over so far
backwards in its attempt to escape odious Victorian flaccidity that
it had become 'Futurist'.* To see Futurism in *Georgian Poetry* II is
to carry its anti-Victorian proclivities to absurd extremes. Robert
Bridges rather more correctly analysed the real nature of the Georgian's anti-Victorian bias while at the same time pointing out the
principal danger it posed to the new poets. 'I do not wish to
criticise,' he wrote Marsh after having read *Georgian Poetry* I, 'but
I may say that I think I am mainly sympathetic with the psychological tendency of the "school", which is generally, I suppose, a
reaction ag$^{st}$ intellectualism. As far as a new moral position is
deduced from this, I feel that the necessity of its being subordi-
nated to aesthetic beauty is in danger of being lost sight of. I feel
sometimes as if I were being reminded of postimpressionists' pictures. You know however that I am not opposed to novelties and
that I welcome any assault against dead conventional bondage.'[18]
Bridges made no mistake. In its time and place *Georgian Poetry* I
was an 'assault'—albeit a polite one—'against dead conventional
bondage'. It was also an implicit 'reaction against intellectualism',
against the kind of 'intellectualism' which was displayed in *Marius*

* *Land and Water*, 4th Dec. 1915, p. 17. Absurd as the accusation may sound, one
nevertheless recalls the assertion of Mayakovsky regarding the wide generic use, or
misuse, of the term by 1916: 'Futurism has died as a particular group, but it has
poured itself out in everyone in a flood. Today all are futurists.' See above, Ch. 2.

or the 'Conclusion' to the *Renaissance* and which had produced the infirm verse of the nineties.

The reviewer for the *Times Literary Supplement* remarked much the same tone in *Georgian Poetry* I. For the first time in many years, he observed, poets seem again to have become the active shapers of experience, not merely passive, delicately tuned receivers of impressions. With *Georgian Poetry* I as a harbinger, it was clear, he predicted, that modern poetry will be something more than a mere record of subtle impressions and ephemeral emotions. It will be a product of mental activity. 'A poet who is afraid to use his brains', he wrote, 'seems nowadays to be as rare as was a poet twenty years ago who trusted anything but his sensibilities.' Some of the new experimental verse is not entirely successful, but, he concluded, 'the desire, however wild its aim may be at first, to clarify and shape experience, rather than sit receptively awaiting its impact, promises more for poetry than the power of writing now and then an exquisite lyric'.[19]

The revolt against late-Victorian tediousness was reflected not only in a Georgian tone but also in a characteristic Georgian form: the dramatic poem, 'the dramatic handling, in some form or other, of life and character'.[20] Almost all the Georgians were intent upon restoring drama to poetry. Several also attempted to restore poetry to the drama. It is no accident that in the work of such Georgians as Abercrombie and Bottomley the verse drama was revived in the pre-war years, for the Georgian temper was essentially dramatic. The Georgians' quarrel was not, of course, with the major Victorian poets who, like Browning, had excelled in dramatic verse, but with the poets of the nineties. *Fin de siècle* verse, as many Georgians thought, had been written too exclusively for the study; it had been allowed to become too cerebrated, too nearly inert. Poets of the modern world 'must decide whether they are writing for the stage or the study', cried Harold Monro; they cannot do both. He left little doubt which kind of poetry he preferred: 'Poets of the modern world! write us plays, simple, direct, dependent for their beauty, not on outward decoration, but on inward force of the spirit that conceives them.'[21] Lascelles Abercrombie agreed. The verse play gets 'closer to "life" ' than the prosaic drama of ideas currently in fashion, he argued, because the prose play seeks primarily to 'diagnose the diseases of life, and suggest cures ... putting ... problems—economic, moral, sociological—into concrete and impressive form'. The aim of drama should not be thus to inform or to preach, but to 'intoxicate' us into a heightened consciousness of 'spiritual reality . . . emotional reality'. Only by using poetry can drama assert its 'fundamental power . . . of forcing us into a state of astonishment—astonishment that glows to perceive with unexpected force that terrific splendid fact, the fact *that we do exist*'. Poetry on the stage is 'the alcohol to which the human organism answers with an intoxication of sense, mind, and emotion, bringing them into a unity of triumphant and delighted self-consciousness'.[22]

Even when not writing specifically for the stage—and only a few of them did—the major Georgian poets habitually wrote dramatic verse. In *Georgian Poetry* I, Rupert Brooke's 'Old Vicarage, Grantchester' and 'Dining-room Tea' are conceived within the framework of a dramatic situation skilfully woven into the fabric of each poem. Walter de la Mare's 'The Listeners' and 'The Sleeper' depend for their ultimate effects largely upon the reader's awareness of a small, suggestive, though fully imagined, dramatic situation. Wilfrid Gibson's 'Devil's Edge' and 'The Hare' are more fully developed pieces. Long narrative-dramatic poems phrased in the first person, they both relate one episode in sequence from beginning to end. Lascelles Abercrombie's 'Sale of St. Thomas' is an even more apt example. In conception it is a rudimentary poetic drama, with one setting and three characters who converse in poetic dialogue. It also poses a specific dramatic problem: shall St. Thomas carry the Gospel to India in spite of his fear of the land and of the barbarities practised upon foreigners? In more general terms, Thomas's problem is the problem of Everyman: shall one face life guided by prudence, or shall he, 'Knowing the possible . . . try beyond it / Into impossible things, unlikely ends'? Thomas decides upon the prudent course but as an ironic result is immediately sold into slavery. The stranger who buys Thomas speaks Abercrombie's characteristically Georgian theme:

> Now, Thomas, know thy sin. It was not fear;
> Easily may a man crouch down for fear,
> And yet rise up on firmer knees, and face
> The hailing storm of the world with graver courage.
> But prudence, prudence is the deadly sin, . . .
> For this refuses faith in the unknown powers

Within man's nature; shrewdly bringeth all
Their inspiration of strange eagerness
To a judgment bought by safe experience;
Narrows desire into the scope of thought.
But it is written in the heart of man,
Thou shalt no larger be than thy desire.

(*Georgian Poetry* i, pp. 20–1)

The tendency towards dramatic poetry was even more pronounced in *Georgian Poetry* ii. In addition to short dramatically conceived poems like those which had appeared in the first volume, *Georgian Poetry* ii contained two full-fledged poetic dramas, Abercrombie's 'End of the World' and Bottomley's 'King Lear's Wife'. That *Georgian Poetry* i and ii should have shown such a marked predilection for dramatic poetry was not simply a matter of individual poetic temperament nor even of Marsh's taste. Dramatic poetry was rather, one feels, the natural result, in the realm of form, of the Georgian's deliberate attempt to escape as thoroughly as possible from the poetic enervation of the late-Victorian age.

Another facet of the Georgian revolt against Victorianism is to be discerned not so much in tone or form as in poetic diction. The Georgians were by no means such extreme innovators as the Imagists or the Futurists, but in diction they showed themselves to be blood relatives to their more extreme contemporaries. Or so, at least, many of the observers of the time took them to be. Not that all the young poets in *Georgian Poetry* i and ii wrote in an identical style; but whether the poet was de la Mare or Masefield, Davies or Brooke, common to most of the Georgians was an attempt to achieve truth of diction. They consciously contrived to write in the accents of common speech while at the same time avoiding, for the most part, an unattractive and unpoetic flatness. In spite of its un-Georgian 'ere' and 'doth', Davies's 'Days Too Short' caught a moment of perfection in words as simple and uncomplex as the experience itself:

When primroses are out in Spring,
    And small blue violets come between;
    When merry birds sing on boughs green,
And rills, as soon as born, must sing;

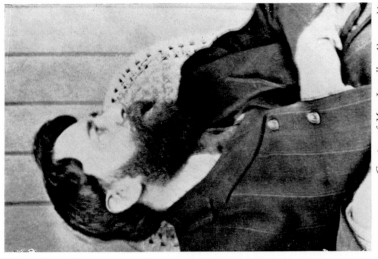

Gordon Bottomley, during a visit to the
Lascelles Abercrombies, 1917

Lascelles Abercrombie at Ryton, Dymock,
Gloucestershire, Spring 1914

Lascelles Abercrombie (*left*) and Gordon Bottomley and
Abercrombie's sons, 1917

When butterflies will make side-leaps
    As though escaped from Nature's hand
    Ere perfect quite; and bees will stand
Upon their heads in fragrant deeps;

When small clouds are so silvery white
    Each seems a broken rimmèd moon—
    When such things are, this world too soon,
For me, doth wear the veil of Night.

                                (*Georgian Poetry* I, p. 60)

Walter de la Mare could not only capture the sense of the strange, touched by the macabre, in such poems as 'The Listeners' and 'The Mocking Fairy', but he was also capable of the utmost simplicity of diction.

    One night as Dick lay half asleep,
        Into his drowsy eyes
    A great still light began to creep
        From out the silent skies.
    It was the lovely moon's, for when
        He raised his dreamy head,
    Her surge of silver filled the pane
        And streamed across his bed.
    So, for awhile, each gazed at each—
        Dick and the solemn moon—
    Till, climbing slowly on her way,
        She vanished, and was gone.

                    ('Full Moon', *Georgian Poetry* II, p. 82)

At its worst the characteristic Georgian antipathy towards 'decorated' verse, rhetoric, and archaic diction led to poetry which seems ingenuously banal. But at its best, Georgian diction can be deceptive, for its very simplicity may sometimes lull a reader into failing to recognize the high order of technical mastery implied. In their diction, indeed, many of the Georgians were successfully reviving one of the primary articles of the preface to the *Lyrical Ballads*. The secret of their diction was in truth no secret at all; it was 'their birthright, inherited from those predecessors who from Wordsworth and Coleridge onwards have worked for the assimilation of verse to the manner and accent of natural speech'.[23]

To be Georgian in 1912–15, then, connoted several things. It meant to be 'modern', in the sense that the Georgian shared with most pre-war poets the prevailing spiritual euphoria and the confidence that poetry was being infused with a new, vital release of creative energy. It meant also to be anti-Victorian, to write poetry which, in tone, form, and diction, was free of both *fin de siècle* weariness and Victorian 'painted adjectives'. But above all, Georgianism in 1912–15 was synonymous with realism.

Poetic realism, or truth to life, was the one feature which distinguished *Georgian Poetry* I and II from other contemporary anthologies and which gave the Georgians their most nearly unique hallmark.* As it was exemplified in *Georgian Poetry* I and II, realism connoted two qualities, the first a state of mind in the poets themselves, the second a technique of writing verse. As a state of mind among the Georgian poets, realism came to mean primarily anti-sentimentalism. As a technique of verse writing it came to mean the inclusion in poetry of details, however nasty, which presumably possessed truth to reality as it was perceived by the five senses.

*Georgian Poetry* II stirred up a critical storm because of the alleged coarseness and brutality of some of the selections Marsh chose for inclusion; but although many critics in 1915 were shocked, they could scarcely have been surprised, for *Georgian Poetry* I had already pointed the way. In early 1913 the *Times Literary Supplement* had taken the Georgians to task for their 'affected and self-conscious brutality'.[24] Edmund Gosse had observed the same tendency. The poets collected in Marsh's first volume, he had written, 'exchange the romantic, the sentimental, the fictive conceptions of literature, for an ingenuousness, sometimes a violence, almost a rawness in the approach to life itself'.[25] And in the same vein J. C. Squire had claimed that the chief tendency of *Georgian Poetry* I

---

* Among recent critics of the Georgians perhaps only Alan Pryce-Jones is sufficiently emphatic in his insistence upon realism as the major, pre-eminent Georgian hallmark. 'It is impossible to imagine Sir William Watson writing a poem about sea-sickness,' Pryce-Jones points out, 'yet the subject came quite naturally to Rupert Brooke. After all, people *are* sea-sick; why, then, should they not write poems which —in Eddie Marsh's phrase—are disquieting to read at meals ?' In subsequent volumes of *Georgian Poetry*, the Brooke-Masefield-Abercrombie strain of realism was seized upon and further developed by such poets as Sassoon, Graves, and Nichols in their battlefield poems (see below, Ch. 7). 'But at the start,' Pryce-Jones quite rightly asserts, 'what Marsh called Georgian poetry was no more than poetry which avoided as its first enemy the insipid.' The point must be insisted upon because the inert, bloodless verse of some of the poets who appeared in Marsh's two post-war volumes, in 1919 and 1922, 'made much Georgian poetry appear to later readers hardly less insipid than the schools of writing which it was trying to supplant' (see below, Ch. 10). Alan Pryce-Jones, ed., *Georgian Poets*, pp. 5–6.

'seemed to be . . . towards the realism, sometimes informed with a conscious brutality, of Mr. Masefield, Mr. Gibson, and Mr. Abercrombie'.[26] 'Biography', the Masefield poem Marsh chose for his first volume, certainly contained no 'conscious brutality', but here and there in a flashing image one sees the realist's eye—in the description of London, for instance:

> Dull Bloomsbury streets of dull brick mansions old
> With stinking doors where women stood to scold
> And drunken waits at Christmas with their horn
> Droning the news, in snow, that Christ was born.
>
> *(Georgian Poetry* i, p. 121)

Gibson's contribution, 'The Hare', recounted the adventures of a young moorlands wanderer with a gipsy girl. If realism is to be described only as truth to detail or the faithful rendering of scenes from the lives of the lower classes and social outcasts, perhaps 'The Hare' fits the description; but nowhere in the poem does one encounter any 'self-conscious brutality'. Gibson's realism in *Georgian Poetry* i was rather more infused with a love of the beautiful than of the ugly, the sordid, or the brutal.

Lascelles Abercrombie was perhaps the foremost practitioner of the more brutal kind of realism. In his 'Sale of St. Thomas' in *Georgian Poetry* i Abercrombie's attempts at truth to life centred around several particularly repellent pictures of India. The ship's captain described the sadistic pleasure of the Indian King, for example, in this passage:

> There was a merchant came
> To Travancore, and could not speak our talk;
> And, it chanced, he was brought before the throne
> Just when the king was weary of sweet pleasures.
> So, to better his tongue, a rope was vent
> Beneath his oxters, up he was hauled, and fire
> Let singe the soles of his feet, until his legs
> Wriggled like frying eels; then the king's dogs
> Were set to hunt the hirpling man. The king
> Laught greatly and cried, 'But give the dogs words they know,
> And they'll be tame.'
>
> *(Georgian Poetry* i, p. 12)

Or he described the fate meted out to missionaries like St. Thomas in this passage:

> Another stranger
> Who swore he knew of better gods than ours,
> Seemed to the king troubled with fleas, and slaves
> Were told to groom him smartly, which they did
> Thoroughly with steel combs, until at last
> They curried the living flesh from off his bones
> And stript his face of gristle, till he was
> Skull and half skeleton and yet alive.
>
> *(Georgian Poetry* i, p. 12)

But the passages which called greatest attention to themselves
were those in which Abercrombie described the flies of India, for
in them it became apparent that the poet was using realistic detail
with 'self-conscious brutality', for no well-defined artistic effect,
that is, but rather simply for its own sake.

> And flies! a land of flies! where the hot soil
> Foul with ceaseless decay steams into flies!
> So thick they pile themselves in the air above
> Their meal of filth, they seem like breathing heaps
> Of formless life mounded upon the earth; . . .
> I abhor flies,—to see them stare upon me
> Out of their little faces of gibbous eyes;
> To feel the dry cool skin of their bodies alight
> Perching upon my lips!
>
> *(Georgian Poetry* i, p. 16)

*Georgian Poetry* ii brought the issue of poetic realism to a head.
The tendency towards disagreeable descriptions of animal life
begun by Abercrombie continued. In a poem which managed to
be extremely effective in spite of its realism, Ralph Hodgson
described a wild bull, deposed leader of a herd, awaiting death at
the edge of a jungle lake.

> Pity him that he must wake;
> Even now the swarm of flies
> Blackening his bloodshot eyes
> Bursts and blusters round the lake,
> Scattered from the feast half-fed,
> By great shadows overhead.
>
> And the dreamer turns away
> From his visionary herds
> And his splendid yesterday,

148

Turns to meet the loathly birds
Flocking round him from the skies
Waiting for the flesh that dies.

('The Bull', *Georgian Poetry* ii, p. 142)

And into his short play 'Hoops', Wilfrid Gibson managed to
inject a mildly revolting description of camels. A deformed,
crippled stableman was given the lines:

And then consider camels: only think
Of camels long enough, and you'ld go mad—
With all their humps and lumps; their knobbly knees,
Splay feet, and straddle legs; their sagging necks,
Flat flanks, and scraggly tails, and monstrous teeth.
I've not forgotten the first fiend I met:
'Twas in a lane in Smyrna, just a ditch
Between the shuttered houses, and so narrow
The brute's bulk blocked the road; the huge green stack
Of dewy fodder that it slouched beneath
Brushing the yellow walls on either hand,
And shutting out the strip of burning blue:
And I'd to face that vicious bobbing head
With evil eyes, slack lips, and nightmare teeth,
And duck beneath the snaky, squirming neck, . . .
I felt that muzzle take me by the scruff,
And heard those murderous teeth crunching my spine,
Before I stooped—though I dodged safely under.

(*Georgian Poetry* ii, pp. 121–2)

Most of the attack and parry, however, centred around the two
major verse plays that the volume contained, 'End of the World'
and 'King Lear's Wife'. The former had been published in early
1914 in the second issue of *New Numbers*, but the latter was
published for the first time and even given the place of honour in
*Georgian Poetry* ii. Most of the objections to Abercrombie's 'End
of the World' were directed not so much to the poet's use of
realism *per se* as to its artistic irrelevancy and the apparently deliberate brutality of Abercrombie's conception. Such passages as
that in which one of Abercrombie's rustics described how frogs
were crushed under cartwheels seemed only, as D. H. Lawrence
said, 'nasty efforts at cruelty'.

> When I was young
> My mother would catch us frogs and set them down,
> Lapt in a screw of paper, in the ruts,
> And carts going by would quash 'em; and I'ld laugh,
> And yet be thinking, 'Suppose it was myself
> Twisted stiff in huge paper, and wheels
> Big as the wall of a barn treading me flat!'
>
> *(Georgian Poetry* ii, p. 200)

The objections to Bottomley's 'King Lear's Wife' were of much
the same order: the brutality was too deliberate, too conscious.
The clearest evidence of this tendency lay in the corpsewasher's
song Bottomley had inserted at the end of his play. The body of
Hygd, Lear's queen, lay newly dead on a bed at the front of the
stage. Two women, one young, one elderly, were assigned to lay
out the corpse for burial. While the younger woman straightened
the Queen's feet, tied them together, and knotted the hair, the
elder sang a particularly revolting parody of the nursery song 'A
Frog He Would a-Wooing Go':

> A louse crept out of my lady's shift—
> Ahumm, Ahumm, Ahee—
> Crying 'Oi! Oi! We are turned adrift;
> The lady's bosom is cold and stiffed,
> And her arm-pit's cold for me.'
>
> 'The lady's linen's no longer neat;'—
> Ahumm, Ahumm, Ahee—
> 'Her savour is neither warm nor sweet;
> It's close for two in a winding sheet,
> And lice are too good for worms to eat;
> So here's no place for me.'
>
> The louse made off unhappy and wet;—
> Ahumm, Ahumm, Ahee—
> He's looking for us, the little pet;
> So haste, for her chin's to tie up yet,
> And let us be gone with what we can get—
> Her ring for thee, her gown for Bet,
> Her pocket turned out for me.
>
> *(Georgian Poetry* ii, pp. 41, 42, 47)

Not that Marsh had lacked warnings that in publishing such
plays he was likely to bring the critical roof down on his head.

Even before their appearance between the covers of *Georgian Poetry* ii both plays had amply demonstrated their power to provoke controversy. When 'End of the World' had been published in 1914 in *New Numbers*, there had come an angry polemic from D. H. Lawrence that might have served to make Marsh more cautious had he not possessed such complete faith in his own poetic tastes. 'I expected Abercrombie's long poem to be great indeed,' Lawrence wrote Marsh, but 'I think I have never seen him at worse advantage' than in this play. 'The spirit of the thing altogether seems mean and rather vulgar. . . . No, but it is *bitterly* disappointing. He who loves *Paradise Lost* must don the red nose and rough-spun cloak of Masefield and Wilfrid. And you encourage it—it is too bad. . . . I hate and detest his ridiculous imitation yokels . . . I loathe his rather nasty efforts at cruelty, like the wrapping frogs in paper and putting them for cartwheels to crush.' Abercrombie's most serious disability was not merely artistic; it was spiritual. He was afflicted with a sickness of soul, Lawrence concluded, which had made his poetic creations 'mean and rather sordid, and full of rancid hate. He talked of *Sons and Lovers* being all *odi et amo*. Well, I wish I could find the "*amo*" in this poem of his. It is sheer "*odi*", and rather mean hatred at that. . . . What has happened to him? Something seems to be going bad in his soul. . . . The feelings in these late things are corrupt and dirty'.[27]

The warning signals were equally unmistakable in the case of 'King Lear's Wife'. John Drinkwater, who was assisting Barry Jackson with the Birmingham Repertory Company, had obtained Bottomley's permission to produce the play in the summer of 1915, and the premier performance took place in Birmingham on 25th September of that year. A gala foregathering of Georgian poets was planned to celebrate the occasion, but though Marsh had planned to join the group, he was kept away by other business. Bottomley, Abercrombie, and Gibson were on hand, however, and knowing Marsh's great interest in the play reported the performance in some detail. Without exception each declared himself greatly impressed. ' "King Lear's Wife" duly made her appearance on Saturday night,' Drinkwater wrote, 'and very proud I am to have been the cause of it. . . . That Gordon and Wilfrid were delighted there is, I think, no doubt, and in work of this kind it is the opinion of the two or three that outweighs the world.'[28] Abercrombie was even more enthusiastic. The power of the play 'came out in an amazing way', he reported. 'It seemed to me the high water mark of modern drama, apart from its lovely poetry. The interest is so astoundingly various and shifting, yet so superbly unified.'* The author declared himself entirely satisfied. 'We had a charming time,' he wrote; 'I sat in a box with my feet on purple cushions, and Lascelles and John and Barry Jackson supported me below.'[29]

But had he chosen, Marsh might also have read some danger signals between the lines of his poets' comments. The play was, to say the least, controversial. The corpsewasher's song was too much for the stomach of the censor, who refused to allow its inclusion in the acted version of the play; the press notices were unanimously unfavourable; and the houses were disappointingly small. 'The audience loathed the play,' wrote Abercrombie succinctly.[30] Drinkwater agreed: 'The houses have been bad, but that's not surprising. A "fit audience find though few"—to do this is all the poets can yet hope to do in the theatre, but it doesn't matter. Those who do care, care very much.'[31] In something of the same spirit both author and producer shook off the bad press. Commercial failure, they agreed, was virtually prima facie evidence of artistic success. Drinkwater reported after the first performance:

> The papers to-day are brutal and obscene, to poet and play and instigator of this event alike. No one escapes, tho' the hardest fury falls on Gordon [Bottomley] and Kathleen [Drinkwater]. . . . Gordon himself laughs at them out of his great beard, and I console myself by blaspheming in my loudest voice. And we are all a contented party in the middle of it all. The Censor added to our gaiety by sending horrified protests on Saturday about the louse and the lady's shift, in a letter which I have given as an heirloom for ever to the clan Bottomley.[32]

Bottomley professed himself nothing but amused by the Philistinism of the Birmingham press. 'I feel sure you will be as delighted as I have been,' he told Marsh, 'to know that Mrs. Lear is a gifted mistake, a beastly drama of blood and lust—, that it dragged

---

* In Abercrombie's view, however, the acting was not quite up to the play. Mrs. Drinkwater as Queen Hygd 'spoke magnificently', he conceded, but Margaret Chatwin's efforts as Goneril left something to be desired: 'Goneril, for some strange reason, assumed the costume and the manners of an Irish washerwoman with a broken heart. I kept expecting her to break off her long speech about her hunting with—"Of course it's the drink, sir. I'm not always like this, but it's the drink comes over me: I can't put it by somehow"—or something of that kind' (Lascelles Abercrombie to E. M., 2nd Oct. [1915], MLC).

Shakespeare into the Divorce Court, and that it is an offence to all rightminded men in this time of national sorrow and mourning.' The whole matter was simply 'too comic to be upset about. . . . I couldn't have minded the press notices while I was seeing how my play had built itself up into such a rich romantic thing under John's producing hands, or while Lascelles and Wilfrid and John were praising it so splendidly. I felt it was a rare thing to be there with them'.[33]

In spite of the fact that storm signals were flying from several quarters, however, Marsh persisted in publishing both 'End of the World' and 'King Lear's Wife' in *Georgian Poetry* II. There is every evidence that he published them not because he thought it in any sense an anthologist's duty to do so, but simply because he admired them. In fact, he seemed more enthusiastic about these two plays than about the work of any other Georgian poets—Brooke excepted—in the history of the anthology. When he first heard Abercrombie read 'End of the World' in early 1914, Marsh wrote to Rupert Brooke: 'L[ascelles] read out of his *End of the World*, now finished, and to appear in the 2nd *N[ew] N[umbers]*. It's a sublime work, in its fusion of poetry and comedy there has been nothing like it.' And when he heard that the poem would be dedicated to him, Marsh predicted that the dedication 'will in itself assure me of immortality'.[34]

About 'King Lear's Wife' Marsh waxed even more enthusiastic. It is the 'only one really great literary event' of 1914, he wrote Brooke. 'The poetic drama is born again, of that there is no doubt. It is short, but the action, the character drawing, and the verses are all the work of a master. There are lines that are like nothing but the famous things in Webster.'[35] Upon reading the play for the first time he even felt impelled to send Bottomley a telegram of praise.[36] He also set about immediately devising means of getting the play on the boards in London, and he approached both Granville Barker and Basil Dean as possible producers.* Above all he

* Gordon Bottomley to E. M., 23rd June 1914, *MLC*. The war put a temporary stop to E. M.'s efforts to get the play produced, but he was eventually successful when, on 19th May 1916, it was performed at a 'Georgian Matinee' at His Majesty's Theatre, along with Rupert Brooke's one-act play 'Lithuania' and Gibson's 'Hoops' (Hassall, *Edward Marsh*, pp. 392–3). Lady Tree took the title role, but the play was even more thoroughly bowdlerized than it had been at its initial performance in Birmingham because, as Bottomley wrote, Lady Tree 'shrank from expressing too many early British feelings' (Gordon Bottomley to E. M., 24th Jan. 1916; 27th May 1916, *MLC*).

was eager to distinguish his anthology by printing the play within its covers, to which end he offered Bottomley twice the profits which would normally have accrued to him if the poet would permit the initial publication of 'King Lear's Wife' in *Georgian Poetry* II. Bottomley could but gratefully accept.

Not only did Marsh print the play for the first time, but he also gave it pre-eminent place as the initial piece of his second volume, which facts he was careful to call to the attention of his readers in a prefatory note. With a remarkable unanimity, the reviewers who did anything beyond stroking surfaces quickly centred their attack on 'End of the World' and 'King Lear's Wife'. The two most forthright and, to Marsh, distressing reviews appeared in the *Times Literary Supplement* and the *New Statesman*.

In tone at least the former was more a warning than a blast. Though they had started in Volume I as a more or less heterogeneous group of young poets who had rebelled in various ways against Victorian sentimentalism, the reviewer (probably Gosse) pointed out that the Georgians of Volume II, unfortunately, showed signs of a more homogeneous attitude. No longer content to rebel in their own individual ways, the Georgian poets had fallen victim to 'a *mechanical* reaction against the fashions of the past'. They seemed to be in the first stages of hardening into a coterie. As the primary symptom of the incipient disease the reviewer pointed to the excessive realism with which *Georgian Poetry* II was informed. In 'King Lear's Wife', for example, a characteristically 'Georgian' convention was becoming apparent: nastiness purely and simply for its own sake.

> Now undoubtedly there are unpleasant people and horrible things in the real world, but we feel that there is too much method in Mr. Bottomley's madness. He is out to write a new kind of poetry, a poetry which is not romantic. He is not going to get a cheap effect, like Tennyson in the 'Idylls of the King', by drawing blameless prigs. But he does get a cheap effect by the opposite method. . . . He draws ugliness, as the Victorians drew beauty, for the sake of the ugliness, as if it were interesting in itself quite apart from what it is made of. This is mere reaction from the notion that beauty is interesting in itself; and his King Lear is no more interesting, no more alive and growing, than Tennyson's King Arthur. He is as rigid and unreal in his own conventional baseness as King Arthur in his conventional loftiness.

Abercrombie, the reviewer charged, achieved much the same effect in 'End of the World'. Like Bottomley, he, too, 'is determined above all things not to be sentimental. Not one of his rustics shall show a glimmer of decent feeling; and they too become rigid in their conventional baseness'. In both poets 'the fear of sentimentalism has gone so far that [they] are determined to eliminate it even from their characters'. Not even Rupert Brooke escaped; the reviewer took him to task, too, for his 'mechanical reaction' against sentimentalism and for his 'scepticism'.[37]

Reviewing *Georgian Poetry* II in the *New Statesman*, J. C. Squire was a bit more caustic. Although the volume contained more good poems than *Georgian Poetry* I, it suffered from the artificial and excessive realism of the two poetic dramas. He was particularly harsh on 'King Lear's Wife'. The language, he conceded, had 'a peculiar, clean, hard bite', but no amount of technical adroitness could cover up 'the poverty of the main conception and the wrong-headedness of the general treatment'. Again the main bone of contention was Bottomley's realism: because the poet applied it simply as décor, the play was in its final effect artificial. Bottomley's 'characters have no complexity', Squire complained, 'and one feels about the horror, not that it is a natural and inevitable growth, but that he is *putting* it there all the time'. Like the reviewer in the *Literary Supplement*, Squire also detected, in the 'curious similarity between the writing of several of these poets who are sick of stale beauties', unmistakable signs of the onset of the coterie spirit. One does not object to realism, he argued, even to morbidity; indeed, 'anything is better than chrysolites and roses'. One objects, rather, to artificiality in poetry: 'An unconventionally ugly image is not necessarily illuminating, and descriptions of grotesques and gargoyles have their limitations like other descriptions. One hopes that the poetical pursuit of insects and bachtrians will not become a habit.'[38]

These two reviews piqued Edward Marsh perhaps more than he was willing openly to admit. His Georgians loyally rallied round him, however, and spread balm over their editor's wounded feelings. Abercrombie, for example, defended himself vigorously against the *Literary Supplement's* review: 'I honestly did not know what the Times man was talking about in several things he said about me and Gordon. I thought my characters were very nice people, and I really do not believe that I am reacting against anything. Probably I admire the Victorians a great deal more than he does.' About 'King Lear's Wife' the reviewer was also 'quite abysmally off the track', Abercrombie complained; 'I never read anything less like a mechanical reaction than Lear's Wife—never anything more like creation governed entirely by its own powers'.[39]

Squire's review raised Georgian hackles even more successfully. In the remarkable unanimity of viewpoint expressed by the Georgians, moreover, Squire might have seen convincing evidence of the truth of one of the allegations in his review: the coterie spirit had indeed touched several of the Georgian poets by 1915. Wilfrid Gibson was the first to declare his opinions. 'Rupert once said to me', he wrote Marsh, 'that Squire didn't know a poem when he saw it—and I, naturally enough, am inclined to think the remark true.'[40] John Drinkwater was equally blunt: 'I saw the N[ew] S[tatesman] article, but I have never had much opinion of J. C. S.'s judgment about poetry. . . . "Lear's Wife" and "End of the World" are neither of them flawless . . . but they are both rare works of genius, and a man like Squire ought to see it, and be damned glad that he has a platform from which he can cry out the good news. Instead of which he identifies himself with the poor journalists of the local press, who can't be expected to know greatness when it comes along.'[41] Bottomley assumed the mantle of artistic aloofness. 'If you don't mind' such unenlightened criticism as Squire's, he wrote Marsh, 'I truly don't. I am as proud as ever of my play having made its first appearance in G. P. and under your care, and as content as ever too. I never received so much misrepresentation and injustice from critics before, but I find it easy to support in such noble company.' And he closed his letter with a historical comparison which must have made Marsh's heart glow with a spark of pardonable pride. 'I suppose there hasn't been such an outburst since Poems and Ballads and Rossetti's 1870 poems. That is something!'[42] The comparison is perhaps not too far-fetched.

Marsh was not content to discuss Squire's review only with his poets. His zeal for 'King Lear's Wife' particularly impelled him to attempt to convert the reviewer himself to the beauties of modern realistic verse. All Marsh's protestations were fruitless. 'Unhappily, we shall have to agree to differ,' Squire replied; 'I don't think we do that very often about verse.' But Marsh's attacks forced Squire to a cogent defence and an admirable summation of the position taken by a considerable body of contemporary critical opinion regarding Georgian realism.

> Bottomley's failure with me was certainly not due to the fact that his characters were wicked people or that he himself expounded no views as to the flagitiousness of murder. My feeling was that the people weren't human; that I didn't care what happened to them. . . . The work in fact strikes me as a sombre and harmonious decoration pretending to be a play with people in it. Isolated pieces of just observation about human nature and destiny don't save it.
> If . . . you mean that we shouldn't be tolerant of slipshod and inaccurate workmanship merely because writers express worthy and congenial sentiments, I am wildly with you. . . . Really great art can't help being morally useful, but certainly the notion of teaching is the wrong one to start with. A man must start from a deep emotion in himself provoked by something in the outer or inner worlds, and express himself as nearly perfectly as he can.
> Bottomley I don't feel started from anything of this sort. I feel he merely wanted to write a play, and invented some puppets to write it round, disguising the barrenness of his conception with the beauties of his execution and incidental riches of a penetrating mind.[43]

Obviously little more remained to be said. Marsh retired from the field, his opinions intact but his mission unaccomplished.

Marsh was not the only one to underestimate the critical storm warnings run up against *Georgian Poetry* II. After all, two influential groups of people seemed to approve his taste: his own Georgians and the reading public. Ignore the critical jibes, Bottomley advised Marsh: 'as long as plenty of people acquire the book, the critics are spoilt of their only chance of hurting us'.[44] John Drinkwater's advice was similar: so long 'as people are taking a proper interest in the book, let the goblins howl never so prettily, it's all one'.[45] That the public was indeed taking a 'proper interest' seemed obvious; the reports from Harold Monro showed the second volume surpassing even the first in sales. The high summer of *Georgian Poetry* was at hand. *Georgian Poetry* II precisely fitted the taste of the public it was designed for. In the realism of Masefield or Brooke, Bottomley or Abercrombie, readers could see tangible evidence that from out of the slough of aestheticism and languor poetry had finally come abreast of the times.

Always available to Marsh, moreover, in the frequently expressed opinions of his Georgians, were several other perfectly adequate—and within limits accurate—explanations for the chilly critical reception accorded his second volume. One could conjure up, as Drinkwater did, the traditional picture of the literary critic as not only blind and deaf but also cowardly: 'the attacks on G.P. ii . . . are, I think, perfectly intelligible. To say that a thing is very interesting, full of great possibilities and even of achievement up to a point is quite easy and comfortably safe, and this the critics could do about the first volume and still seem to be generous enough. But to say that here is a body of work by men most of whom will help make their generation a famous one in poetry is quite another thing, needing uncommon courage, and of G.P. ii folks must either say this, or that it doesn't fulfill the promise of the other'.[46] Equally persuasive was Harold Monro's argument that a good press could hardly have been expected for *Georgian Poetry* ii because by 1915 the critics had had time to pick out their favourites for inclusion in the anthology, and they reacted with hostility when those favourites were excluded. In fact, Monro concluded, it would have been 'dangerous' had *Georgian Poetry* ii received the same kind of enthusiastic notices as the first volume.[47] In spite of such attractive explanations, however, there is no evidence that reviews like those in the *Times Literary Supplement* and the *New Statesman* were actuated by either jealousy or critical favouritism. They resulted rather from an aesthetic revulsion against what was thought to be an insincere use of realism solely for its own sake.

To the historical eye, the critical flurry stirred up by the Georgians' realistic proclivities is significant, for from it at least two important conclusions emerge. First, by late 1915, when *Georgian Poetry* ii appeared, the Georgian poets were beginning to copy one another; in their excessive reaction against sentimentalism, they were slowly and perhaps unconsciously beginning to harden into a coterie. Given their baptism of critical fire when 'King Lear's Wife' was presented to Birmingham and again when the reviewers attacked *Georgian Poetry* ii, the Georgians rallied round their editor and their injured comrades in a fashion which spoke well for their loyalty if not always for their taste. Almost alone D. H. Lawrence retained some discrimination, but in doing so he became, as someone remarked, a Jonah in the Georgian boat.

Secondly, after publication of *Georgian Poetry* ii a considerable body of English critics and reviewers had become, if not hostile to the anthology, certainly wary of ever again doling out the kind of extravagant praise which they had accorded the first volume. No large segment of influential critical opinion was turned against Edward Marsh's anthology at this relatively early date, but from 1915 on through 1922 each successive volume would have to stand on its own poetic merits. Never again was *Georgian Poetry* to enjoy the unclouded weather it had had in the halcyon days of 1912–14. From the point of view of public support, in late 1915 and 1916 it was still high summer for the anthology, but there were unmistakable signs that a long and lean critical winter might soon set in.

# 7

## War and the Georgians

To the Georgians, as to most other English poets, the outbreak of war brought a sense of instant and devastating shock. It seemed to put a too cruel and ironic end to all their hopes for themselves, for poetry, and for humankind which had flowered so briefly and extravagantly in the pre-war years. It put a final, malicious period to the time of youth. They expressed themselves differently but all to the same effect:

> To people who were fifty when the war broke out it came as an interruption, however long, terrible and fraught with change. To us, who were thirty or less, it came as an end. We had no careers or long associations behind us, only beginnings, first sortings and plans, discoveries of friendship. The war broke on us, destroying, invalidating. Our youth went prematurely, we were scarred before our time by the griefs of age, we had to face a new world when we were just beginning to be acclimatized to an old one. And for half of us the parting from youth was more bitter and final, for to those bones there is no return, even in imagination, to lost things; no remembering, with every pang and outline softened in the gold-dusty air of illusion, the joys and sorrows that were, and the faces, serious or laughing, of those who strayed through courts that strangers now inhabit and by streams that still so brightly and indifferently flow.[1]

Searching his heart and conscience during the first grim weeks, Rupert Brooke found unutterable grief and bewildering confusion. In an unusually revealing meditation the young poet mused upon the friends he had known in Germany such a few short months before, upon the great 'primitive abyss of hatred and lust for blood' which is war; and he could find no hatred in his heart,

A group of Georgians outside the Birmingham Repertory Theatre after a performance of *King Lear's Wife*, September 1915. *Left to right*: Wilfrid Gibson, John Drinkwater, Lascelles Abercrombie, Mrs. Gibson, Mrs. Abercrombie, and Edward Marsh

The grave of Rupert Brooke on Skyros in the Aegean, 1915

only pain. He found a deep abiding love of England, her fields and hills, her peaceful homes, her quiet beauty hallowed by time. But he found no fervent patriotism. He could only conclude half-heartedly, 'Well, if Armageddon's *on*, I suppose one should be there.'*

The shock did not last long. After the first numbness wore off, most of the younger Georgians plunged desperately into new work or volunteered for the armed services. Brooke himself joined the Royal Naval Division and went off to Armageddon singing, 'Now, God be thanked who has matched us with his hour, / And caught our youth, and wakened us from sleeping'. Brooke was never quite so well matched with his hour as when he died in April 1915 in the Aegean, for, ironically, he was to have a more pronounced effect on English poetry dead than he had ever had living. In Rupert Brooke dead for the homeland, buried on Scyros, the isle of Achilles, an English public starved for heroes saw not only the tragic archetype of youth sacrificing itself for England but also the epitome of the poet gone to war. Unconsciously Brooke had prepared the way for his own apotheosis in his war sonnets. 'If I should die, think only this of me.' Dean Inge quoted the sonnet from the pulpit of St. Paul's. Winston Churchill wrote a letter to the *Times* expressing the sense of national loss at the poet's death:

Rupert Brooke is dead. A telegram from the Admiral at Lemnos tells us that this life has closed at the moment when it seemed to have reached its springtime. A voice had become audible, a note had been struck, more true, more thrilling, more able to do justice to the nobility of our youth in arms engaged in this present war, than any other—more able to express their thoughts of self-surrender, and with a power to carry comfort to those who watch them so intently from afar. The voice has been swiftly stilled. Only the echoes and the memory remain; but they will linger.

During the last few months of his life, months of preparation in gallant comradeship and open air, the poet-soldier told with all the simple force of genius the sorrow of youth about to die, and the sure triumphant consolations of a sincere and valiant spirit. He expected to die; he was willing to die for the dear England whose beauty and majesty he knew; and he advanced towards the brink in perfect

---

* *NS*, III (1914), 638–40. Brooke wrote the piece in the third person as the thoughts of 'a friend of mine', but the opinions were quite obviously the poet's own.

serenity, with absolute conviction of the rightness of his country's cause and a heart devoid of hate for fellow-men.

The thoughts to which he gave expression in the very few incomparable war sonnets which he has left behind will be shared by many thousands of young men moving resolutely and blithely forward into this, the hardest, the cruellest, and the least-rewarded of all the wars that men have fought. They are a whole history and revelation of Rupert Brooke himself. Joyous, fearless, versatile, deeply instructed, with classic symmetry of mind and body, ruled by high undoubting purpose, he was all that one would wish England's noblest sons to be in days when no sacrifice but the most precious is acceptable and the most precious is that which is most freely proffered.[2]

Brooke's friends vied with one another to write poetic tributes to him, some—notably those of his close friends among the Georgians—genuinely moving, others merely banal and maudlin.* And countless young subalterns fresh to the mud of Flanders from the public schools were powerfully moved to emulate their national poet-patriot hero. Almost alone, Brooke's death resuscitated the

* Among Brooke's poetic peers Ezra Pound was one of the few who kept his head during the period of Brooke's canonization. Writing a hurried note to Harriet Monroe on 25th Apr. 1915, he reported the news of Brooke's death and admitted that Brooke 'was the best of all that Georgian group' (*Letters of Ezra Pound*, ed. Paige, p. 103). Sometime early in 1914, however, he had written a small poem attacking Brooke and insinuating that the motive for Brooke's journey to the South Seas in 1914 was something less admirable than mere romantic wanderlust. He gave the poem to Wyndham Lewis for publication in *Blast*. Unfortunately, it was published not in the first but in the second number of *Blast*, which of course appeared shortly after Brooke's death, at a time when the lionizing of the dead poet was at its height. At such a time it was considered by many to be in extremely poor taste.

When Harriet Monroe rebuked her 'London correspondent' for permitting the poem to be published, Pound defended himself. The poem had been written many months before Brooke's death, he pointed out; the second number of *Blast* was supposed to have been printed in December 1914, when Brooke would still have been alive. Moreover, Pound wrote, 'Brooke would have been amused at the lines, at least I hope and suppose he was man enough to have been entertained by them. If he wasn't God help him in limbo.'

What Pound most strenuously objected to were the maudlin attempts of Brooke's literary friends to deify the poet (and in the process to associate themselves in the mind of the public with the dead poet-hero). 'Now that his friends have taken to writing sentimental elegies about his long prehensile toes,' Pound wrote Miss Monroe, 'it might seem time for him to be protected by people like myself who knew him only slightly.' If Brooke 'went to Tahiti for his emotional excitements instead of contracting diseases in Soho,' Pound continued, 'for God's sake let him have the credit of it. And for God's sake if there was anything in the man, let us dissociate him from his surviving friends. Something ought to be done to clear him from the stain of having been quoted by Dean Inge, and to save him from his friends who express their grief at his death by writing such phrases as (yes, here it is verbatim): "in fact Rupert's mobile toes were a subject for the admiration of his friends"!' (*Letters of Ezra Pound*, ed. Paige, p. 110).

lagging poetic revival. But more than any other single event, it also opened the gates to a flood of sentimental poetry from the amateurs, the stay-at-home patriots, and the soldier-poets with little more reason for writing than the uncontrollable urge to express themselves in verse. The result was an unmistakable increase in the quantity of verse published but an equally unmistakable decrease in the quality.

From the first only a handful of poets and reviewers were taken in by the deluge of patriotic verse which the war loosed upon England. To be sure, the initial upsurge of patriotism immediately after England's declaration of war occasioned, as Frank Swinnerton observed, a number of fatuous 'articles by professors, near-professors, and literary romantics who detested Realism, Futurism, *Blast*, and tranquillity. They said, with one accord, that the war would prove the salvation of English letters. It would purge us of evil humours, and release the stream of pure poetry which had been too long muddied by science, meticulousness, and nonsense'.[3] And as late as five months after the outbreak of war a reviewer for the *Times Literary Supplement* could still claim that the war was exerting a beneficent effect on British verse because it had made poetry 'more impassioned and more manful'.[4] Most of the poets themselves were a good more realistic. Only one month after the war had begun Harold Monro declared bluntly, 'The sentiment of patriotism has never produced much poetry. Modern warfare will be likely to produce less.' The emotions encouraged by war, he conceded, sometimes 'stimulate poetry, but they do not necessarily produce it, and in a civilised age they will more probably be revealed after than during the event'.[5] At the same time J. C. Squire protested, in the name of poetry, the flood of shoddy patriotic verse the first month of war had produced:

> What is wrong with most of these patriotic versifiers is that they start with a ready-made set of conceptions, of phrases, of words, and of rhymes, and turn out their works on a formula. Put England down as 'knightly', state her honour to be 'inviolate' and her spirit 'invulnerable', call her enemies 'perjured' and branded with the 'mark of Cain', refer to 'Trafalgar' (which has always done good service as a rhyme to 'war'), summon the spirits of Drake and Grenville from the deep, introduce a 'thou' or two, and conclude with the assertion that God will defend the Right—and there's the formula for a poem.*

* NS, III (1914), 737. Not long after Squire also wrote a short poem satirizing the

The critics also withstood the temptation to confuse poetry and patriotism in reviewing the anthologies of war poetry which began to appear as early as October 1914. Writing in the *Egoist*, John Gould Fletcher scathingly dismissed one of the earliest anthologies pretentiously entitled *Poems of the Great War* (1914), demolishing in the process some of the most sacred names of the Establishment, Watson, Newbolt, Binyon, Noyes, Chesterton, and Bridges.* In December 1914 the *Egoist* also published what must surely have been the earliest satiric poem to come out of the war. Written by 'Herbert Blenheim', it made exquisite use of the very metre, versification, and diction of the correspondence-column poets:

### SONG: IN WARTIME

At the sound of the drum,
Out of their dens they come, they come,
The little poets we hoped were dumb,
The little poets we thought were dead,
The poets who certainly haven't been read
Since heaven knows when, they come, they come,
At the sound of the drum, of the drum, drum, drum.

At the sound of the drum,
O Tommy, they've *all* begun to strum,
With a horrible tumty, tumty, tum;
And it's all about you, and the songs they sing
Are worse than the bullets' villainous 'ping',
And they give you a pain in your tumty-tum,
At the sound of the drum, of the drum, drum, drum.

At the sound of the drum,
O Tommy, you know, if we haven't all come
To stand by your side in the hideous hum,

---

stay-at-home amateur poets who habitually published in the editorial pages of the daily press. Appended to a letter to E. M. (16th Apr. 1915, *MLC*), the poem read:

> O to be in Flanders
> Now that April's there
> Where the water's drying up in the trench
> To make more room for the summer stench
> With General Joffre and Marshal French
> In Flanders now.

* *Egoist*, I, no. 21 (2nd Nov. 1914), 410–11. See also a review of a second war-poetry anthology by Fletcher written two weeks later in which he attacked, among others, Kipling and de la Mare (*Egoist*, I, no. 22 [16th Nov. 1914], 424–6).

It isn't the horrors of war we fear,
The horrors of war we've got 'em here,
When the poets come on like waves, and *come*
At the sound of the drum, of the drum, drum, drum.*

Critics like Fletcher and Squire were only a short step ahead of
their time, for by mid-1915 the triviality of most wartime verse
had become apparent to all but the most obtuse. By July the *Times
Literary Supplement* had experienced a change of heart. Far from
repeating the earlier claim that wartime poetry was 'more impassioned and more manful', a reviewer could now grant that to
date most war poetry had been unspeakably shoddy: 'With a few
exceptions, rhetoric and invective, loftiness of aim and an inadequate expression of it, have been the mark of the verse that has
been poured out in such abundance.' It is not in the fires of war
but 'in the peace that is surely coming that poetry, we may hope,
will renew its youth'.[6] But the wartime reading public was not to
be deterred from its plunge into bathos. By mid-1916 booksellers
were reporting that the public was eagerly buying slender volumes
of works by the less well-known poets, especially if the authors
had been killed in action. Unfortunately, 'the spectacle of "whom
the gods love" dying young has always fascinated mankind', and
in spite of the best efforts of critics, reviewers, and professional
poets, the public was pathetically eager to sentimentalize over
these memorials of promise unfulfilled, ambition frustrated, high
hopes and ardent passions effaced at a breath'.[7]

One of the effects of the first two years of war, then, was to
quicken the poetic revival which had begun in the pre-war years.
But the war also worked a change upon the essential character of
the pre-war renaissance. It created a large body of amateur would-
be poets, in and out of uniform; and it created an emotional
culture in which the virus of bad popular verse could multiply
unchecked. But the spirit of the times was perhaps only partially
to blame. Faced with a wartime paper shortage, publishers liked
the notion of small volumes at high prices and so encouraged talk
of the poetic revival. By 1916 there were still a few prophets
abroad in the land to cry shame on their times, 'a few obstinate
people who declined to allow their critical faculties to be chloro-

* *Egoist*, I, no. 23 (1st Dec. 1914), 446. I have been unable to penetrate the
pseudonym, though I suspect the deft hand of Richard Aldington. Mr. Hassall
informed me that he suspected Squire. In any case, the matter is scarcely crucial.

formed by popular sentiment, who continued to believe that although death on the field of battle might gain for the hero instant admission to Valhalla, it was not necessarily a qualification for Parnassus. Such ironsides clung to the notion that it is quality, not quantity, which makes a golden age in literature'.[8] But they were prophets without influence. Even in late 1915 and 1916, and certainly by 1917, when Edward Marsh began to contemplate the possibility of a third volume of *Georgian Poetry*, there seemed some danger that the serious work of professional poets would be swept from public view by the flood of puerile rhymes from public school subalterns and patriotic effusions from armchair patriots and bloodthirsty old ladies from Bath.

But poetry—serious, professional poetry—was not to die so easily. To be sure, the wartime efforts of the older generation, whose reputations had been established before the war began, were almost universally third-rate. From the pens of such poets as Watson, Hardy, Bridges, Noyes, and Kipling only a handful of war poems seem worthy of recall: Hardy's 'In Time of "The Breaking of Nations" ', 'The Pity of It', and 'A New Year's Eve in War Time'; Noyes's 'Victory Dance' and 'The Wine Press'; and perhaps Kipling's 'Nativity'. In fact, many of Kipling's excursions into war poetry were so feeble that a practical joker was able to hoax the *Times* into publishing a burlesque of them in good faith that the poem had been written by Kipling himself.[9] Fortunately the work of the older generation did not come within the purview of *Georgian Poetry*. And so when Edward Marsh set out to compile *Georgian Poetry* III in mid-1917, he had before him the work of three significant groups of younger poets from which to choose. First, there were Marsh's 'regulars', the poets who had formed the hard core of the first two volumes, men like Bottomley, Davies, de la Mare, Hodgson, or Monro. Then, there were the war poets. This group comprised the poets in uniform, men like Graves, Rosenberg, Nichols, and Sassoon, who were even younger than Marsh's original contributors—second-generation Georgians, so to speak—whose serious work could scarcely be denied admission to an anthology published in the midst of wartime. Finally, there was a considerable group of new, young stay-at-home poets just beginning to emerge into some prominence in the middle war years. Contemporaries of the Graves-Sassoon-Rosenberg group, for one reason or another most of them had not put on the uniform by mid-1917. Though cast in a rather different vein from the work of either the Georgians or the war poets, their work seemed promising enough to entitle them to a hearing. This body was composed of men like W. J. Turner, John Freeman, and J. C. Squire. Since part of Marsh's aim in publishing *Georgian Poetry* III was to demonstrate that in spite of the war English poetry was continuing to put on 'new strength and beauty', he would obviously have to choose verse representative of at least these three groups.

None of the first group—Marsh's regulars of *Georgian Poetry* I and II—could legitimately be called a 'war poet'. Even by mid-1917 none of them had turned his talents wholly to war poetry; indeed, only two had published a volume of predominantly war poems. John Drinkwater's *Swords and Ploughshares* (1915) was only mediocre; far more considerable was Wilfrid Gibson's *Battle* (1915). The majority of the Georgians turned their backs on war as a direct subject for poetry, preferring to keep in remembrance the things of peace; they continued to write poetry in spite of war, not about war. In holding up before wartime England the poetry and the values of peacetime, the work of such poets as de la Mare, Lawrence, Davies, and Hodgson made an indirect but devastating commentary upon the degradation of the human spirit and the loss of aesthetic standards in war which was the more effective because it was more subtle than the hammer blows of the patriotic versifiers.

The most impressive poetry in *Georgian Poetry* III was to come, however, not from the Georgian regulars, but from the second group represented in the volume, the soldier poets. Beginning in late 1913 Edward Marsh had befriended these young men in many ways and had given unstintingly of his advice and experience in poetic matters. When war came these poets—Graves, Sassoon, Nichols, Rosenberg—were among the first to go. Fortunately, they corresponded frequently with Marsh, and in letter after letter written from the trenches of France, they recorded how the essential personality of the poet was preserved amid the gigantic impersonality of war. As early as 1915 and 1916, long before Sassoon's ultimate burst of white-hot anger in *Counter-Attack* or Wilfred Owen's quintessential statement of the pity of war, the letters to Edward Marsh gave evidence that the initial patriotic sentiments expressed by Rupert Brooke or Julian Grenfell had worn off. Months of first-hand contact with the brutality of trench warfare had effectively dispelled whatever noble notions the soldier-poet may have begun with. The problem of the poet in the trenches in the middle war years was far more basic: how was he to manage to keep alive at all a poet's awareness of a spiritual world or a sensitivity to the unremembered beauties of this world upon which the creation of any poetry ultimately depended? The letters to Edward Marsh show how the impossible was achieved.

The young Graves perhaps best expressed the keen sense of unreality which initially beset the poet in the trenches.

> I feel exactly like a man who has watched the 'Movies' for a long evening and then suddenly finds himself thrown on the screen in the middle of scalp-hunting Sioux and runaway motor cars: and rather surprised that I am not at all frightened, and that the noise doesn't disturb me at all yet. You may disbelieve the following, but I swear to you, Eddie, it's a true bill, that a violent artillery duel going on above my dugout two night ago simply failed to wake me at all though I was conscious of the whole place rocking but, when this ceased, I was awoken by a very persistent lark which hung for some minutes on my platoon trench swearing at the Germans.

Even in such an environment, however, he was writing poetry, for in the next paragraph he quoted three stanzas of 'a recent improvisation' which eventually turned out to be the first and the final stanzas of 'It's A Queer Time', and he enclosed for Marsh's criticism what must have been most of the text of 'The Poet in the Nursery'. And then the abrupt switch from poetry back to war as Graves closed his letter:

> Tomorrow we go, they say, into some trenches where we and the Boches are sitting in each other's pockets, the whole place mined and countermined, complete with trench mortars, gas, and grenade throwing parties. So now for a little sleep.
>
> Yours in the Muses<br>ROBERT GRAVES[10]

Graves frequently found the physical dangers of war less onerous than the spiritual aridity it engendered. In a desolate, angry letter to Marsh he complained of the isolation he felt among his fellow-officers, whom he called 'offensive, quarrelsome and bumptious'.[11] The fortunes of war frequently threw Graves and his friend Siegfried Sassoon together. Even in the brief intervals when they were assigned to the same battalion and when, consequently, the poetic shop-talk could have flowed freely, the two poets were inhibited by the determinedly chilly attitude of their fellow-officers towards the arts. Graves recorded the subterfuge in which the poets had to indulge in order not to seem unduly strange to their mess-mates:

> S. S. and I have great difficulty in talking about poetry and that sort of thing together as the other officers of the batt. are terribly curious and suspicious—If I go into his mess and he wants to show me some set of verses he says 'Afternoon, Graves, have a drink . . .; by the way I want you to see my latest recipe for rum punch.' The trenches are worse than billets for privacy. We are a disgrace to the batt. and we know it: I don't know what the C.O. would say if he heard us discussing the sort of things we do. He'd probably have a fit. His saying is that 'there should only be one subject for conversation among subalterns off parade'. I leave you to guess it. It's a great standby to have S. S. here in such society.[12]

Out of such difficulties and from such an environment came Graves's *Fairies and Fusiliers* (1917). The spirit of poetry was as stubborn as the human will to create.

Sassoon also complained to Marsh of much the same kind of intellectual isolation and spiritual aridity, and from his letters emerges even more clearly than from Graves's the poet's eye for beauty and for detail which kept poetry alive in Sassoon through almost two years in the trenches. 'I have just seen Robert [Graves],' he wrote Marsh:

> his Battn. came along and bivouacked 300 yds away. And we sat among the thistles under the cloudy night sky lit with flashes and the hidden moon, with dull stars of camp fires burning all around in the wide dark countryside—and guns booming along the valleys. And talked of how we'd go to the Caucasus, or any old place, après la guerre, while his men snored under their piled rifles a little way off. And there he sleeps now. And tomorrow I suppose we'll both be up in the show. Germans been pushed back another mile or two they say.[13]

Sassoon's eye for detail which was to etch the bitterness of his war poems with a distinct and unforgettable realism is clearly evident from the start.

> How I long to be a painter of some skill; everything out here is simply asking to be painted or etched: it is wildly picturesque. Soldiers in barns with one candle burning, and wintry evening land-

scapes with guns flashing and thudding. I put 'angry guns that *boom* and *flash*' in my poem [i.e. 'To Victory'], but really they flash and thud. The flash comes first, they only boom when they are very near in some valley. The other evening up in the trenches with only 20 yards of mine craters between us and the other side, there was an evening sky overhead with all the stars on parade and the young moon in command (on her back!), and some owls flitting across the lines. It seemed so strange, with the men ancle-deep [*sic*] in clay peering from under their round steel caps, very tired after a day of strafing with trench mortars and 'oil-cans', and the rattle of machine-guns on the left in the luminous dusk.[14]

For Sassoon, as for all the professional soldier-poets, the writing of poetry was a serious matter to be undertaken carefully, deliberately. It was not to be achieved, as it was with so many of the amateurs, merely by allowing powerful emotions to overflow spontaneously on to a piece of paper in whatever ragged form happened to come most readily to hand. Even in the midst of trench warfare Sassoon laboured over his poems, corrected, inserted, emended, to bring them as near to perfection as he was able; he constantly made notes of the scenes he saw and the emotions he experienced so that the poems he would write from them later might have the ring of authenticity; he carefully stored to overflowing both his memory and his notebooks. From the inclusion of a small excerpt from one of his notebooks in a letter to Edward Marsh one gets some insight into the self-consciousness and the sensitivity of the poet at war:

I am going up to the trenches very shortly; . . . and I mean to suck in all I can when I get up there. I am always trying to impress things on my memory, and make as many notes as I can. This is the usual sort of thing, but it is good training—

'Then I rode out toward Albert with larks carolling very clear and 2 solemn black and white dogs staring at me from outside an R. E. hut on the ridge where the reserve trenches are being finished. From the slope, looking N. W. the country rises and falls, sparse—green, and drab, and brown, to a skyline of trees in tiny, delicate silhouette with occasional dark lines of woodland,—the white seams of trenches dug in the limestone, and here and there a road climbing away to nowhere, the German territory, unexplored and sinister. Albert, with 2 or 3 chimney stacks and the ruined basilica tower, shows above a line of tall trees by the river,—a medley of roofs, looking peaceful enough from far away, but in reality a town deserted and half in ruins,—in places utterly smashed. Everywhere the rural spirit has been chased away by shells and soldiers and supply sheds and everything new: the very skies have lost their once bird-held supremacy of whiteness and clarity.'[15]

In Sassoon, too, the sensitivity of the poet was kept alive, laboriously, deliberately, amid the anguish and impersonality of war. Out of Sassoon's distant view of Albert, out of his compassion for his men ankle-deep in trench mud, dog-tired under their round steel caps, came *To Any Dead Officer* (1917) and *Counter-Attack* (1918).

Surely there was no more pitiable sacrifice to the stupidity of war than Isaac Rosenberg. One of the most promising poets of them all, Rosenberg was the least fitted of any to become a soldier. Physically a very slight man, and suffering always from fragile health, he endured unspeakable pain in the trenches from both a chronic weakness of the lungs and severe trench-foot during over two years of active service in France until he was killed on 1st April 1918. Temperamentally, too, he was as thoroughly unfitted for military life as any man in the British Army. To withstand the brutality of the military system required every ounce of spiritual stamina the poet could muster. Even while still training in England, he complained to Edward Marsh: 'I find that the actual duties though they are difficult at first and require all one's sticking power are not in themselves unpleasant, it is the brutal militaristic bullying meanness of the way they're served out to us. You're always being threatened with "clink".'[16] Unlike Sassoon and Graves, Rosenberg served in the ranks and as a private soldier was forced to endure several kinds of hardships which officers were spared. Once in France, he was to meet a new form of frustration which to a poet was disheartening in extreme: 'I have been forbidden to send poems home,' he wrote Marsh, 'as the censor won't be bothered with going through such rubbish.'[17]

Though Marsh tried upon at least one occasion to use his influence towards getting Rosenberg assigned to less strenuous duties, his efforts were unsuccessful, and Rosenberg remained on arduous and hazardous duty in France.[18] Rosenberg was not often stung to anger or self-pity in his comments about his condition. The understatement with which he characteristically described his trials, especially those he endured during the winter months, makes some of the more angry and violently phrased letters of other war poets sound almost contrived. 'This winter is a teaser for me,' he wrote from France, in early 1917, 'and being so long without a proper rest I feel as if I need one to recuperate and be put to rights again.' But 'I suppose we'll stick to it', he added almost flippantly; 'and if we don't, there are still some good poets left who might write me a decent epitaph'.[19] Perhaps Rosenberg's correspondence with Marsh most clearly reflected the characteristic attitude of the English poet at war, a combination of hope and despair, pride in his work and desolation over his own and the general human condition. His letters are a pastiche of comments on the future and the present, poetry and trench-foot:

> My sister wrote me you have been getting more of my 'Moses'. It is hardy of you, indeed, to spread it about; and I certainly would be distressed if I were the cause of a war in England; seeing what warfare means here. But it greatly pleases me, none the less, that this child of my brain should be seen and perhaps his beauties be discovered. His creator is in a sadder plight; the harsh and unlovely times have made his mistress, the flighty Muse, abscond and elope with luckier rivals; but surely I shall hunt her and chase her somewhere into the summer and sweeter times. Anyway this is a strong hope; lately I have not been very happy being in torture with my feet again. The coldness of the weather and the weight of my boots have put my feet in a rotten state.[20]

But from out of his misery Rosenberg too was creating poetry; he too was approaching the task professionally, seriously, conscious that the creation of good poetry required not only the impulse but also an act of creative will. More than most of the soldier-poets—Wilfred Owen perhaps excepted—Rosenberg retained a stringently critical eye towards his own verse. He worked and re-worked his war poems. 'I've written some lines suggested by going out wiring,' he told Marsh, 'or rather carrying wire up to the line on limbers and running over dead bodies lying about.' But his first effort did not impress him: 'I don't think what I've written is very good but I think the substance is, and when I work on it I'll make it fine.'[21] Work on it he surely did, and he made it 'fine', for in its final form it became 'Dead Man's Dump', one of the most poignant poems to come out of the war. To the extent to which he was able, through volumes sent him by his sister, Marsh, Gordon Bottomley, and other friends, Rosenberg also kept an alert eye on the progress of poetry back in England, and his critical faculties were in no wise dulled by his condition. 'Gibson's "Battle" was sent to me and delighted me. It is as good as Degas,' he wrote Marsh. 'In a way it seems a contradiction that a thinker should take a low plane as he does there instead of the more complex and sensitive personality of a poet in such a situation. Most who have written as poets have been very unreal and it is for this reason, their naturalness, I think Gibson's [war poems] so fine. The Homer for this war has yet to be found—Whitman got very near the mark 50 years ago with "Drum Taps".'[22]

Perhaps the best evidence of Rosenberg's success in keeping alive within himself the spirit of the poet and the poet's ability to mould raw experience into moments of transcendent beauty is in his final letter to Marsh. Writing only four days before his death (the letter was postmarked one day after he was killed), he spoke of being up in the trenches again and of trying 'to write a battle song for the Judeans' he had met. In the draft of a new poem which he enclosed one could find no more fitting tribute to the spirit of the English poet gone to war or to the human will to create amid times of evil:

RETURNING, WE HEAR THE LARKS

Sombre the night is.
And though we have our lives, we know
What sinister threat lurks there.

Dragging these anguished limbs, we only know
This poison-blasted track opens on our camp—
On a little safe sleep.

But hark! joy—joy—strange joy.
Lo! heights of night ringing with unseen larks:
Music showering our upturned listening faces.

Death could drop from the dark
As easily as song—
But song only dropped,
Like a blind man's dreams on the sand
By dangerous tides,
Like a girl's dark hair for she dreams no ruin lies there,
Or her kisses where a serpent hides.*

* Isaac Rosenberg to E. M., 28th Mar. 1918, *MLC*. Though most of the Rosenberg letters to E. M. are printed in *The Collected Works of Isaac Rosenberg*, eds. Gordon

It was the poets in uniform, then, who afforded the most dramatic evidence that serious poetry would not die, for they kept the spirit and the craftsmanship of the professional poet alive under the most forbidding conditions. But in addition to the war poets and the original Georgians of volumes I and II, by 1917 a third group of young poets also afforded Edward Marsh some evidence that serious poetry had not been lost in the flood of bad, popular wartime verse. Not all the young men of the poetic generation just behind the first Georgians had donned a uniform. Some remained at home and were writing verse which, though it was of a very different order from the war poems of their coevals, was to gain them access to *Georgian Poetry* III. Their major representatives in that volume were to be Turner, Freeman, and Squire. Freeman had published two volumes in 1916, *Presage to Victory* and *Stone Trees and Other Poems*; Turner had published *The Hunter and Other Poems* (1916); and Squire *The Lily of Malud* (1917). As it was to turn out, their contributions were to be more significant for the future of *Georgian Poetry* than even those of the soldier-poets, for it was their kind of verse which came to exert the dominant influence over the last two volumes of the anthology and made *Georgian Poetry* IV and V markedly different from *Georgian Poetry* I and II. *Georgian Poetry* III was the watershed volume, the one in which the dividing line between the 'early' and the 'late' Georgian movements first becomes apparent.

*Georgian Poetry* III cost Marsh more effort and worry than any

---

Bottomley and Denys Harding (London, 1937), pp. 304, 312, 314–15, 316, I have nevertheless preferred to cite holograph letters in the Marsh Collection for at least two reasons. In the first place, the undated letter from which I quote a passage on p. 173 (concerning Gibson's *Battle* and commenting on Whitman as a war poet) was apparently overlooked by the editors of the *Collected Works*; in any case, it is nowhere printed in that volume. According to my observation, however, when I saw the Marsh Collection in 1955, this letter was definitely among the Rosenberg papers. Secondly, the poem which Rosenberg enclosed in his final letter to E. M. (dated 28th Mar and postmarked 2nd Apr. 1918) was, according to the editors of the *Collected Works*, 'Through these Pale Cold Days' (*Collected Works*, p. 322). According to the evidence of the letter I saw in 1955, the poem was 'Returning, We Hear the Larks', as I have indicated in my text.

It should also be added that the *MLC* contains other letters written by Rosenberg, Graves, and Sassoon from the trenches in addition to the few that I have used. The three poets' accounts of their wartime experiences are often equalled, however—and sometimes excelled—by Edmund Blunden's moving and more finished record of the poet at war, *Undertones of War* (London, 1928). Though an appendix contains many of Blunden's poems occasioned by specific events in France, the book is largely a prose autobiography. Perhaps more than any other prose account of the war, however, Blunden's book causes one to see, feelingly, the quintessential truth of Wilfred Owen's dictum: the poetry is in the pity.

other volume of the series. The enthusiasm with which he had entered upon his task in 1912 and the certainty of judgment he had displayed in his choices of poems in 1915 were notably lacking in 1917. In the beginning, in fact, Marsh himself was subject to some doubts about whether the quality of the verse published during 1916–17 warranted a new anthology. *The Lily of Malud*, he wrote J. C. Squire, was one of the few volumes of new verse which made him contemplate *Georgian Poetry* III.[23] Initially Harold Monro was even less sanguine than Marsh about the wisdom of publishing a new volume. When Marsh first broached the subject to his publisher in mid-1917, Monro immediately pointed out that materials would be scarce and expensive, that advertising costs had risen steeply, and that in his opinion the book trade in general would be in a slump by the end of 1917.[24] Moreover, he confirmed Marsh's own doubts about the quality of recent verse. 'I heard you mention 2 or 3 names,' he wrote, 'but I wonder if they were of people you would really want to include *much* of. You've been so jolly careful in the past. It would be much better to have something completely good at the end of 3 years than open to doubt for the sake of publishing one at the end of 2 years [*sic*]. The thing I'm thinking is that only very few of the principal people represented in the last 2 G.P.'s will have published anything new of value.'[25] Such old hands as Lascelles Abercrombie also questioned Marsh's decision to publish, though more mildly than Monro. 'I am interested to hear you have thoughts of a third G.P. this year,' Abercrombie wrote. 'Do you think the public would stand it?— But there certainly is a good deal of quite new and quite good stuff going about.'[26]

Despite the marked lack of enthusiasm in many quarters and his own lukewarm feelings in the beginning, Marsh resolved to piece together a third volume of his anthology and announced its publication for November 1917. He succeeded in convincing Monro not only that the volume would be financially successful but also that the new verse from poets not represented in either of the first two volumes was sufficiently promising to warrant publishing it.[27] Again Marsh proved an astute judge of the public temper, for to Monro's amazement, by early August—three months before publication—orders for *Georgian Poetry* III were beginning to come in to the Poetry Bookshop.[28]

*Georgian Poetry* III was different from its two predecessors in

175

several ways. It was a book of new poets. Of the eighteen poets represented half were new, a far larger proportion than in any other volume of the series after the first one. The older Georgians were quick to note the change. When Wilfrid Gibson read that the projected volume would include the verse of Sassoon, Rosenberg, Squire, Graves, Turner, and Freeman, he wrote that although he had to confess ignorance of most of the work of the young men, he presumed it fitting that such 'old fogies' as himself should make way for newer blood.[29] And when Gordon Bottomley read the roster for the new volume, he suggested to a fellow-Georgian, tongue in cheek, that the 'old' Georgians might soon find it necessary to form 'a society of George the Firsts'.[30]

Moreover, with *Georgian Poetry* III Marsh appears to have altered the principles upon which he compiled his anthology. In the preface to both volumes I and II he had specifically disavowed any intention of broad catholicity. *Georgian Poetry* III, on the other hand, was more nearly representative of all kinds and conditions of poetry than any other volume of the series. The question is obviously one of degree, for an anthologist is not a curator. At some point or another he must exercise personal taste; he must define limits which by their very nature are exclusive. Obviously, Edward Marsh's poetic canons would not allow the inclusion of such *avant-garde* poets as, say, the Sitwells. But within the limits of his own taste—and at several points, indeed, by stretching his tolerance to the utmost—Marsh made *Georgian Poetry* III a reasonably representative anthology.

Why should Marsh's third volume have differed so greatly from either *Georgian Poetry* I or II? The answer lies, one suspects, in Marsh's reaction to the critical flurry stirred up by *Georgian Poetry* II, particularly by 'King Lear's Wife' and 'End of the World', in which Marsh had seen only the stark beauties of the new realistic verse, but several critics only striking evidence of an incipient coterie spirit. In preparing *Georgian Poetry* III Marsh went out of his way to avoid laying his anthology open again to the coterie charge.

Marsh's new-found caution was reflected in the fact that he tolerated—in fact, sought out—a good deal more advice in 1917 than he had in either 1912 or 1915. To be sure, on at least one occasion he turned down an unsolicited recommendation with customary firmness. Several poets, among them Walter de la Mare,

Siegfried Sassoon, while on leave from the
Front, 1916

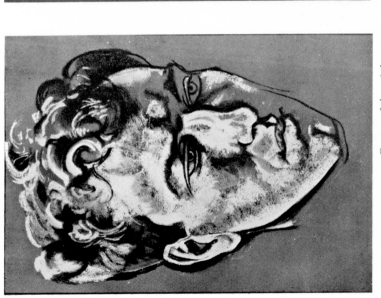

Robert Graves, *c.* 1921. From a drawing
by Eric Kennington

Edmund Blunden, 1924

Isaac Rosenberg, a self-portrait, 1915

John Freeman, and W. J. Turner, suggested that *Georgian Poetry* III would be strengthened by the inclusion of some work by Edward Thomas. Though they may have been unaware of it, Thomas's advocates had hit upon one of Edward Marsh's unfortunate blind spots. Even though in 1914 and 1915 Thomas had been on quite intimate terms with several of the major Georgian poets—Gibson, Abercrombie, and Brooke—and even though, on de la Mare's urging, Marsh had obtained a financial grant from government funds for Thomas in 1916, Marsh remained 'largely ignorant of him as a poet, and never appreciated his quality until too late'. Marsh therefore politely but firmly declined the three poets' suggestion on the grounds that Thomas was no longer living. Writing to Freeman, Marsh explained that he had been compelled to make it 'a strict rule never to represent any writer for the first time posthumously'.* The tone of Freeman's reply was remarkable in its restraint and in the implications of what it left unsaid:

> I quite understand now the difficulty with regard to Edward Thomas's work. I didn't know before the principle which restricted your choice—perhaps it's unfortunate that fine work should be permanently excluded from representation. I've had the privilege of seeing probably the whole of his verse; . . . and I only made the suggestion because as far as my own opinion might stretch or be worth anything, it would be splendid if the next Georgian book included any other new poetry of comparable individuality and power.[31]

But Marsh showed himself far more complaisant in other instances. He was eager to include the work of a woman poet in his third volume, and when he approached Monro for suggestions, Monro strongly urged Charlotte Mew's 'The Farmer's Bride'.[32] Unconvinced, Marsh sought out the advice of Walter de la Mare, who responded with a frank, and negative, opinion: he found the

---

* Christopher Hassall, *Edward Marsh*, p. 422. For a detailed account of Thomas's friendship with Abercrombie, Gibson, and Brooke—as well as with Robert Frost, his poetic mentor—see Elizabeth S. Sergeant, *Robert Frost: The Trial By Existence*, pp. 135–47. In the course of an informal conversation about the Georgian poets at my home in Delaware, Ohio, in March 1960, Mr. Frost reminisced at some length about his relations with the Georgians and spoke particularly of his close friendship with and admiration for Edward Thomas. One of Mr. Frost's phrases in particular spoke so eloquently of the identity of interest between the two poets that I set it down verbatim immediately after the conversation. Of himself and Edward Thomas Mr. Frost said: 'We were very close. His mockery was my mockery, and we felt the same about war and peace.'

protagonist inconsistent ('dialectical in the first stanza and literary in the last'), the rhymes 'rather doubtful' in several instances, and the rhythm unsuccessful.[33] Marsh was willing to accept de la Mare's estimate, and Miss Mew was excluded from *Georgian Poetry* III. Monro expressed his dissatisfaction: 'you couldn't really want my opinion', he wrote, 'seeing that you reject it in the one case in which I give it with real emphasis'.[34] His conclusion was unsound; in mid-1917, far from being deaf to the opinions of others, Marsh was simply giving preference to one man's judgment over another's. Marsh also solicited opinions from Monro on a tentative list of poems and poets for the third volume, and on this occasion editor and publisher found themselves more nearly in agreement.*

Marsh also showed himself remarkably receptive to the repeated importunities of J. C. Squire on behalf of W. J. Turner. Squire even went so far as to suggest to Marsh several specific poems of Turner's which he felt Marsh should print, a course of action which in 1912 or 1915 would have earned for its promoter only the firmest of refusals.[35] Nevertheless, by the first part of August Turner had accepted Marsh's invitation to contribute to *Georgian Poetry* III.[36] Squire was delighted: 'I can't tell you how glad I am you appreciate [Turner's] stuff,' he wrote. 'I feel he was a discovery. His first verse appeared here [i.e. in the *New Statesman*], and I have egged and egged him on.'[37]

Even more significant than Marsh's willingness to heed advice regarding a specific poet or poem was his willingness to reconsider his own basic principles of anthologizing. In a series of letters in April 1917—several months before he set about seriously collecting material for his third volume—Marsh sought to discuss first principles with his long-standing friend Maurice Baring, absent in France with the B.E.F. and himself an experienced anthologist. Though Marsh's side of the correspondence is unavailable, he obviously placed himself in the ironic position of arguing for representativeness, the very canon which he had specifically disavowed in the preface to *Georgian Poetry* I five years earlier. And Baring, in arguing for intrinsic poetic merit as the anthologist's lodestar, espoused the principle upon which Marsh had deliber-

---

* Harold Monro to E. M., 26th–29th July 1917, *MLC*. In the exchange of letters E. M. made it clear that he was considering including the work of both Maurice Baring and J. C. Squire in *GP* III. Monro objected more or less strenuously to both inclusions, but in spite of his objections both Baring's and Squire's poems appeared in the volume.

ately constructed his first two volumes. Clearly, in 1917 Marsh was suffering from a temporary failure of nerve. 'I utterly disagree with you about the Gepäck,' Baring wrote Marsh.

I am certain that once you begin to try and make a peerage you are lost. That is *just* what you must *not* try and do. It is impossible because the field of choice is infinite and inexhaustible, and not limited like the peerage. Once you begin to say, 'But if you have this you *must* have that,' you are lost. Because this is the wrong principle. And wrong because impossible: a mirage. You do not, at least I do not, want to make a *nursery garden* or a *Museum* but a nosegay (Anthologia, in fact) and when you make a nosegay, you don't say 'If you have that rose and those violets, you *must* have *that* tuberose and that gardenia or that crocus'.

It doesn't matter what you have as long as they smell sweet and are pretty. But if you try to have a specimen of every single remarkable flower you will find that your bouquet is impossibly big, and in that case it is much better not to pick the flowers at all but to leave them in the garden and the conservatories.[38]

The exchange of letters continued over several months, and even as late as July 1917 Baring had not given up the attempt to save his friend from the dark wood of anthological error into which he had strayed. 'Axiom applicable to all Gepäcks,' he warned, 'never to be forgotten by the Gepäck maker, who should repeat it day and night. Le mieux est l'ennemi du bien. LE MIEUX EST L'ENNEMI DU BIEN.'[39]

Despite the fact that he did not entirely accept the advice of Baring—and the promptings of his own better judgment, too, one feels—Marsh was never before, and never after, so open to suggestion or so willing to compromise as he was in 1917. 'Are you a little more inclined nowadays to be influenced by other people's views or by general opinion?' Monro questioned Marsh in midsummer 1917. As if unwilling to give credence to such an assumption, he quickly added, 'It may be only an idea I've got for the moment, partly through your mentioning several times what other people think of the poems you are selecting. I don't see you nowadays, but I expect you are just as strong-minded as you were about the other two [volumes]—which is the only way.'[40] Monro's first surmise was more accurate than he knew: by 1917 Marsh was something less than 'strong-minded'. How else can the inclusion of such a poem as Herbert Asquith's 'Volunteer' in *Georgian Poetry*

III be explained? His friend Edmund Gosse attacked Marsh in a particularly vulnerable spot in suggesting quite frankly that in case of Asquith something other than poetic achievement entered into Marsh's choice. 'How you can bring yourself to include Herbert Asquith in your "Georgian" passes my comprehension,' Gosse complained. 'I read him forward and I read him backward, and I see nothing. If he were a Herbert Snooks . . . no one would ever have looked at his verses. And people say that the "age of privilege" is passed!'[41]

At least *Georgian Poetry* III met with no such strictures as had attended the début of its predecessor in 1915. To most critics it seemed precisely what Marsh had intended it should be: adequate and uncontroversial. The *Athenaeum* gave it an uncomfortably brief dismissal, only listing the names of the eighteen posts represented and noting that nine of them were new to this volume.[42] Holbrook Jackson, writing in *To-day*, reached the not very startling conclusion that *Georgian Poetry* III was proof that good poetry exists not only in the great periods of literature which scholars label and minutely study but also in the intervals between. In a sufficiently modest fashion, he concluded, the volume fills one of those intervals.[43]

In the comments of reviewers who treated the volume at greater length one finds, understandably, a remarkable diversity of opinions. *Georgian Poetry* III was the most difficult of the entire series to review, for it contained little to provoke discussion and less to provoke argument. Even from the viewpoint of the conservative *Times Literary Supplement* the volume appeared too traditional, too conservative. If the third volume of *Georgian Poetry* is to be taken as representative of English poetry in 1917, the *Supplement* reviewer wrote, then

> there is nothing in the poetry of our young writers to alarm or distress the most conservative. Not only youth, but example and, more than either, new conditions of life might offer them the excuse for impatient rejection of the established and for the playing of all sorts of pranks in the effort to get expression for their youth and their strange and violent being. And what they are found for the most part to be doing is pouring their new wine into the old bottles; or—to use a more homely and perhaps more 'Georgian' simile—thrusting their proud young feet into old boots, and finding them good to march or to dance in.

For this lack of originality the reviewer was willing to blame the times; charitably, he left unspoken the possibility that it might have arisen by design on the part of Edward Marsh. 'Where, in the restlessness that heralded the war strange experiments were tried and the old means were contemptuously or angrily thrown away, the new conditions, enforcing sincerity, have maintained the old ways.'[44]

In an inconsistent review, Edward Shanks managed to straddle the fence. *Georgian Poetry* III shows 'that modern inspiration has not altered appreciably since 1912', he argued. 'The new-comers to the gathering have as much in common with the original contributors as the originals have in common among themselves.' On the other hand, he claimed that the nine new poets represented in the volume afforded conclusive evidence that *Georgian Poetry* III marked 'a break in the continuity of the series' and should therefore disprove once and for all the allegations of coterie poetry which had begun to appear in 1916.*

T. S. Eliot was at least more consistent. In spite of the nine new poets in the volume, he argued, *Georgian Poetry* III showed essentially the same tone as its predecessors. 'In Georgian Poetry there is almost no crossing visible,' he wrote; 'it is inbred. It has developed a technique and a set of emotions all its own.' What diversity there was in the volume was confined largely to such minor matters as syntax. The characteristically Georgian attitude which Eliot professed to see in all three volumes of *Georgian Poetry* was 'pleasantness'. In Georgian poetry, he wrote, 'there are two varieties of pleasantness: 1] the insidiously didactic, or Wordsworthian (a rainbow and a cuckoo's song); 2] the decorative, playful or solemn, minor-Keatsian, too happy, happy brook, or lucent sirops. In either variety the Georgians caress everything

* *NS*, X (1917), 280–1. In fairness to Shanks it should be added that he laboured under many difficulties in writing this review. By late 1917 J. C. Squire had become literary arbiter of the *NS*. His conservative tastes were well reflected in those of Shanks and Freeman, both of whom became, from mid-1917 on, increasingly frequent reviewers for that journal. Because each had been represented in *GP* III, obviously neither Squire nor Freeman could write the review of that volume. As Squire wrote Marsh on 11th Dec. 1917: 'It is obviously impossible for me to puff G. P. myself this time, but I tried to do my bit beforehand' (*MLC*). Shanks was therefore given the review but required to work under a handicap. When Marsh wrote Shanks mildly disagreeing with those sections of the review which had attacked his Georgians, Shanks replied: 'But it is really rather absurd to criticize such a book at all. No doubt you could be as destructive about it as any reviewer. We ought to recognize your difficulties more. My chief difficulty, of course, was that I was forbidden to say anything about Squire' (29th Dec. 1917, *MLC*).

they touch'. It is unfortunate that Eliot chose to distort one of the secondary qualities of *Georgian Poetry* I and II under the pretext of reviewing volume III. The charge of 'pleasantness' is far more easily supportable against volumes I and II than against III. Moreover, 'pleasantness' was no more than a minor tendency even of *Georgian Poetry* I and II, being confined largely to such poets as Drinkwater, Stephens, Monro, and (to a much lesser extent) perhaps Davies and de la Mare. *Georgian Poetry* III was precisely the one volume of the series in which 'pleasantness' was at a minimum. It is difficult to understand what Eliot found either 'insidiously didactic' and 'Wordsworthian', or 'decorative, playful' and 'minor-Keatsian' in Sassoon's war poem ' "They" ':

> 'We're none of us the same!' the boys reply.
> For George lost both his legs; and Bill's stone blind;
> Poor Jim's shot through the lungs and like to die;
> And Bert's gone syphilitic;
>
> *(Georgian Poetry* III, p. 45)

or in Graves's 'It's A Queer Time'; or Nichols's 'Assault', a vers-librist rendering of the stream of consciousness:

> Bullets a stream.
> Devouring thought crying in a dream.
> Men, crumpled, going down. . . .
> Go on. Go.
> Deafness. Numbness. The loudening tornado.
> Bullets. Mud. Stumbling and skating.
> My voice's strangled shout:
> *'Steady pace, boys!'*
> The still light: gladness.
> *'Look, sir. Look out!'*
> Ha! Ha! Bunched figures waiting.
> Revolver levelled quick!
> Flick! Flick!
> Red as blood.
> Germans. Germans.
> Good! O good!
> Cool madness.
>
> *(Georgian Poetry* III, p. 61)

The charge of 'caressing all they touched' might have set well against only one of the major groups of poets in *Georgian Poetry* III: the Squire-Turner-Freeman school. But curiously Eliot saw fit specifically to exempt the archetypical poem of that group from his strictures. ' "The Lily of Malud" ', he concluded, 'is an original and rather impressive poem which deserves better company.'[45]

Marsh's friends were no more successful than the reviewers in discerning the real significance of *Georgian Poetry* III. They confined themselves largely either to innocuous congratulations or to comments on specific poets and poems which they liked or disliked. Having received the book in France, Maurice Baring admitted that his taste did not exactly parallel Marsh's. He liked the selections from Turner, Monro, Davies, Bottomley, and Hodgson; he had reservations about Squire, Sassoon, and Rosenberg. Masefield, he declared, 'bores me stiff. He always has and I think always will, but I think you were right to include him for variety and width's sake'.[46] Edmund Gosse, to whom *Georgian Poetry* III was dedicated, acknowledged the honour with a potpourri of comments. He 'delighted' in Turner, chided Marsh gently for not including Graves's 'Fox Hunter', hazarded that Isaac Rosenberg must surely be a young Dane because 'his verses are so like those which come to me from young bards in Copenhagen', called Squire's work 'rather odd to be in this galère', and disagreed over the inclusion of James Stephens because 'his buttermilk is getting very thin and sour'.[47] Even those poets chosen for inclusion were not universally happy at the varied company into which they had been cast. John Freeman wrote Gordon Bottomley: 'I've not seen anything in the *Nation* on the new Georgian book. Do you refuse any personal application and agree that the book isn't very good? Much of it I can't read, or can't read with pleasure.'[48]

Even the most acute contemporary observers could hardly be expected to have assessed the real significance of *Georgian Poetry* III, for its importance emerges only with historical perspective. It was the volume which marked the dividing point between the dominance of the 'old' Georgians of volumes I and II and the 'new' Georgians who were to become increasingly important in volumes IV and V. One may more conveniently call these two schools the Georgians and the Neo-Georgians.* *Georgian Poetry* III

* The Neo-Georgian label is not entirely my own. It has been used by other critics, though only infrequently, with the specific intent of distinguishing between Georgian poets, 1912–17 vintage, and Georgian poets, 1917–22 vintage. As far as I can determine, the word was first used more or less with this intent by Alec Waugh in 'The Neo-Georgians', *Fortnightly Review*, CXV, n.s. (1924), 126–37. The distinction was elaborated upon by Herbert Palmer in *Post-Victorian Poetry*, p. 197 and *passim*. Here, as in subsequent chapters, I am indebted to Palmer for the general concept of not one but two schools of Georgian poets and poetry.

was the only volume of the series which comprised the work of both groups but showed the dominance of neither.

For the moment, in 1917, the ascendence of the Neo-Georgians was blocked by the war poetry of Sassoon, Graves, and Nichols. Their work, dramatic and bitter, with its emphasis on bloodshed and death, seems at first glance to put *Georgian Poetry* III squarely in the major tradition of volumes I and II. In fact, the war poetry seems to give the screw of anti-sentimentalism yet one more turn. 'Channel Passage' and 'King Lear's Wife', 'The Everlasting Mercy' and 'End of the World', seem unreal, the result only of over-wrought poetic imaginations, when compared with the first-hand observations of genuine horror in Sassoon or Nichols. In a sense, therefore, the young war poets of *Georgian Poetry* III can be viewed as building upon the precedent of the realists, those poets who strove for truth to life, in the first two volumes—Abercrombie, Bottomley, Masefield, and Brooke.\* But with historical perspective one is compelled to look through the more immediately striking war poetry to the quieter verse of the Neo-Georgians, Squire, Turner, and Freeman, for it was this group which was to dominate the last two volumes of the series.

At least three Neo-Georgian harbingers appeared in *Georgian Poetry* III, portents which even those who run may read: Freeman's 'Happy Is England Now', Squire's 'Lily of Malud', and Turner's 'Romance'. They were representative of a large segment of British poetry which, by 1917, was attempting either to ignore or escape from the brutality of a spiritually disastrous and too-long-protracted war. Freeman's was a war poem of sorts, but it evaded the real war of Rosenberg or Sassoon, the war of blood and mud and trench-foot, and substituted instead a sentimentalized vision of war, 'a meditative rusticity' which domiciled 'the western front among the lanes and fields of England'.[49]

> Happy is England in the brave that die
> For wrongs not hers and wrongs so sternly hers;
> Happy in those that give, give, and endure

---

\* Some notion of the influence of Brooke on some of the younger poets of realistic proclivities can be derived from a comment of Robert Graves to E. M. Graves took it upon himself to speak for his entire group as he wrote Marsh: 'How wrong about Rupert: we all look up to him as to our elder brother and have immense admiration for his work from any standpoint, especially his technique on which we all build. I know it is fashionable in some low quarters to pretend to dislike him; but nobody does really, least of all R. N[ichols]., S. S[assoon]., or R. G[raves].' (Robert Graves to E. M., 18th Mar. [1918?], *MLC*).

The pain that never the new years may cure;
Happy in all her dark woods, green fields, towns,
    Her hills and rivers and her chafing sea.

                            (*Georgian Poetry* III, p. 138)

Perhaps Freeman's spurious view of war may be said to have had
some precedent in *Georgian Poetry* II, in Brooke's war sonnets, but
the precedent is shadowy. Moreover, Brooke wrote in 1914. By
late 1917, a picture of England as 'Happy . . . in the brave that
die / For wrongs not hers . . ., / Happy in all her dark woods, green
fields, towns, / Her hills and rivers and her chafing sea', was
pitifully unrealistic. Three protracted years of bloody, dirty trench
warfare had made bitter mockery of such sentiments. Late 1917
was the age of *Counter-Attack*:

The barrage roars and lifts. Then, clumsily bowed
With bombs and guns and shovels and battle-gear,
Men jostle and climb to meet the bristling fire.
Lines of gray, muttering faces, masked with fear,
They leave their trenches, going over the top,
While time ticks blank and busy on their wrists,
And hope, with furtive eyes and grappling fists,
Flounders in the mud. O Jesu, make it stop!

'The Lily of Malud' was even more obviously a poem of escape,
though of a different kind. It turned completely away from the
subject of war and as a relief from horror sought beauty in the
exotic moon-drenched landscape of the jungle.

The lily of Malud is born in secret mud.
It is breathed like a word in a little dark ravine
Where no bird was ever heard and no beast was ever seen,
And the leaves are never stirred by the panther's velvet sheen.

It blooms once a year in summer moonlight,
In a valley of dark fear full of pale moonlight:
It blooms once a year, and dies in a night,
And its petals disappear with the dawn's first light;
And when that night has come, black small-breasted maids,
With ecstatic terror dumb, steal fawn-like through the shades
To watch, hour by hour, the unfolding of the flower.

                            (*Georgian Poetry* III, p. 30)

In the cultivation of the strange and the exotic Squire was matched,
and frequently excelled, by W. J. Turner, a poet enchanted by the

sound of the names of far-off places. Turner's 'Romance' was on the first page of *Georgian Poetry* III:

> When I was but thirteen or so
> I went into a golden land,
> Chimborazo, Cotopaxi
> Took me by the hand.
>
> My father died, my brother too,
> They passed like fleeting dreams,
> I stood where Popocatapetl
> In the sunlight gleams.

Again, there was some precedent for Squire and Turner in *Georgian Poetry* I and II, in the Eastern exoticism of Flecker's verse, or in the curious, unique blend of strangeness, beauty, and mystery in the verse of de la Mare. But again the differences appear more striking than the similarities; again the Neo-Georgians gave the screw an extra turn. Their verse seems too cultivated, too obviously unreal, their beauty too lush, too patently contrived. Ironically enough, poems like 'Romance' and the 'Lily of Malud' —and there were to be many of them in *Georgian Poetry* IV and V— are the best possible evidence of the genius of Walter de la Mare, for they demonstrate unmistakably that his poetic mode is essentially inimitable.

In leading *Georgian Poetry* down the path of the moonlit, exotic jungle the Neo-Georgians were beginning to force the anthology into a cul-de-sac. Already by late 1917 their misty escape poetry was an anachronism, but within the next five years it was to become even more obviously out of step with the age it lived in. The Neo-Georgians were poets of the moon; their verse was washed white with the pale beams of Diana. Compared to the best of the Georgians the Neo-Georgians were pallid, lifeless, and monotonous. And they were to take Edward Marsh's anthology eventually from the real world of men and things, the world of truth to life, to an eternally moon-washed land of tropic nights. With such poems as the 'Lily of Malud', 'Happy is England Now', and 'Romance', *Georgian Poetry* took the first step towards verse that was increasingly trivial, unreal, and irrelevant to the late war years and the violent post-war period.

The decline of *Georgian Poetry* can be blamed directly or indirectly upon the war. The anthology began to founder when, after three years of war, it began to substitute 'agreeableness' for 'truth'. The war had made it impossible to combine the two qualities, and 'as might be expected, truth was the first to be sacrificed'.[50] The sacrifice was begun—though barely begun—in *Georgian Poetry* III. But the blame cannot be placed on the war alone; it must be placed in part on Edward Marsh as well, for surely some of the weakness of his third volume resulted from Marsh's deliberate substitution of a principle of anthologizing which was radically different from the one he had followed in compiling *Georgian Poetry* I and II. Following the principle of representativeness, Marsh succeeded not only in making *Georgian Poetry* III a potpourri but also in opening the gates of his anthology to new poets and new forces which were in subsequent years to exert more influence than he had bargained for. In 1912 and 1915 'Georgian' had implied vigour, revolt, and youth. After 1917 it was to imply retrenchment, escape, and enervation.

# 8

# The Literary Scene: 1918-1922

---

If the years 1912–15 can be said to have seen the high summer of *Georgian Poetry* and 1917 the first premonitory light frosts, then with the period 1918–22 the anthology fell full upon the years of winter. Despite the war poetry it contained, *Georgian Poetry* III had shown some evidence that Edward Marsh's anthology was beginning to lose touch with the environment of the late war years. *Georgian Poetry* IV and V, published in 1919 and 1922 respectively, were to demonstrate this even more conclusively. But if *Georgian Poetry* itself changed character between 1912 and 1919, the literary atmosphere into which volumes IV and V were cast had changed even more drastically. Indeed, the post-war anti-Georgian reaction which began to set in about 1918 resulted as much from the temper of the times as from hostility towards the contributors to *Georgian Poetry* IV and V or resentment over specific acts of omission or commission on the part of Edward Marsh. And so to understand adequately the reasons for the decline of *Georgian Poetry* one turns temporarily from the historical account of the series to a depiction of a few of the more pertinent literary features of the post-war age. It is just as important to see *Georgian Poetry* IV and V in their proper context as it was to see *Georgian Poetry* I and II in theirs.

## I

By 1918 many of the landmarks of the pre-war poetic renaissance had been swept away. Marinetti and Futurism were dead issues, historical curiosities to be conjured up nostalgically over a post-prandial glass of port as a happy memory of the uncomplicated days before the war. Vorticism, and with it Wyndham Lewis's *Blast*, had also passed into the limbo of half-forgotten causes of half-forgotten days. *Rhythm* and *Blue Review* had been early casualties of the war, and their editor, Middleton Murry, after serving as a reviewer for the *Times Literary Supplement*, became editor of the *Athenaeum* in 1919. In the strange, violent world created by the war new movements were a-borning, new literary high priests emerging: the Sitwells, T. S. Eliot, Aldous Huxley. Four momentous years of war had considerably changed the tone of literary London.

That is not to say that the break between the modern poetic movements of 1912-15 and those of 1918-22 was complete. In some respects pre-war and post-war coteries appear to have differed more in degree than in kind. New work and new personalities did not spring full-blown upon the post-war scene. It is well to be reminded, for instance, that Eliot's 'Prufrock', a poem from which some choose to date the beginning of 'modern' poetry, had been written before the war, and had been published for the first time in mid-1915; that his 'Preludes' and 'Rhapsody of a Windy Night' had been printed in the second number of *Blast* (July 1915); and that although his first book of verse, *Prufrock and Other Observations*, had not been published until 1917, many of the pieces in it had already been printed individually from 1915 to 1917, in *Poetry*, *Blast*, the *Egoist*, or the *Catholic Anthology*.[1]

Moreover, a few of the same poetic controversies that had rent the air in 1912 were still live issues in the late war years and after. Even the war failed to dampen arguments over free verse. With an air of exasperation, T. S. Eliot set forth in 1917 to slay the preposterous dragon of *vers libre* once and for all. As a strictly definable poetic form, *vers libre* was a prosodic will-o'-the-wisp, he argued; 'the division between Conservative Verse and *Vers Libre* does not exist, for there is only good verse, bad verse, and chaos'.[2] Far from settling anything, Eliot's dicta seem only to have set the pot simmering again, for reviewers continued damning or praising *vers libre* just as if it had not been declared a fiction. One of the most consistent sufferers at the hands of the anti-verslibrists was D. H. Lawrence whose *Look! We Have Come Through* (1917) received several scathing reviews because of its failure to use conventional rhythms.[3] As late as 1919 Lawrence himself re-entered the controversy with a series of arguments in favour of free verse which precisely echoed those he had championed so eloquently in correspondence with Edward Marsh in 1913.[4]

The Poetry Bookshop not only survived the war but also extended its influence into the post-war years. But in comparing the pre-war and post-war activities of the Bookshop and of its founder, Monro, one begins to see evidence of the changed tone of post-war literary London. Monro and the Bookshop were perceptibly drifting away from the poetry and poets of the Centre towards those of the Left. Poetry readings had continued at the Bookshop during the war on a more or less sporadic basis even while Monro was absent in military service. By mid-1919, however, the readings had once again become weekly events, and the readers were chosen increasingly from among the more controversial and experimental poets of the Left.* Monro performed an even more valuable service to post-war poetry by a series of informal parties which he inaugurated in the spring of 1919. Ostensibly intended to launch his new periodical, the *Chapbook*, these parties achieved much more by affording poets torn from their art by war a pleasant means of becoming reacclimated to the London literary world. 'They formed a meeting place for old friends who had lost touch with one another during the war years, as well as providing those who frequented them with opportunities of making new acquaintances. Almost everyone who had ever published any verse turned up at them.' It was at these parties, too, that the new literary alliances of the post-war era began to take shape and the new battle lines began to form, for over a glass of Monro's wine 'warfare between the Left Wing literary rebels and the "stuffed shirts" of the Establishment, who had formed themselves into a racket and controlled most of the post-war reviewing, was carried on with enormous gusto'.[5]

Perhaps the *Chapbook* affords the clearest evidence of Monro's swing towards the Left. In all, Monro edited forty issues of the *Chapbook* from July 1919 to July 1925. It appeared regularly as a

---

* Among them was Vachel Lindsay. One hopes that the boom in Lindsay's poetic reputation among English poets during 1919 and 1920 may become the subject of a detailed investigation, for such a study might lead to interesting conclusions regarding his influence upon British poetry of the 1920's. *General William Booth Enters into Heaven* (1913) and the *Congo* (1914) were apparently 'discovered' by Robert Nichols during a trip to America in 1919. When Nichols trumpeted his new-found discoveries to the British literary world, Lindsay's work became the *dernier cri* for several years among some *avant-garde* circles. Among the enthusiasts in 1919 and 1920 were, strangely, such diverse poets as Masefield and Yeats.

monthly journal for approximately the first two years of its life, but by early 1922 it had run into financial difficulties and from that time until its demise in 1925 was published irregularly, apparently whenever the material warranted or the spirit moved Harold Monro. The sub-title of the first number was 'Poetry and Drama, New Series', and Monro's prospectus announced that it 'replaced' Poetry and Drama, which had suspended publication at the end of 1914. But even a cursory comparison between the poets who habitually contributed to the Chapbook and those whose work had formed the backbone of Poetry and Drama suggests some major differences in emphasis and tone in Monro's two journals. The Chapbook reflected the post-war literary scene just as Poetry and Drama had reflected the pre-war. The contributors to the very first number tell something of the story. A few Georgians appeared among the twenty-three poets whose work was represented: de la Mare, Turner, Davies, even Sturge Moore. But they were far outnumbered by poets of the newer schools: Herbert Read, W. P. Ker, the three Sitwells, 'H. D.', Flint, and Aldington. In subsequent volumes the tide turned even more markedly against Centrist verse. The three critics whom Monro chose to review the state of contemporary English poetry in early 1920, far from being Georgians, were T. S. Eliot, Aldous Huxley, and F. S. Flint. In 1920 and 1921 Monro began increasingly to take notice of the more modern American poets. The May 1920 number comprised only John Gould Fletcher's review of contemporary American poetry, and the August number of the same year was entirely given over to Edna St. Vincent Millay's Aria Da Capo. The Chapbook became increasingly precious from 1922 to 1925 as it began more frequently to indulge Monro's passion for 'discovering' minor poets; but for two years, from mid-1919 to mid-1921, it presented a reasonably adequate mirror of post-war literary London, along with evidence that the new environment was working a change in the tastes of even so essentially a Centrist poet as Harold Monro.

The situation of the Imagists in the post-war world presents interesting parallels. Essentially a pre-war poetic force, Imagism had extended its influences well into the war years. Three successive volumes of the Imagist anthology, Some Imagist Poets, were published from 1915 through 1917.* When Richard Aldington

* Some indication of the waning force of the Imagists, the enfants terribles of the

entered military service in mid-1916, the *Egoist* appeared to have been safely left in the hands of 'H. D.', who took over her husband's assistant-editorship. But it is doubtful that Imagism survived the war as an organized coterie; or if it did it was bereft of its most effective platform. Around the middle of 1917, owing to the influence of Pound (who had long since been read out of Imagist ranks) the *Egoist* began to change its tone, and new contributors who would more faithfully reflect the post-war poetic scene began to make increasingly frequent appearances in its pages. Herbert Read and T. S. Eliot began to receive more critical attention. In May 1917 the Egoist Press published *Prufrock*, which Pound reviewed in the journal with fulsome praise. In June 1917 Eliot's name appeared on the masthead for the first time as an assistant editor, and the Aldingtons' names were absent (though both husband and wife subsequently contributed to the journal). After Eliot's accession to office, poems and reviews by Pound became markedly more frequent, and in August 1917 there appeared for the first time in the journal a contribution from the young Aldous Huxley. And so perceptibly throughout 1917 and 1918 the Imagists lost their hold over the *Egoist*; they were replaced by poets and reviewers of newer schools who, though they were sympathetic to Imagism and though their work bore unmistakable traces of its influence, nevertheless were not within the Imagist coterie. Huxley, Eliot and Read were predominantly men of the post-war, not the pre-war, era.

A few of the pre-war issues, institutions, and coteries, then, survived into the post-war years, though they were severely altered. The post-war spirit is better observed in those movements indigenous to the climate of the late war years and the period immediately following. By late 1916 new coteries began to appear, more partisan, more scurrilous, more thoroughly dedicated to the destruction of their poetic enemies than their counterparts in 1912 had ever been. New poetic coteries meant new coterie anthologies and little magazines. *Georgian Poetry* had pointed the way, as many poets conceived it: corporate publication of verse was the surest means of achieving fame and fortune. And so London was bombarded with partisan, and usually ephemeral, publications of verse

pre-war years, can be gathered from the fact that even a *TLS* reviewer could find nothing to complain of in their 1916 anthology. In fact, he spent a large part of his allotted space in welcoming new forms to modern poetry (*TLS*, 11th Jan. 1917).

for several years after the war. Though they were in a sense eloquent testimony to Edward Marsh's success in making poetry pay, most of the post-war anthologies and little magazines were adamantly, bitterly hostile to *Georgian Poetry*. Again, as in the years before the war, the journals, and the poets who edited and contributed to them, can be conveniently classified as Left, Centre, and Right.*

The first sally against Georgianism from the Leftist camp was mounted by the anthology *Wheels*. In its beginnings it was not, in fact, a post-war publication, but though three of its numbers appeared during wartime, it was the first harbinger of the post-war spirit. Six annual numbers of *Wheels* were published, the first in late 1916, the last in 1922. Featuring the contributions of such young poets as Osbert and Edith Sitwell, Aldous Huxley, Herbert Read, Nancy Cunard, Arnold James, and Iris Tree, *Wheels* was self-consciously *avant-garde*. Like *Blast* and several other pre-war little magazines, a part of its aim was surely *épater la bourgeoisie*; and to do it, moreover, with as much insolence as possible.

But in tone *Wheels* belonged unmistakably to the post-war world: it was brilliant on the surface, but underneath there lurked a dominant mood of bitterness, cynicism, and flippancy. The *Wheels* coterie threw over poetic convention with a fine and studied insolence, but they substituted for it nothing but a cynical and epigrammatic brilliance which, though it coruscated, quickly burned out to cinders and ashes. The major contributors to *Wheels*, as a contemporary critic observed, share a poetic mood which is 'on the whole dour and morose; they see nothing bright in the present, and no bright hopes in the future'. Most of them profess only 'a dolorous morbid hopelessness'.[6] That is not to condemn the contributors to *Wheels*. Hopelessness was a far more genuine reflection of the post-war temper than the Georgian 'too happy, happy brook, or lucent sirops' kind of 'pleasantness'. Moreover, the Cyclists tended towards excessively precious poetry. They 'have a little the air of smattering', T. S. Eliot complained. They represent an opposite extreme from the Georgians, but an extreme nevertheless. 'Instead of rainbows, cuckoos, daffodils, and timid hares, they give us garden-gods, guitars, and mandolins,

---

* Again one must warn against any temptation to extend a convenient poetic label to matters in any sense extra-poetical. No political allusion whatever is implied (see above, Ch. 1).

Lancret rather than Watteau, though they seem to have thrown Pierrot overboard. They need Catullus, Homer, Heine, Gautier; for they have extracted the juice from Verlaine and Laforgue.'[7]

The *Wheels* coterie put a high premium on cleverness; they were too self-consciously rebels. Any poetic practice which smacked of tradition had to be rejected out of hand not because it was poetically good or bad, useful or useless, but simply because it was traditional. Had the great English poets of the past approached their art with high seriousness? The *Wheels* coterie would approach it flippantly. Had English poets, especially those of the detested Victorian age, eschewed cleverness in verse? The *Wheels* coterie would be excruciatingly clever.

> The school of poets of whom Miss Sitwell is a leader are essentially of the sideways- or backwards-turning variety. It is terrible to them to think that they are practising an art which Milton, Wordsworth, Shelley, Swinburne and Tennyson practised before them. All those highbrows! We have become accustomed to think of . . . a kind of holy seriousness as a condition of poetry; how pitifully antique! Detachment, nonchalance are new requirements; and the object of *Wheels* is to get effect from such use of words as shall have least in common with the uses to which they have been put by previous poets. Verse becomes in this way an admirable vehicle for the communication of cleverness, and everybody in Miss Sitwell's company is clever. . . . They are bright and they are independent.[8]

Even forty years after the last volume was published, the poems in *Wheels* seem almost invariably amusing, but they remain unconvincing. One's sympathies are not engaged, not even those sympathies usually engaged by the best satirical verse.

*Wheels* itself, however, was perhaps not so influential as its editor, Edith Sitwell. The acknowledged leader of the *Wheels* coterie, she led her oddly assorted band in a slashing assault against the Georgians. *Wheels* was her first blow but by no means her only one, for she seldom overlooked an opportunity, however remote, to snipe at the enemy and to harass him from every quarter. She was able to turn every defence of her own kind of poetry sooner or later into an attack on every other kind. For Midas-eared post-war critics she had only scorn. Accused of failing to see the value of tradition in verse, she countered by telling the critics that they did not recognize a tradition when they saw one; rather, they recognized only one, the Wordsworthian. Her poetry returned, she explained, to the Elizabethan. For the general reader of poetry, too, she could shed few tears. The fresh views of post-war poetry came as a shock, she admitted, but the horrified reader was getting no more than he deserved for allowing his emotions to vegetate and preferring to take his poetic impressions second-hand. The best modern verse, especially as written by Miss Sitwell, Miss Sitwell claimed, forced the reader to perform an act of creative imagination required by almost no poetry since the seventeenth century: the fusion of the activities of the senses and of the brain. Modern verse made a reader think. No wonder it excited hostility.[9]

On the subject of the Georgians Miss Sitwell waxed wonderfully, scornfully eloquent, though looking behind the withering sarcasm and the purple prose one may well question whether her implied definition of 'Georgian' is either entirely sound or entirely complete. She excluded Davies, de la Mare, and Hodgson from her strictures *in toto*, and Masefield and Gibson in part; but for the rest, they were only minor nature-lovers, week-end poets, and scribblers 'who seem obsessed by the predilection for sheep'. On Rupert Brooke as an archetypical Georgian she was particularly trenchant. Some of his poems have a mercurial shimmer to them, she conceded—which is more than can be said for his imitators in later *Georgian* volumes—'but they have, at the same time, a faintly spurious flavour. . . . They lie flat on the page, and are painfully unobtrusive'. What emotion they succeed in bodying forth is pretended emotion. It was this quality in particular, the pretence of emotion instead of the real thing, which Miss Sitwell condemned not only in Brooke but also as the single pre-eminently Georgian trait.[10]

There is just enough truth in F. R. Leavis's ill-tempered dictum that in their early years 'the Sitwells belong more to the history of publicity than the history of poetry' to make Miss Sitwell's judgments of the Georgians suspect, but surely she was no reluctant warrior. She was a master alike of the thrust, the parry, and the free-swinging slap with the side of the blade, and she enjoyed her mastery hugely. She was the first to attempt to reduce the Georgians with ridicule, a tactic which was to be frequently employed, though never so well, by less adept critics in subsequent decades. Miss Sitwell gave Georgian poetry one of the most scathing—and masterly—dismissals it has ever had:

Mr. Housman was followed by a school of poets, rather loosely held together by their sub-Wordsworthian ideals. To these men rhetoric and formalism were abhorrent, partly, no doubt, because to manage either quality in verse, the writer must have a certain gift for poetry.

In the age of which I speak, we find the first shy buds of those full-flowered transcriptions of Robert Elsmere into blank verse which enliven the pages of a certain monthly arbiter of our taste. In that verse . . . the praise of worthy home life alternated with swollen, inflated boomings and roarings about the Soul of Man. These beauties reigned triumphant, together with healthy, manly, but rather raucous shouts for beer, and advertisements for certain rustic parts of England, to the accompaniment of a general clumsy clod-hopping, with hob-nailed boots. Birds became a cult. Any mention of the nest of a singing-bird threw the community into a frenzy. Dreamy plaster-faced sheep with Alexandra fringes and eyes like the eyes of minor German royalty, limpid, wondering, disapproving, uncomprehending, these were admired, as were bulldogs weeping tears of blood. Nor was Romance absent. At one moment, any mention of 'little Juliet', 'Helen of Troy', or of Troy itself roused a passionate interest. The names alone were sufficient. Again, any allusion to a violin— although this must be called a fiddle—any simple description of a gaffer doddering in the village alehouse, melted the audience to tears. Yet with all this romantic simplicity, the business man's careful logic was never absent, combined, strangely enough, with the legendary innocence of the country clergyman (this last trait being a tribute to the memory of the unfortunate Wordsworth).[11]

One of the Leftist little magazines of the post-war period in which Miss Sitwell and her brother Osbert had a direct hand was *Art and Letters*. In original intent a quarterly, the journal was published intermittently from July 1917 to 1920. Its editor was Frank Rutter. One of the major contributors to the first number was Herbert Read, whose influence remained strong throughout the life of the journal, but especially during 1917 and 1918. With the 1918 and early 1919 numbers *Art and Letters* turned almost exclusively towards work from the *Wheels* coterie, and with the issue of Summer 1919, Osbert Sitwell became poetry editor. In that number, and subsequently, the journal's poetic preferences seemed to broaden a little. It published some excellent posthumous work of Isaac Rosenberg, Eliot's 'Burbank with a Baedeker' and 'Sweeney Erect'; and it distinguished itself head and shoulders above almost all the literary journals of the era by being among the first to recognize the poetic stature of Wilfred Owen, three of whose poems appeared posthumously in the Spring 1920 number. But the major poetic contributors remained the Sitwells, Eliot, and Pound, whose poems, towards the end of the journal's existence, came to be printed with increasing frequency.

In spirit *Art and Letters* was not so much anti-traditional as anti-democratic. It carried on into the post-war years something of the tone of Middleton Murry's *Rhythm* and *Blue Review*, but with more finesse and considerably greater hauteur. The feeling for the natural superiority and exclusiveness of the artist breathed through every number of *Art and Letters*, and with it the implied assumption that by definition no popular art can be good art. In his 'Nine Propositions' Frank Rutter caught some of the scorn for the Philistine with which *Art and Letters* was infused:

I   There can be no art without life.
II   There can be no life without growth.
III   There can be no growth without change.
IV   There can be no change without controversy.
V   Vital art-work is controversial and displeasing to the majority.
VI   Uninformed opinion is always hostile to the unknown.
VII   Of any given subject the number of persons possessing knowledge is smaller than the number of uninformed.
VIII   A minority is not always right, but right opinions can be held only by a minority.
IX   Ignorance triumphs at a general election.[12]

It is small wonder that in its choice of poetry *Art and Letters* sometimes found itself on the edge of the inane. Some of the verse it printed was obviously chosen more with an eye towards infuriating the Bumbles than out of a concern for poetic art. Upon what other supposition can one account for the publication of such a bit of nonsense as Susan Miles's 'My Friend is Crying'?

> My friend is crying.
> Is it because her mother is dead?
> Or because the dust-bin is smelling,
> And the charwoman's little daughter is
>    having whooping-cough in the kitchen?
> She does not know.[13]

Frequently the attack of *Art and Letters* against Bumbledom was more direct. In a poem which clearly expressed the bitterness of the post-war intellectual temper and the scorn of the poet for the

general reader, Osbert Sitwell launched a wonderfully mordant
shaft against the British reading public:

> We will not buy 'Art and Letters',
> It is affected!
> Our sons
> And brothers
> Went forth to fight
> To kill
> Certain things—
> 'All this poetry and rubbish'—
> We said
> We will not buy 'Art and Letters'.
>
> We sent them quite willingly
> To kill
> Certain things—
> Cubism, futurism, and so on.
> There has been
> Enough art
> In the past;
> If they would only turn
> Their attention
> To killing and maiming.
> If they cannot kill men,
> Why can't they kill animals?
> There is still
> Big game in Africa;
> Or there might be trouble
> Among the natives.
> We will not buy 'Art and Letters'.
>
> It is tolerably clear to us
> That the War
> Was due to a German poet—
> All this Nietzsche and nonsense—
> We will not buy 'Art and Letters'.
>
> .     .     .     .
>
> But as the Pharisees
> Approached the tomb
> They saw the boulder
> Roll back
> And the tomb was empty
> And they said:

'It is all very disconcerting,
I am not at all
Narrow-minded:
I know a tune when I hear one—
And I know what I like.
I did not so much mind
That he blasphemed
Saying that he was the Son of God
But he was never a sportsman:
He went out into the desert
For forty days
And never shot anything:
And when we hoped he would drown
He walked on the waters.'

No, we will not buy 'Art and Letters'.[14]

A far better edited publication than either *Wheels* or *Art and Letters* was *Coterie*, a periodical conceived and published entirely within the post-war years. *Coterie* was edited by Chaman Lall from Jesus College, Oxford, and ran for seven numbers at approximately quarterly intervals from May 1919 to December 1920. In make-up the most handsome journal of its time, *Coterie* was an amateur publication, but only in the sense that its editorial staff was unpaid, performing their services for modern poetry as a labour of love. In its initial numbers *Coterie* devoted itself entirely to the publication of new poetry, but it quickly branched out into other genres of imaginative literature, proudly—and justifiably— advertising itself as 'the only periodical of standing in contemporary literature which contains nothing but work of creative imagination'. Though no fiery poetic credos were laid down by *Coterie* (uniquely enough, no editorial comments of any kind prefaced the first number), it was apparent from the beginning that the journal would be decidedly modern. The first, only mildly controversial, number furnished a convenient platform for the 'Oxford Group': T. W. Earp, Wilfred Childe, and its editor, Chaman Lall. But it also published work from, among others, T. S. Eliot and Aldous Huxley. With the second number (September 1919) the subsequent tone of *Coterie* was set. New work from new sources appeared: poems by Edith Sitwell, Herbert Read, Conrad Aiken, and John Gould Fletcher; drawings by Gaudier-Brzeska, Walter Sickert, Nina Hamnet, and William Rothenstein.

In this number Huxley's 'Leda' saw its first publication. Though in several subsequent issues some attempt at catholicity was made by the inclusion of verse from such poets of the Establishment as Gibson and Monro, the new still far outweighed the old in the work of young poets like Sacheverell Sitwell, Edmund Blunden, Babette Deutsch, Robert Nichols, Iris Tree, and Russell Green.

*Coterie* was neither so insolent and provocative as *Art and Letters* nor so strenuously *avant-garde* as *Wheels*. In the eyes of some critics, indeed, it was too solemn, as only the very young could be solemn. Even the *Times Literary Supplement* reviewer could take the first number to task for what he considered an unbecoming excess of decorum among English youth. *Coterie* lacked the 'definite experimentalism' of the Imagist anthologies and the 'rebelliousness' of *Wheels*, and if the work of Eliot and Huxley is excepted, he wrote, 'there is little in "Coterie" to surprise us as original or to thrill us as outrageous. One rather hopes always to find "les jeunes" tweaking the beards of Academicians; no doubt they have as good a right to be solemn as the rest of us—but so much decorum is slightly discouraging'.[15] As *Coterie* progressed it became increasingly adept at tweaking beards among the Establishment.

But *Coterie's* significance lay not so much in its ability to be provocative—a task which *Arts and Letters* performed superlatively well—but in the fact that its very reason for existence demonstrated an important fact of post-war literary life. *Coterie* was begun because many young poets felt that during the war established English literary journals had fallen too exclusively to the control of conservative editors who had banded themselves into an informal guild dedicated to keeping new and modern poetry off their pages and, conversely, printing only the verse of the Establishment. Denied publication, then, the younger poets founded their own journals. *Coterie* was one of them; so, among others, was *Art and Letters*. But *Coterie* was compelled to bring the issue more clearly into the open than most other little magazines, for it attracted the ire of the most influential of the conservative journals, J. C. Squire's *London Mercury*. In the columns of the *Mercury* Squire attacked *Coterie* with greater regularity and more venom than he customarily devoted to any other Leftist journal. He concluded a particularly vigorous attack in the November 1919 issue of the *Mercury* with a scathing one-sentence dismissal:

'It is a pity that so much paper should be wasted on so much rubbish.' Stung finally to reply to an antagonist they had so far ignored, the editors of *Coterie* made amply clear the grievances which young poets felt and the bitterness to which corporate publication of verse had brought poetic warfare by 1920. The kinds of criticism that *Coterie* has received, the editors wrote, are sufficient evidence, if more is needed, that 'in the present conditions governing the production of English literature, an aesthetic quarterly written by volunteers rather than by pressmen cannot hope, despite the obvious sincerity and accomplishment of its expression, to escape the irrelevant invective of crustacean criticasters or the dull malice of philistine sciolists'. *Coterie* gave as good as it got. It accused the *Mercury* and its editors of 'cultural Prussianism', its reviewers of being at best 'renegades from the fraternity of letters' whose sense of professional honour towards the staff of a sister periodical, if it did not make their minds more receptive, should at least have made their tongues less sharp in public print. The editorial concluded with a spirited attack on the Establishment: 'It is not by perpetuating the barrel organs of Georgian poetry that the race of Helicon shall be renewed. Nor is English literature in general likely to rebuild its Parthenon out of the accumulated rubble of a sombre academicism.'[16] The attack was *Coterie's* swan song, but the journal at least died with a magnificent gesture of defiance which pointed up for all to see the immense power exerted over English literature by a few conservative literary journals in the post-war years.

One more post-war journal of the *avant-garde* deserves mention, T. S. Eliot's *Criterion*. By almost any standards the most significant little magazine of the twenties, *Criterion* can only be mentioned in passing because its beginnings (in October 1922) barely fall into the period under consideration. In the beginning *Criterion* continued much the same tone as its predecessor, the *Egoist*; and it made use of many of the same contributors, including Pound and Aldington. But from the start it drew upon more diverse literary schools for its articles and was far less contentious, far less coterieminded, than the *Egoist* had been. In the first few volumes it printed some of Eliot's poetry, short stories of Virginia Woolf, an autobiographical fragment of Yeats, stories by May Sinclair, and critical pieces by Eliot, Herbert Read, Marcel Proust, Middleton Murry, and Osbert Sitwell. It could scarcely be accused of the kind of literary parochialism in which most of the little magazines of the time indulged. But to the historical eye *Criterion* was a poetic bellwether. In its first number, in October 1922, appeared 'The Waste Land'.[17] The next month *Georgian Poetry* v was published. Such a juxtaposition offers striking evidence that—as subsequent chapters will demonstrate—Edward Marsh's anthology had completely lost touch with the temper of the times.

*Wheels*, *Art and Letters*, *Coterie*, and *Criterion*, then, may be said to comprise the most significant post-war journals of the Left. Others of more definitely Centrist persuasion deserve some mention. Most of them made a valiant attempt to avoid being tarred with the coterie brush, Right or Left, but in an era when the partisan spirit was flourishing as never before, their attempts at splendid isolation were by and large unsuccessful. The middle ground was becoming increasingly difficult to discern and almost impossible to hold, for attempts to keep to the middle succeeded only in provoking violent attacks from both sides. Caught in the cross-fire, and impecunious in the extreme, most of the little magazines of the Centre, like Monro's *Chapbook*, were eventually forced either to stretch a tentative foot towards one of the coteries or to suspend publication. Only a few were able to survive long enough or to find sufficient worth-while material to print to render them noteworthy. Almost by the nature of things in the post-war literary world, neutralism meant death.

Among established periodicals perhaps the *Athenaeum* most successfully maintained the position of the Centre. Traditionally a weekly, it had been forced to monthly publication in 1916 by the wartime paper shortage, and it had turned its attention largely away from strictly literary and artistic concerns to those which may be broadly described as political or social. In early 1919, however, Middleton Murry became editor, and with the issue of 4th April of that year it returned to its customary character, being published once again as a weekly and devoting itself almost entirely to literature. In the post-war years the *Athenaeum* was careful to dissociate itself from the more extreme fringes of literary modernism, but at the same time it maintained an attitude which was by no means fusty. By mid-1919, in fact, under Murry's direction it had become the chief antagonist of J. C. Squire's *London Mercury*.[18] The most frequent poetry reviewer in its columns was Aldous Huxley; Murry also contributed important critical articles on poetry; and in late 1919 Katherine Mansfield became the major novel and short story reviewer. By 1919, however, being of the Centre party did not necessarily mean being pro-Georgian. On the contrary, one of the first unmistakably sharp but well-reasoned post-war attacks on the Georgian movement came in a leading article written by Middleton Murry in the *Athenaeum* of 16th May 1919.

Among the memorable little magazines of the Centre was Thomas Moult's *Voices*. It was an eminently uncontroversial journal published by a poet who was himself to be included in *Georgian Poetry* IV. It appeared at approximately monthly intervals from 1919 to 1921. A journal like *Voices*, not strenuously devoted to either Left or Right, had considerable difficulty finding suitable material to publish, and Moult frequently complained to Edward Marsh of the dearth of publishable verse in the post-war period.[19] Consequently *Voices* was too largely filled with the work of minor poets who achieved only a second- or third-rate competence in their brief moment before they sank mercifully back into obscurity. The tone of *Voices* was quiet, and though the poetry it characteristically printed was more frequently than not in the modern style, the harsh post-war note of despair was not to be heard in its pages. The spirit which governed the selection of poetry for *Voices* was perhaps best expressed in one of Moult's dicta on modern poetry. 'Forethought and afterthought are too much with us in contemporary poetry,' he wrote. 'Even when the artist is sufficiently master of himself to shed the shackles of intellect and allow supremacy to vision, which is emotion, there remains the further danger that his expression will be achieved either hastily or with wrestlings too prolonged.'[20] The more extreme kinds of modern verse were obviously too cerebrated, too devoid of emotion, too hard and dry for *Voices*.

A more considerable though much more short-lived little magazine of the Centre was *The Owl*. It comprised only two numbers, the first appearing in May, the second around October 1919. It was edited by Robert Graves, who was abetted and assisted to some degree by J. C. Squire and W. J. Turner. In a brief foreword to the first number the editor of *The Owl* renounced all coterie verse:

> It must be understood that 'The Owl' has no politics, leads no new movement and is not even the organ of any particular generation—

for that matter sixty-seven years separate the oldest and the youngest contributors.

But we find in common a love of honest work well done, and a distaste for shortcuts to popular success.

'The Owl' will come out quarterly or whenever enough suitable material is in the hands of the Editors.

The journal's deeds matched its words: it not only achieved perhaps the highest literary standard of any contemporary little magazine, but it also managed to achieve a degree of eclecticism beyond the power of most. Among the contributors to the first number were Hardy, Beerbohm, Masefield, Davies, Graves, Sassoon, and Squire; to the second was added work by Blunden, de la Mare, Vachel Lindsay, and Shanks. The only unifying concept behind *The Owl* was its dislike of the coterie spirit, 'the love of honest work well done'. On the back cover of each of the two numbers appeared the drawing of an owl and beneath it this quatrain:

> Athenian fowl with feathered legs
> Stand emblem of our will
> To hunt the rat that sucks the eggs
> Of virtue, joy, and skill.

But although Athene's owl of wisdom stood as emblem of the will to avoid the coterie spirit, the will was not enough. That spirit was abroad in the land, and the short life of even so excellent a little magazine as *The Owl* is some evidence that in the post-war environment a journal could perish from an excess of eclecticism just as surely as from an excess of partisanship.

A final Centrist journal which deserves brief attention is *To-day*. A monthly edited by Holbrook Jackson, it appeared for the first time in March 1917 and achieved something of a record in a field where the mortality rate was high by appearing without a lapse until September 1920, when it became a quarterly. It, too, eventually succumbed to the disease of the little magazines, financial anaemia, and after appearing briefly on a monthly basis again, beginning in July 1923, it finally expired. During its first year it was undistinguished, but by 1918 poems by many Georgians as well as by poets of more modern proclivities began to appear. Perhaps no contemporary journal published so much poetry or so many different kinds of poetry as *To-day*. During 1918 and 1919, little by little *To-day* began to lean towards the Left. An article by Pound, ostensibly on Chinese poetry but actually defending obscurity in verse, appeared, as well as an article on Pound written by Eliot, and numerous poems by Osbert Sitwell and others of the modern school. But editorially *To-day* stated both frequently and vigorously its declared policy of avoiding the coterie label at all costs. Holbrook Jackson made explicit the policy which placed *To-day* squarely with the Centre in 1919:

> The contributors to the following pages are not drawn entirely from a single generation any more than they are drawn from a particular school. Attention is drawn to this point, because a little while ago I heard somebody remark that *To-day* was a literary journal that 'gave young writers a show'. Let me be quite frank and quite brief on that point: *To-day* does not. As an editor I am no specialist; I specialize neither in periods nor poses, youth nor age. Good writing happens in all circumstances, and takes little account of age or sex or breed. I am content with the best of that coming my way which gives me pleasure in the sure faith that the best is nearly good enough for *To-day* and its readers.[21]

The conservative Right-wing of the post-war literary scene is far more readily definable than either Left or Centre. The Centrists were by and large amorphous; the Leftists advanced to battle with a bewildering variety of ammunition—*Wheels, Coterie, Art and Letters*—but the banner of poetic conservatism was stoutly defended in its hour of mortal peril primarily by one man. He frequently found a valuable ally in the *Times Literary Supplement*, though its assistance was usually confined to judicious elder-statesmanly counsel, and it did not deign to take an active part in coterie warfare. (By 1919, moreover, even the *Literary Supplement* found itself able to express an occasional liberal sentiment in its reviews and was by no means as antediluvian in attitude as it had sometimes appeared in the pre-war years.) But the self-appointed defender of the Right was J. C. Squire.[22] From the citadel of the *London Mercury* Squire wielded vast literary powers in the post-war period and throughout the twenties. His eminence stemmed not alone from being editor of the *Mercury*, 'one of the most ambitious literary journals that the century has produced', as Harold Monro claimed, but also from the fact that he exerted powerful influence over 'the literary columns of many dailies, weeklies, monthlies, and quarterlies, so that it has often been hinted, rightly or wrongly, that such young poets as are blessed with his favour need not fear to be snubbed, drubbed or neglected by the Press'.[23]

By 1920 Squire was well on his way towards establishing a literary coterie of the Right just as partisan, as militant, and as dedicated as the Leftist coteries. In 1917 Edward Marsh had printed Squire's 'Lily of Malud' in *Georgian Poetry* III, not as an act of far-seeing policy or of literary expediency, but only because he admired the poem greatly (it was one of the few works of 1917 which encouraged him to contemplate a third volume, he had written Squire).[24] Nevertheless, as luck would have it Marsh had also made a powerful friend in days to come, for with his own poetry and that of his friends, Shanks, Freeman, and Turner, safely enshrined in *Georgian Poetry* from volume III or IV on, Squire became sworn champion of the anthology. On the other hand, perhaps no single action of Marsh so completely alienated most of the younger poets of the post-war era as his inclusion of the poets of 'the Squirearchy', as the coterie came to be known. From the third volume on, in the eyes of the younger poets *Georgian Poetry* had been tarred with Squire's brush. Consequently the anthology was injected into a coterie war marked by a spirit of vicious partisanship on both sides.

Almost every school of experimental verse was certain sooner or later to feel the sting of Squire's lash, for his tastes were as conservative as his tongue was sharp. His antipathy to modernism had first become evident in the pre-war years, when he had acquired a position as columnist on *Land and Water* and had subsequently become literary editor of the *New Statesman*. Frequently using the *nom de plume* 'Solomon Eagle', he had expressed only the utmost disdain for Futurism, seeing in it only a stunt for self-advertisement and reminding the Futurists that in attitude and technique alike, far from being new, they were only a *réchauffé* of Whitman—who, he added for their edification, was 'a mid-Victorian American'.[25] *Blast* he found tedious, the Vorticists only 'a heterogeneous mob suffering from juvenile decay tottering along . . . in reach-me-down fancy-dress uniforms . . . trying to discover as they go what their common destination is to be'. He was particularly severe on Ezra Pound, an antipathy which he was to carry on into the post-war years. '*Le Bon Ezra*', he wrote, 'nearly bursts himself in the attempt' to be new, but 'in spite of the abruptness of his phraseology and the unmeaning inequalities in his rhythms, he does not succeed in convincing one that he has discovered anything. . . . When he is comprehensible he is usually silly. . . . Where he is incomprehensible he would not, I suspect, be found much less silly if one had the key to his cipher.'[26] It is to Squire that one is indebted for the last word on *Blast*. It succumbed, he wrote, 'shortly after a hostile critic, consulting his Webster, had discovered the definition: "*Blast:*—a flatulent disease of sheep".'[27]

The post-war years found Squire's opinions still as adamantly conservative, his pen as biting. They gave him, moreover, an opportunity to express his views which was unequalled in the literary world. In November 1919 Squire founded and became first editor of the *London Mercury*, the most influential journal of its time. The *Mercury* was launched with no more than the usual spate of high-minded comments about promoting the cause of literature in a Philistine world; ostensibly, as Frank Swinnerton wrote, Squire and his staff 'stood for vigorous rational criticism without frills, a mean between subservience to established ideas and iconoclasm, and no mercy to slop'.[28] The *Mercury* would never be allowed to succumb to the coterie spirit; it would not become just another partisan journal 'attempting to make universal the shibboleths of some coterie or school', Squire promised in the foreword to his first number. He explicitly disclaimed for his new journal any 'ambition for an infallible pontificate of letters'. Even while he was stating his virtuous aims on one page, however, he was implicitly contradicting them on another. Given the literary conditions of 1919, how could the *Mercury* escape becoming a coterie journal when its editor could dismiss most modern poetry and poets in this fashion?

> Young simpletons who, twenty years ago, would have been writing vapid magazine verse about moonrise and roses have discovered that they have only to become incoherent, incomprehensible, and unmetrical to be taken seriously. . . . Year after year we have new fungoid growths of feeble pretentious impostors who, after a while, are superseded by their younger kindred; and year after year we see writers who actually have some intelligence and capacity for observation and exact statement led astray into the stony and barren fields of technical anarchism or the pitiful madhouse of moral antinominianism.

And how could the *Mercury* hope to become known for the application of 'sound critical standards' when, in his first issue, Squire could accuse fellow literary critics of sheer cowardice because they treated modern poetry with too much respect? 'Everything is treated with respect,' he complained, even when all right-minded critics were bound to agree in the depths of their consciences that most modern poetry was arrant rubbish.[29]

The *Mercury's* antipathy towards Edith Sitwell's coterie was particularly marked. Its review of the third issue of *Wheels* left little doubt where the journal stood. To Miss Sitwell's poetry the reviewer applied the most damning of all epithets: 'incomprehensible'. He gave Wilfred Owen's 'Strange Meeting' a most ignominious dismissal and then turned his attentions to Aldous Huxley. Squire was habitually kinder to Huxley than he was to others of the *Wheels* group (indeed, Huxley was a frequent contributor to the *Mercury*, writing some uncontroversial articles on older English men of letters); but the reviewer made a comparison which could not entirely have pleased the young poet. 'Mr. Huxley', he claimed, 'when these poems were written . . . seems to have been in the same sort of revulsion against sentimentality as Rupert Brooke was in when his first book was being composed.' And he bestowed on Huxley the same patronizing pat on the head that Brooke had received from his early reviewers: Huxley 'can see things with his own eyes, and has a powerful intelligence, and when he has discovered something to write about he may become a very good poet'.[30] In 1921, when an anonymous parody of *Wheels*, compiled by 'Obert, Sebert, and Ethelberta Standstill' and entitled *Cranks*, was published, the *Mercury* again seized upon the opportunity to deride the contributors to *Wheels*. 'The worst of it is,' Squire wrote, that the verses in *Cranks* 'are unlikely to be permanently readable owing to the nature of the subjects [the author] has chosen to burlesque. The book is a parody of the annual collection *Wheels*, the contents of which are not popular enough to be worth attacking and not good enough to keep a parody alive. . . . Ten years hence, should any of [the *Wheels* coterie] run across detached poems from *Cranks* they will find it difficult to say whether themselves or a parodist wrote them.'[31]

Squire's opinions of other *avant-garde* poetic schools were equally hostile and just as caustically expressed. His antipathy towards the Imagists was of long standing. He dismissed Amy Lowell summarily: 'Miss Amy Lowell is, in America, the most vigorous propagandist of the revolt against what are deemed old-fashioned kinds of poetry. Having tried to turn verse into prose, she is now trying to turn prose into verse.'[32] His distaste for the poets who contributed to *Coterie* has already been remarked. In his reviews of that journal he surpassed himself in aspersion, being particularly harsh on Herbert Read.[33] For the *avant-garde* European literary movements he had only profound scorn. In the 'New and Recent Periodicals' section of the *Mercury* short notices like this were not infrequent: 'The publisher of a Dadaist organ apparently called "391" has sent us a copy of it, for which we are profoundly grateful. The price seems to be two francs, but this figure may possibly be one of the poems.'[34]

Squire rang the changes in the *Mercury*, as before the war, on a few dominant themes: modern poetry is only an amusing fad; it results only in prosodic stunts and verbal legerdemain; it will one day pass, and all will once more be well with the queen of the arts. But above all, for Squire, poetry had to communicate. With him, as with most of the post-war Right Wing, incomprehensibility was the poetic sin of sins. The premise that an incoherent world demanded an incoherent poetry was beyond his limits of tolerance. Rather, incomprehensibility was only a trick, a means of self-advertisement for versifiers who could attract attention in no other way.

Perhaps it was not so much Squire's conservatism which irked the younger post-war poets as it was the tone in which he expressed his ideas. About almost all new verse he characteristically adopted the tone of an omniscient father of gods handing down his observations to wayward children as if from Olympus. Hostility was one thing; the modern poets could expect that and take it in their stride. But scorn was quite another; and it earned for Squire and the *Mercury* bitter attacks from the younger generation almost without exception. Most modern verse, he pontificated in 1920, 'has ceased to be amusing'; but, he added, 'we don't think that anybody need be alarmed; nobody can like it, and in the end those who . . . have pretended to will revolt against a diet of wind and sawdust and return to something more palatable'.[35]

Faced with such sentiments expressed in such a tone, it is small wonder that the young men declared war on the *London Mercury*. Their fury was increased by the fact that Squire obviously sat in a position of great power and could, if he chose, dominate the tone of a sizeable number of reviews of their own poetic efforts. And so the battle was joined between the rebels and the Establishment; and though it frequently may not have seemed so amid the dust and the shouting, the new poets were fighting on the winning side, for they were fighting with, not against, the spirit of the age.

## II

Given the literary environment of the post-war world, it was to be expected that a severe anti-Georgian reaction would set it. By late 1919 or 1920 two facts about modern poetry were beginning to emerge with reasonable clarity. In the first place, if the modernists won the day—and they were beginning to—modern poetry would be obscure. Incomprehensibility, or incoherence, the whipping-boy of the conservative critics, was not, the modern poets claimed, a stunt to attract attention but the most effective means for transmuting the spiritual and social incoherence of the post-war world into poetry. And it was to become a more or less permanent condition of poetry throughout the twenties and thirties. Secondly, modern poetry, like other forms of twentieth-century art, was well on its way to becoming a private not a public art. The shift towards private poetry had begun, of course, in the pre-war years, and by the end of the war it was becoming increasingly clear that poetry was either retreating into the scholar's study or becoming the expression only of the poets' private world. Both obscurity and privateness ran directly counter to the tendencies of *Georgian Poetry*, especially to the mystery-cum-moonlight tendencies which began to overtake the anthology with the third volume. They also ran directly counter to Edward Marsh's poetic canons. Obscure verse had been anathema to Marsh from the beginning, and in the post-war period he was to become even more hostile to poetry which he considered eccentric or incomprehensible. *Georgian Poetry* was therefore almost bound to become an anachronism by 1919 and 1922. And the reaction against it is in part attributable to the fact that it was looked upon by many of the newer poets and critics as being not only un-modern, but positively anti-modern.

Another reason for opposition to *Georgian Poetry* among many post-war poets rested upon more personal considerations. By the laws of human nature an anthology must make an enemy of almost every poet whom it excludes. *Georgian Poetry* was no exception. By 1918 the work of twenty-eight poets had been represented in the three volumes of the anthology. But how many times that number had been excluded, even of the professional poets whose level of competence might have admitted them to serious consideration? Personal rancour against the anthology, against its editor, and against the major poets represented in it was bound to grow with each volume. An ever-increasing antipathy could have been expected and planned for—as in fact it was by both Marsh and Monro—but the situation was aggravated by 1918 or 1919 by the fact that the coterie spirit was hardening on all sides, but particularly among the Leftist poets whose aesthetic convictions normally placed them in opposition to the Georgians. In such an environment each exclusion from *Georgian Poetry* was likely not only to pique the pride of the individual poet barred from paradise but also to bring down upon the head of the anthology the wrath or scorn of the entire coterie to which the excluded poet belonged.

Nor was pride alone involved; financial considerations also played their part. The reaction against *Georgian Poetry* was part of a post-war reaction against anthologies in general. The initial effect of at least the first two volumes of *Georgian Poetry* had been to increase sales of the poets' individual volumes. Indeed, the anthology had been almost too successful in its aim of pushing the new poetry, for during the war years the anthology boom showed scant signs of quieting; on the contrary, as anthologies began to increase in number they began to compete with one another rather severely for the reader's shillings. The competition occurred not only between *Georgian Poetry* and some of the more modern anthologies like *Wheels* but within each camp as well. One particularly close rival to Marsh's anthology was R. C. Trevelyan's *Annual of New Poetry* (1917), which contained the work of many of Marsh's Georgians—Gibson, Davies, Drinkwater, Sturge Moore, and Bottomley—as well as poems by Robert Frost and Edward Thomas.* To the stream of competing anthologies must also be added the innumerable collections of war poetry published from 1914 to 1918. The result was that a movement which in 1912 and 1915 had succeeded in helping to increase poets' individual sales was in many cases having a decidedly opposite effect in the post-war era, for the public was refusing to purchase expensive individual copies of poets' works when ade-

---

* The rather over-close resemblance of Trevelyan's anthology to the *Georgian Poetry* series was not overlooked by the reviewers. Cf. *TLS*, 29th Mar. 1917, p. 151; *NS*, VIII (1917), 617.

quate samples were at hand for the same money in an abundance of anthologies.[36]

The professional poets' and critics' hostility towards the anthology system was expressed largely in private utterance, or if it appeared in public print, it became more frequently a matter of tone than of direct attack. One of the first public blows was struck, however, by Middleton Murry in mid-1919 in the *Athenaeum*. The anthology system, he admitted, 'with its perturbations and aberrations, its wheels within wheels . . . is now a familiar feature of the intellectual heavens', but unfortunately, the 'stability and brilliance of this new system mainly depend upon its nebular structure'; they depend, that is, upon anthologies, regularly appearing, because most of the anthology poets are mildly impressive only when seen *en masse*. Mediocrity and a comfortable sameness are the natural results, Murry reasoned, for poets who want to be published must write minor, occasional verse for the anthologies. If post-war poetry is to have any vitality, he concluded, the poets 'must break up the anthological system in which their comfortable revolutions are at present pursued [and] shoot off into the invisible unknown' on their own orbits.*

By 1921 the poets themselves were more willing to speak out publicly against the anthology system. Criticized in the *Times Literary Supplement* for allowing certain of his works to be printed in Untermeyer's *Modern American Poetry*, T. S. Eliot replied, in a letter to the *Supplement*, that he had not been consulted regarding selections for the anthology; 'in short', he wrote, 'the whole production is a surprise to me'. To avoid such incidents in the future, Eliot suggested that poets must take a strong stand against the anthology system. 'The work of any poet who has already published a book of verse is likely to be more damaged than aided by anthologies,' he argued, because short anthology selections almost perforce misrepresent the nature of a poet's complete canon. And he closed his letter with the hope that other poets might come forward and publicly express their views on the matter.[37] The next

---

* *Athenaeum*, no. 4,646 (16th May 1919), pp. 325–6. Though I have attributed the article to Murry, the author cannot perhaps be quite so positively identified. Because of the particular brand of anti-Georgian sentiments expressed in the course of the article, however, and for other reasons as well, Middleton Murry seems the likely author. A contemporary reader guessed that Lascelles Abercrombie had written it, an attribution which Abercrombie quickly and emphatically denied (ibid., no. 4,647 [23rd May 1916], p. 374; no. 4,649 [6th June 1916], p. 438).

week Robert Graves enthusiastically commended Eliot's position, adding an objection to anthologies which might well have been aimed squarely at *Georgian Poetry*. 'A poet who once gets marked by the reviewers with the ranch-brand of the anthology in which he first appears', Graves claimed, 'is thereafter made to suffer for the failings of the other weaker members of the herd, with whom he may have nothing further in common.'* The motto of the professional poet in the face of the anthologist must be: 'Nothing for Nothing and Mighty Little for Sixpence.'† The occasional instances when the struggle was brought out into the open suggest something of the bitterness against anthologies which many poets were expressing privately. *Georgian Poetry* was the chief target of the anti-anthology movement, for by common consent it was looked upon as the father of the anthology system; and even in the years of its decline it remained, in terms of sales, the most considerable anthology of the times.

The post-war anti-Georgian reaction expressed itself in a number of ways. *Coterie*, *Wheels*, and other partisan little magazines and anthologies were one avenue through which hostility found an outlet. Parodies were another. As the Georgian poets came increasingly to assume a 'Georgian' manner they invited parody; and as the coterie spirit of the Left solidified in 1919 and 1920 they were assured of getting it. Much of the anti-Georgian occasional verse of the post-war period was not, strictly speaking, parody, but rather broadly satiric verse which administered the lash to the Georgians for their coterie proclivities. The Georgian penchant for log-rolling, for instance, was made the subject of an anonymous poem in *Coterie*:

* This objection is partially explained by the fact that by late 1921 Graves was engaged in more or less strenuous attempts to cast off the 'Georgian' label which had been affixed to him by reason of his appearance in *GP* III and IV. He had little in common with the poets of the 'Squirearchy' and was concerned lest the 'ranch brand' of their Neo-Georgian drenched-in-moonlight school should be applied to his own work. Nevertheless, he was to permit his work to appear in *GP* V.

† The case against Eliot and Graves was pursued in subsequent issues of the *TLS* by two self-styled 'ordinary lovers of poetry', one of whom argued that the poets were biting the hand that fed them. 'The reader who, meeting a poet in anthologies, does not trouble to search him out,' he wrote, 'would hardly be likely to buy his works in any case so no sale is lost.' The second correspondent threw Eliot's argument back in his face, asserting, 'I bought Mr. T. S. Eliot's "Prufrock" entirely on account of the poems from it contained in "Catholic Anthology", published by Mr. Elkin Matthews in 1915.' There the matter was allowed to rest, each side having made its point (*TLS*, 17th Nov. 1921, p. 746; 24th Nov. 1921, p. 771; 1st Dec. 1921, p. 789; 8th Dec. 1921, p. 827; 15th Dec. 1921, p. 853).

PERPETUUM MOBILE: A PANTOUM, MORE OR LESS

Pilk lauds the verse of Jobble to the skies,
And Jobble says that Bibson's Dante's peer;
Bibson is great on Pagg,—'What Art!' he cries
While Pagg is sure that Dubkin is a seer.

While Pagg is sure that Dubkin is a seer,
Dubkin swears Botchell's odes will never wane;
Botchell commands: 'Watch Pimpington's career!'—
Pimpington writes a book on Trodger's brain.

Pimpington writes a book on Trodger's brain,
And Trodger shrieks: 'Glabb's genius stirs my soul!'
Glabb raves of Cringeley's rhymes with might and main;
Cringeley pens Gummitt's name on glory's scroll.

Cringeley pens Gummitt's name on glory's scroll,
And Gummitt sees in Sludd new worlds arise.
Sludd bids us hear Pilk's mighty rhymes roll;
Pilk lauds the verse of Jobble to the skies. . . .[38]

Another more finished poem shed crocodile tears over the situation of the displaced Georgian in early 1920. Written by Douglas
Goldring, it depicted the unfortunate pre-war Georgian as leaderless and without artistic haven in the cruel post-war world. In its
tone, as in its very title, it skilfully suggested what many young
poets keenly felt: Georgianism was a dead poetic movement by
early 1920.

POST-GEORGIAN POET IN SEARCH OF A MASTER

I had been well brought up: I liked the best.
My prose was modelled on Rebecca West,
My 'little things' erstwhile reflected tone,
My brother poets claimed me as their own.
In those blithe days before the War began—
Ah me, I was a safe young Georgian!
Now all is chaos, all confusion.
Bolshies have cast E. M. from his high throne:
Wild women have rushed in, and savage Yanks
Blather of Booth and Heaven; and T. S. E.
Uses great words that are as Greek to me.
Tell me the Truth, and ah, forego those pranks—
Whom must I imitate? Who's really It?
At whose embroidered footstool should I sit?

There's Podgrass now—*he* seems a coming man;
Writes unintelligible stuff, half French, half Erse,
He told me Philomela had technique
But not much feeling; Crashaw knew his trade,
But Keats had no idea of writing verse . . .
The thing to read (he said) had just come out,
His latest work, entitled 'Bloody Shout'.

And then there's father Michael, Secker's pal,
Who's left dear Sylvia for the Clergy-house.
Michael lives sumptuously: silver, old oak,
Incunabula, the Yellow Book, Madonnas, Art;
Excited wobblings on the brink of Rome;
The 'Inner Life', birettas, candles, Mass;
Fun with *Church Times* and Bishops; four hair shirts,
And Mr. Percy Dearmer's Parson's Book.
He talked to me of Antinominianism
And stirred the incense, while two candles burned.
Then read aloud his works, with eye upturned,
(Somehow I felt I'd heard it all before—
When I was 'boat-boy' in a pinafore).

Are Sitwells really *safe*? Is Iris Tree
A certain guide to higher poesy?
Can Nichols be relied on, for a lead;
Or should I thump it with Sassoon and Read?
Or would it not be vastly better fun
To write of Nymphs with Richard Aldington?
Or shall I train, and nervously aspire
To join with Edward Shanks and J. C. Squire
—A modest 'chorus' in a well-paid choir?

I've thought of middling Murry and Sturge Moore,
I've thought of Yeats (I thought of him before).
I've toyed with Aldous Huxley and Monro—
I don't know where I am, or where to go.

Oh, mighty Mr. Gosse! Unbend, I pray!
Guide one poor poet who has lost his way. . . .[39]

The most persistent and masterful parodies of the Georgians
came not from the Left, however, but from the pen of E. V. Knox,

who under the pseudonym 'Evoe' published his works in *Punch*.* Knox began his parodies early, during the years when the Georgians were at the height of their power and pre-eminence, and he precisely hit off both their characteristic manner and matter. He parodied John Drinkwater's sedate pastoralism in the ponderous blank verse that the poet was so fond of using. And he nicely satirized W. H. Davies, one of the most susceptible of the early Georgians to parody:

#### COMPANIONS

When I go in to ask for ale
  At Stratford pubs in lamplight gleam,
More sweet than any nightingale
  The sounds of men do seem.

I rub my hands, I laugh, I smoke,
  I tap my coins upon the bar,
Like woodpecker that strikes an oak
  When woods most tranquil are.

But when I see two men that fight
  Outside the pub for all the world
As though they'd clench their hands more tight
  Than bracken fronds uncurled.

Thereat my heart gives such a prick,
  I feel the wound for months and months.
I take my library and stick
  And leave West Ham at once.

In fields where tiny daisies grow
  And throstles sing I then do drowse
And often see small birds that go
  Quite close to hooves of cows.

The titmice perch upon my thumbs
  And cock their heads to ask for food;
More sweet than any urban slums
  Is then my solitude.[40]

* His parodies were collected in two volumes, *Parodies Regained* (London, 1921) and *These Liberties* (London, 1923), from which all subsequent examples of Knox's work will be cited.

In several poems Knox was able to satirize the work of de la Mare, a poet who did not lend himself to parody as readily as many other Georgians.* And one of the most delightful thrusts was 'The Snail', a parody of Ralph Hodgson's 'The Bull'. Taking for his subject, as he said, 'the only horned livestock on my premises, which are snails', Knox playfully reduced to absurdity one of the most popular poems ever published in *Georgian Poetry*:

> See the sick and wounded snail
>    Sick in body and mind both,
>    Travelling through the undergrowth
> Of asparagus and kale,
> Exiled from the herd (or horde)
> Where he once was overlord.
>
> See him as his eyeballs glaze;
>    Nasty sorts of flies and things,
>    Such as every poet brings
> Into poems nowadays,
> Buzz about the eyes and tail
> Of this old unhappy snail.
>
> Ants arise to greet the dawn,
>    Beetles burnish up their mail,
>    But this old unhappy snail
> Creeps toward the croquet lawn
> Where the loathly blackbird jumps,
> Looking out for slithery lumps.
>
> .    .    .    .
>
> Now how altered! Now he's been
>    Broken like the one before;
>    All his face is smeared with gore;
> Showing undisguised chagrin
> He is crawling, as I said,
> Through the vegetable bed.
>
> Soon to meet the blackbird grim
>    Perching on the fateful tree
>    While the last snail (Number Three),
> Having now defeated him

* See especially an exquisite shaft at de la Mare entitled 'The Lost Bus' (*These Liberties*, pp. 131–5). See also 'The Mocking Navy' and 'Questions' (*Parodies Regained*, pp. 15–17).

Lords it, till in turn he fails,
And a fourth—
    Oh!—these snails.[41]

The Neo-Georgians did not escape 'Evoe's' shafts. Perhaps the soft verse of the drenched-in-moonlight school was best satirized in a parody of John Freeman, who, Knox claimed, belonged to 'the school of the wistful, the dreamy, the unsatisfied and the faint'. The poem, in which the poet rejects earthly for ideal love, is entitled simply 'Go':

GO. . . .

I would not that you should stay;
Your lips and your eyes confound me;
I want you to go away
And not keep coming round me.

There is a love of the mind
That holds, never loosens,
More sweet than the bodily kind
And much less of a nuisance. . . .

We should glimpse and pass on
And remember the glimmer,
Like the pool that grows wan
When the twilight glooms dimmer;

But you creep so close
When I crave but your image;
Kissing makes me morose;
It resembles a scrimmage. . . .

I would make you my own,
Blossom sweet and enthralling,
But alone, but alone. . . .
And you *will* keep on calling.

What was fire in the brain
Turns, touched, to a statue;
Don't come here again
Or I'll set the dog at you.
Get away. . . .*

* E. V. Knox, *Parodies Regained*, pp. 37–40. The young poets who contributed to *Wheels* and *Coterie* could scarcely have hoped to escape an occasional satiric shaft. One satirist, J. B. M[orton]., aimed almost an entire volume of parodies at the

Whether the satire was predominantly good-natured, like that of Knox, or in the more derisive vein of Douglas Goldring, parody was one of the most amusing avenues for expression of anti-Georgian sentiment. But it cannot be claimed that the parodies of the Georgian poets were in any sense the cause of the anti-Georgian reaction. They were rather a symptom of it. They did not start the fire, but they succeeded in adding a good many more faggots to the already warm blaze.

Perhaps the most significant feature of the post-war literary scene, however, was not the reaction against Georgianism *per se*, but rather the perceptible hardening of the coterie spirit which took place from 1918 to 1922 and which resulted too frequently in an attitude of mind among poets and critics that can only be described as literary intolerance. The situation presented its mildly humorous aspects, for, as Harold Monro observed, by 1920 literary London had come to resemble nothing so much as the Left Bank, with all the 'factional acrimonies, jealousies, and scandal-mongerings' of French coteries, but with an important difference: the British were too deadly earnest in their partisanship; their coteries commonly lacked the light Gallic touch, the 'pleasant and private inner qualities' of their French counterparts.[42] The intensi-fication of literary partisanship had its serious implications, too, both for *Georgian Poetry* and for the immediate future of English letters. It made the struggle against the Georgians more bitter and perhaps more protracted than it might otherwise have been. Geor-gianism was not to be allowed to die a peaceful death in the natural course of poetic affairs but was to be hooted to its grave by the unnecessarily derisive jeers of those self-appointed poets and critics who had mounted a death watch over Marsh's antho-logy. Moreover, the sneers uttered in the heat of partisan battle in large measure set the tone for critics in years to come so that a balanced estimate of Georgian poetry became impossible for almost three decades.

From all sides came anguished recognition of the danger to letters posed by coterie warfare, but from no quarter came an

Leftist coteries (*Gorgeous Poetry, 1911–1920* [London, 1920]). And J. C. Squire, who was one of England's truly great parodists, launched many a poetic attack against the verslibrists whom he so cordially detested. One of his best—and a genuinely great parody—was his attack on Ezra Pound entitled 'Very Libre' and subtitled 'If A Very New Poet Had Written "The Lotus Eaters" '. Squire's parodies have been collected in *Tricks of the Trade* (London, 1917). Squire also edited one of the best anthologies of verse parodies ever assembled: *Apes and Parrots* (London, 1928).

effective solution. Like almost every war, no one seemed to want it, but no one seemed to be able to propose a means of avoiding it. Even Harold Monro, genuinely fired with idealism and hope for the future of English poetry in the pre-war days, turned cynical as he surveyed the post-war poetic scene. 'Verse writing in the year 1920 is a professional occupation,' he wrote. The love of work well done is gone; success no longer comes from merit but through advertising, and the coterie is obviously the most effective advertising medium. Thus the clique fulfilled a function: it was a 'support to individuals not strong enough to stand alone'. Mediocrity was the only possible result, and originality, the most precious possession of poetry, was snuffed out.[43]

Some turned against the Georgians, seeing in *Georgian Poetry* the first cause and the prime mover behind the solidifying of the coterie spirit. Even though he published the anthology, Monro himself candidly admitted in public print that, although 'in its infancy the "Georgian Movement" was uncharacterized by evidence of design, that is, it did not, like other schools, preach or practise a special dogma of the poetic art', the poets included in its latter volumes 'devoted much energy to narrowing and hardening what had begun as a spontaneous co-operative effort. They sought to establish . . . "a form of literary tyranny", demanding of its own disciples a complete conformity to certain standards, and seeking to exclude altogether those who refuse to do homage to those laws'.[44] Others, recalling the pre-war literary scene, were willing to place a large share of the blame for post-war partisanship at the door of the verslibrists or, more specifically, the Imagists.[45]

Still others were willing to blame not so much the poets as the conditions surrounding post-war reviewing. 'It is not poetry at all that stands in peril,' wrote Gerald Gould in 1922; 'poetry cannot die. Poetry cannot even "have a bad time" or "be in a bad way". At some times there are more great poets than at others. But there are always poets; and in so far as they *are* poets, they will always quietly go on their way, saying nothing when they have nothing to say, and, when they cannot help saying something, saying it in a form they cannot help.' It was contemporary reviewing that was at fault, for it was too obviously partisan, too ready to judge a poem according to its coterie hallmark rather than on its intrinsic merit.[46] The practice of using signed reviews, common to all but a few of the best post-war journals, also nourished literary animosity. Such reviews were usually solicited only from among the more famous literary figures of the time. The results of the 'star system', as Douglas Goldring called it, were obvious: 'those whom the "star" attacks are tempted to form an offensive and defensive alliance against him. Those whom he praises rally at once to his side. . . . Thus the cliques come into being'.[47]

Whichever direction they turned, all agreed that coterie warfare was fraught with real and present danger, for it was tearing the craft of letters apart, reducing the individual poet to impotence, and stifling creative originality. Moreover, in coterie warfare the artists were dissipating their energies on the wrong front. 'Concerted effort . . . is the effort to justify art to the Philistines,' Frank Swinnerton warned the embattled cliques, 'not to destroy its examples for the banal amusement of Dilettanti.'*

But English poetry was to become a good deal more coterie-minded before it became very much less. 'Verse writing in the year 1920 is a professional occupation': Monro spoke cynically, but the facts bore him out. For most poets it was simply a case of fight or die, coterie warfare or poetic oblivion. The slow, often halting development of the individual poetic genius along lines determined by its own uniqueness, which had been the priceless jewel of English poetry for generations, seemed likely by 1920 to become a thing of the past, a sacrifice to the collectivist urge and the relativistic spirit of the onrushing twentieth century. But as one observer concluded, 'even the war that was to end war ended, and so also will the war that is going to end pre-war poetry; and just as the war-that-was-going-to-end-war has not ended war, so the war-that's-going-to-end-pre-war-poetry will not achieve its heart's desire. Wars never do'.[48] For a few years, amid shouts and jeers, behind dust and tumult, the post-war coteries succeeded in obscuring the voice of English poetry, but they could not choke it into silence. The real poets, the poets who, 'when they cannot help saying something, say it in a form they cannot help', were still writing amid the shouting; and from the twenties was to emerge a new kind of verse which was as adequate to its age as that of any other era of English poetry.

---

* Frank Swinnerton, 'Coteries', *Athenaeum*, no. 4,675 (5th Dec. 1919), pp. 1,281–2. Swinnerton was one of the most persistent fighters against the coterie spirit in the post-war years, launching several unusually frank and heated attacks in 1919 and 1920. Other critics, however, also warned against the dangers of coterie warfare in much the same tone (e.g. *TLS*, 19th Aug. 1919, p. 434).

# 9

# Decline and Fall

The editing and publishing of *Georgian Poetry* IV and V followed the familiar pattern set up with the first three volumes. In mid-April 1919 Harold Monro sounded out Marsh on the prospects of a fourth *Georgian Poetry*. Though the volume was financially feasible, he reported—in fact, a number of pre-publication orders had already been placed with the Poetry Bookshop—Monro expressed his customary doubts as to whether the material at hand warranted a new volume. It might be wise and discreet, he suggested, to allow a three-year rather than a two-year interval between volumes. Marsh did not agree. Though second thoughts were to assail him a few months later, he decided in April to go ahead with his fourth volume. Monro replied, only partly convinced, that he was glad to hear the decision had been taken, but he was 'as usual . . . a little diffident about the material'.[1] Both editor and publisher set to work, and by the end of September the first proofs were in Marsh's hands. Monro set the price of the new volume at 6s. per copy, almost double the 3s. 6d. that *Georgian Poetry* I had cost and a small testimony to post-war inflation.*

The book was published on schedule in November and, Monro wrote, had sold almost 6,000 copies by the second week in December. 'I'm not sure how much I like this popularity!' he added. 'I *am* sure that I think it the worst G.P.—but that's in confidence. The second one set such a very high standard.' Monro was almost as unhappy with the reviews of *Georgian Poetry* IV as he was with

---

* Harold Monro to E. M., 26th Sept. 1919, *MLC*. Not one to overlook an opportunity, Monro also raised the price of *GP* III to 6s. in November 1919, 'so as to get a bit more on it', he wrote Marsh (loc. cit.).

the volume itself, being particularly displeased with Middleton Murry's comments in the *Athenaeum*. Murry was not entirely qualified to write such a review, he claimed; 'he should have given it to Eliot!'[2]

On the timing of *Georgian Poetry* v both editor and publisher agreed. When Monro advised Marsh against publishing a new volume at the end of 1921, Marsh readily assented to a three-year interval between volumes IV and v.[3] By May 1922, however, poems for *Georgian Poetry* v were being chosen, and by mid-August— somewhat earlier than had been the case with previous volumes —the fifth volume had reached the proof stage. Again Monro expressed reservations about the quality of the book, and between the lines of his correspondence with Marsh one reads his concern over the deterioration of the entire series. The inclusion of little 'jingles' like Richard Hughes's 'Poets, Painters, Puddings', he wrote Marsh, only made the absence of first-rate work the more painfully obvious.[4] *Georgian Poetry* v was put on sale in November 1922 and sold, as Edmund Blunden wrote, 'like scandalous revelations—though surely', he added, 'this time it is the mirror of innocence'.[5] Compared to the sales of the previous volumes, however, those of *Georgian Poetry* v were unimpressive. Even *Georgian Poetry* IV had a total sale of 15,000 copies, but its successor sold only 8,000. As Marsh himself conceded, such an obvious 'falling-off in public receptivity' in 1922 afforded 'a pretty strong hint' that *Georgian Poetry* had outlived its day.[6]

The editorial problems Marsh encountered with *Georgian Poetry* IV were not greatly different from those he had met in compiling his first three volumes. Only one situation seems to have arisen for which no clear precedent existed. By 1919 the success of *Georgian Poetry* had made entrance to its pages a prize ardently coveted by many poets, and Marsh was therefore made the object of several solicitations by poets on their own behalf. The approaches were in some cases surprisingly direct. Thomas Moult, the editor of *Voices*, was moved to submit his own work for *Georgian Poetry* IV. Being a stranger to the editorial policies governing the anthology, Moult explained, he did not know precisely how Marsh's attention was drawn to new poets' work. Nevertheless, the extraordinary honour he would feel at being chosen for inclusion in *Georgian Poetry*, Moult continued, impelled him to run the risk of seeming too brash. Though Marsh was a bit taken aback by such a frontal assault, Moult's verse fortunately met with his approval, and the poet was included in *Georgian Poetry* IV, though not until he agreed to undertake revisions of several of the poems Marsh had chosen.[7] Other poets who approached Marsh in the same fashion were not so fortunate. They received kind words, but very little else.[8]

On the question of whether a woman poet should be included in *Georgian Poetry* IV Marsh was on more familiar ground. Again, as in 1917, he was eager to include a poetess provided one could be found whose work appealed to his tastes. The task which had proved fruitless in 1917 was to be successful in 1919. For the second time Monro strongly urged the candidacy of Charlotte Mew; Edward Shanks argued for the work of Rose Macaulay; and both Shanks and Sassoon suggested Edith Sitwell. The suggestion of Miss Sitwell must have afforded Marsh only a moment of amusement. Indeed, none of the advocates prevailed, for Marsh favoured the work of Fredegond Shove.* Shanks deferred to Marsh's judgment on Miss Macaulay, but he could not resist protesting the inclusion of Mrs. Shove. 'I still think that her work is neither strong enough nor, especially, individual enough,' he wrote Marsh. 'Mrs. Shove, I feel, is like a house in which all the fittings for electric light are in position but which is not yet connected with the main. If something happened to her, I believe she might begin to write poetry; but I remain doubtful as to whether she has really done it yet.'[9]

With *Georgian Poetry* IV Marsh's principles of anthologizing once more came under attack. And again the arguments were familiar. For the anthologist, 'le mieux est l'ennemi du bien', Maurice Baring had insisted in 1917. In 1919 an even more formidable voice, that of Marsh's long-time friend Edmund Gosse, arose to remind him of the maxim. Warning Marsh that this number of his anthology was the first to be launched into unmistakably stormy and hostile waters, Gosse argued that it was unwise to anthologize a minor poet on the basis of one or two good poems which appeared to stand out only because of the sodden uniformity of the rest of his work. 'I think you can hardly now be too careful in selecting and winnowing,' Gosse advised. 'I suggest that it is no longer safe to include a poet on the score of one piece which has

---

* Mrs. Shove, wife of Gerald Shove, Lecturer in Economics at King's College, Cambridge, and daughter of F. W. Maitland, jurist and biographer of Sir Leslie Stephen, had recently published *Dreams and Journeys* (1919). She is perhaps better known for a subsequent critical study of Christina Rossetti (1931) than for her poetry.

pleased you, but that there should always be a *body* of work from which you select a poem which meets your standard. One ode does not make a Georgian.'[10]

The editing of *Georgian Poetry* v in 1922 again presented Edward Marsh with several familiar problems. He was faced with the delicate task of excluding from volume v a poet who had been represented in volume iv. Having heard *Georgian Poetry* v was being assembled, Thomas Moult again seized the initiative and offered up any of his work Marsh might care to choose.[11] Marsh replied in a letter which, though it was apparently the apogee of tact, made it clear that Moult would be required to step down. The poet was understandably disappointed, but he bore no grudge.[12]

With *Georgian Poetry* v Marsh was also called upon again to withstand special pleading from a friend on behalf of a poetic protégé. This time he remained firm in the face of a plea from the Poet Laureate himself. On several occasions in June and July 1922 Bridges persuasively stated the case for inclusion of several poems by Herbert Palmer. His poems possessed a 'genuine imaginative quality', the Laureate pointed out, and Palmer had already shown his willingness to accede to Marsh's criticisms by emending a line in the sonnet 'Ishmael' to which Marsh had previously objected because it would not scan. Regarding 'Ishmael' Bridges wrote Marsh quite bluntly: 'I read it with a good deal more pleasure and admiration than I find awakened in me by the average of the poems you print.'[13]

Marsh declined to print any of Palmer's work. Perhaps the major reason for Marsh's refusal was the very quality which the Laureate took to be a virtue: 'the genuine imaginative quality' of Palmer's verse. The 'Ishmael' sonnet was perhaps too 'imaginative', too vibrant (and a good deal too obscure) for Marsh in his Neo-Georgian mood. At any rate, in answering Marsh's letter of refusal, Bridges underlined what he considered Marsh's too narrow tastes.

My dear Marsh,
   Your letter is amusing enough to be in some sort a reward to me for my charitable effort. I am sorry that it didn't succeed, but I did not wish you to go counter to your judgment, which has made your book what it is.
   Still Graves and I w'd say that you do not recognise the *sort* of excellence that this man has. You c'd have pulled Blake to pieces in

much the same way—and Palgrave refused Blake a place in the Golden Treasury. Now he is reckoned next to Shakespeare for his lyrics. He is of course incomparable with the present case, except that in being so much greater he is a stronger example. . . .

With thanks for your patience I am sorry to have caused you trouble.

Yours sincerely,
ROBERT BRIDGES[14]

Bridges was one of the few poets in England who could have written such a letter to Marsh. And the Laureate saw fit to rub it in a little with a comment some months later: 'Did you see', he wrote Marsh, 'that the poet Davies has given Palmer's Ishmael a place in his very *original* anthology?'[15]

Marsh's major difficulty in compiling both Georgian *Poetry* IV and V arose out of a situation which had occurred very infrequently with the first three volumes. Increasingly, many of the poets he approached either agreed to their inclusion only reluctantly or refused altogether to be represented. Even several of his old-line Georgians who had appeared in all the first three volumes were at best lukewarm about volumes IV and V. John Masefield entirely declined Marsh's invitation to contribute to *Georgian Poetry* IV, and although Marsh had succeeded in changing Masefield's mind under similar circumstances in the past, this time all his persuasions were to no avail.[16] Masefield appeared in neither *Georgian Poetry* IV nor V.

Walter de la Mare also expressed doubts about his inclusion in both volumes. He permitted his verse to be printed in both *Georgian Poetry* IV and V, though perhaps more out of friendship than conviction. When approached for a contribution to *Georgian Poetry* IV in 1919 he reminded Marsh that poetic times had changed: 'I feel . . . that I am a rather stale old bird to be chirping in the new nest,' he wrote. In 1922 he not only reiterated his position but also, in his characteristically gentle manner, attempted to give Marsh some sound advice: 'You *must* shed as you go, if you decide to continue. . . . To be in 5 would be monstrous. . . . So, pray, seriously reconsider this. I am quite certain the critics would welcome some removals. "Old ruts"—can't you hear the echoes?' In both instances, however, Marsh pursued de la Mare, and the poet capitulated gracefully though not without misgivings.[17]

Lascelles Abercrombie was also accommodating to an old friend but dubious of Marsh's editorial wisdom in publishing *Georgian Poetry* v. Invited to contribute, he wrote Marsh, 'As to the *general* policy of continuing the G.P. series, I'm doubtful; but you don't ask me about that, and as you *are* anyhow making up a new number I shall be delighted and honoured to be in it.'[18] Gordon Bottomley was less obliging. He declined to contribute at all to volume v on the grounds that his work might 'seem too occasional in the eyes of an increasingly critical world'. This from the poet who in 1915 had 'laughed out of his great beard' at the critical abuse heaped on 'King Lear's Wife'! Perhaps a more cogent reason for Bottomley's refusal may be noted in the reservations he expressed about Marsh's policy of continuing *Georgian Poetry* along customary lines: 'Beside my scanty production during the qualifying period, I feel that the time has come when your memorable standard for the first G.P.—"an accession to power"—ought to be applied again in a re-examination of the whole ground. . . . I am sure that the time has come when you ought to leave me out, and that G.P. can only be valid by keeping its face towards the dawn.'[19]

From among his newer contributors Marsh also encountered several objections and at least two point-blank refusals. Edward Shanks accepted Marsh's invitation to contribute to *Georgian Poetry* IV lukewarmly, and only after having turned him down on the first approach.[20] Sassoon accepted but expressed an implied warning for the future in several frank observations about his coevals between the covers of *Georgian Poetry* IV:

> I think it is very important that the collection should contain nothing half-baked. The danger with G.P. is that it will become too tidy. I hear you are putting in Mrs. Shove. I would suggest that Edith Sitwell ought to be asked, as her work is far stronger, and quite as original. But when you've got people like Drinkwater in, the thing is bound to be more or less an academic hotch-potch. The same thing applies to Shanks—delightful as his verse is—it doesn't excite and is all based on echoes from the past. Turner's stuff (unequal as it is) is on a different plane—*he* has *real* creative imagination.[21]

In 1922 Sassoon saw fit completely to withdraw from *Georgian Poetry* v. 'I am entirely out of sympathy with several of the Georgian shavers in the shade of your laurel-tree,' he told Marsh.[22]

An equally forthright refusal came from W. J. Turner. Though he was invariably polite and grateful for Marsh's efforts in the cause of modern poetry, Turner left small room for doubt as to why he felt impelled to withdraw from *Georgian Poetry* v. The poet had already crossed swords with Marsh in 1919, when Marsh had demurred at including several of Turner's poems in *Georgian Poetry* IV on the grounds of his ancient abomination, obscurity. Far from knuckling under, Turner had defended himself vigorously. He had invoked the aid of Squire, and Marsh had been prevailed upon to print the poems in volume IV.[23] When he was approached for *Georgian Poetry* v, Turner was quite explicit: 'With regard to the new G.P., while fully appreciating the compliment of being asked to contribute—I feel that you do not really like my last book and I would rather on this occasion therefore be out of it.' Marsh candidly admitted in reply that Turner's book had not impressed him because 'there are obscurities in it', but he asked the poet to reconsider his decision to withdraw entirely from the series.[24] His request elicited from Turner a somewhat less formal letter but an equally firm refusal.

> My dear Eddie,
> I hope you will not think me foolishly perverse if I say I feel I must stick to my decision. No one appreciates more than I all you have done for living poets. In fact this personal appeal is so strong that it is with the greatest difficulty, believe me, that I can resist it. But sometimes a devil rises up in me which will not be denied. I cannot properly explain why I want to be out of G.P. this year; it is merely a blind instinct which is too strong even for my admiration and liking for you so I do hope you will be indulgent to my caprice with your characteristic generosity.
>
> Yours sincerely,
> Jim[25]

The inelasticity of Marsh's tastes had played a large part in excluding from his final volume perhaps the foremost poet among his Neo-Georgians.

Most reviewers received *Georgian Poetry* IV and v with a notable lack of enthusiasm, if not downright hostility. *Georgian Poetry* IV attracted some particularly heavy fire. Almost to a man the critics agreed upon two major points: first, that the verse in *Georgian Poetry* IV was characterized by a distinct lack of vigour; and secondly, that in the tedious sameness of much of the verse it contained, Edward Marsh's fourth volume gave ample evidence that the Georgians had become a full-fledged coterie.

In a review significantly entitled 'Georgian Poetry: New Style', the reviewer for the *Times Literary Supplement* deplored the lifeless-ness of *Georgian Poetry* IV. The Georgians, he claimed, have become too greatly enamoured of 'ingenuous poetry', the identifying characteristics of which are unmistakable: 'Some simple mood, perception, or admitted truth is taken and deliberately elaborated upon until it seems portentous; the means employed are tireless repetitions . . . cascading catalogues of nouns and adjectives, and often a repeated reference to secret knowledge of the world known only to the poet.'[26] From across the Atlantic came the voice of Amy Lowell, never a Georgian partisan but now more caustic than ever. 'Weary verse!' she cried. 'It is a profound labour to read this book.' Most of the poetry it contains is only 'stale stuff', wan echoes from the past attenuated by poetic and spiritual 'atrophy'.[27]

The reviewer for the *New Statesman* struck out at the deadly sameness of most Georgian verse, which had been produced, he argued, by the fact that the Georgians had begun to copy one another. Whereas *Georgian Poetry* I and II showed 'no detectable tendency' towards coterie verse, he observed, 'as time has passed the volumes—therein presumably, and we think certainly, reflect-ing the movement of the time—have become increasingly homo-geneous'. It was only to be expected that by 1919 'the weaker of the poets included' in the series should have begun to 'show traces of the influence of the others'; but it was more deplorable that even several of Marsh's original Georgians should have suc-cumbed. With *Georgian Poetry* IV, 'some of those—rather tedious realists originally—who are veterans in the series have now cast off their old habits and become guilty of the sincerest form of flattery'. The result is a flat homogeneity most clearly evident in the Georgians' undue emphasis on landscape verse.[28]

In spite of this hostility towards *Georgian Poetry* IV, however, most critics were willing to make at least two general qualifications to their sweeping condemnations. In the first place, as even Amy Lowell conceded, it was the Neo-Georgians who were primarily to blame for the enervation of *Georgian Poetry* IV, not the Geor-gians. Neo-Georgian verse is largely derivative, Miss Lowell pointed out, and 'it is stuff and nonsense to try and raise such echoes into the dignity of a poetic creed as Mr. Squire and Mr. Shanks are constantly trying to do. All literature is against them; good poets are not echoes, and never were, and that is the long and short of it'.[29] The reviewer for the *Times Literary Supplement* agreed: it is primarily the Neo-Georgians, he found, who 'pause and shrink from the highest themes' and are therefore responsible for the lifelessness of Edward Marsh's fourth volume.[30] Secondly, perhaps more at fault than any group of poets, Georgian or Neo-Georgian, was the post-war age itself. The *New Statesman* reviewer saw in the increasing coterie spirit of the Georgians only a reflection of 'the movement of the time'.[31] The *Times Literary Supplement* took the deterioration of *Georgian Poetry* as unmistakable evidence of 'the lack of spiritual direction of a nation that turns upon itself, leaderless, discontented, and half-hearted'.[32] Similarly, Amy Lowell condemned most of the verse in *Georgian Poetry* IV as not only stale but 'pathological' as well. 'We know what these young men want to say,' she conceded, but the power to say it 'has been weakened by strain. They have not the energy to see personally, or speak with their own voices. The will to do so is strong; the nervous strength necessary for the task ... is lacking.'[33]

The single most influential critic of the entire *Georgian Poetry* series, however, was Middleton Murry. T. S. Eliot, to be sure, ranks close behind him. With his charge that the Georgians possessed an uncommon degree of 'pleasantness', of either the 'Wordsworthian' or the 'minor-Keatsian' variety, Eliot had spoken out for the first time in 1917.[34] And again in 1918 Eliot had elaborated on his thesis. 'What we commonly find among contemporary poets', he had complained, 'is a mentality which has remained in the age of Wordsworth or in the age of Tennyson, with a technique which is actually inferior to that of either of these.... While the mind of man has altered, verse has stood still.' Most contemporary poets are capable only of 'a heavy trifling; they have nothing to say to the adult, sophisticated, civilised mind; they are quite unaware of its tragedies and ecstasies'.[35]

In December 1919, with *Georgian Poetry* IV, Murry attacked. His forthright statement of the post-war anti-Georgian position merely summed up what many other poets and critics were thinking, but no one put the case quite so cogently. As his biographer has remarked, Murry's attack on the Georgians 'was mainly responsible for his reputation at that time'. After his review had appeared, Murry wrote to Katherine Mansfield: 'There's no doubt it's a fight to the finish between us and them. ... Them is the "Georgians" *en masse*. It's a queer feeling I begin to have now: that we're making literary history.'[36] Murry made no mistake; he was indeed making history, for not only did his argument help set the anti-Georgian critical pattern for years to come, but it was his review which, above all others, succeeded in toppling Edward Marsh's anthology from its pedestal once and for all. From this time onward as Marsh's biographer wrote, 'E. M.'s anthologies ceased to hold their position as the acknowledged vehicle for the best in contemporary verse.'[37]

By 1919, Murry pointed out, there could no longer be any doubt that the Georgians had become a coterie; they were only 'individuals-by-courtesy whose flavour is almost wholly corporate'. They had come to share two pernicious hallmarks: 'false simplicity' and 'right-mindedness'. The former Murry defined as being 'compounded of worship of trees and birds and contemporary poets in about equal proportions', and concerning the latter he complained: 'there is nothing disturbing' about the Georgians. They have about them 'an indefinable odour of complacent sanctity, an unctuous redolence of *union sacrée*. . . . You feel, somehow, that they might have been very wicked, and yet they are very good. . . . They sympathise with animate and inanimate nature. They have shining foreheads with big bumps of benevolence . . . and one inclines to believe that their eyes must be frequently filmed with an honest tear, if only because their vision is blurred'. It was only to be expected, then, that the verse in *Georgian Poetry* IV should have been uniformly sodden. If the Georgians have an idea, 'it leaves you with the queer feeling that it is not an idea at all, that it has been defaced, worn smooth by the rippling of innumerable minds'.

It was to the Neo-Georgians, however, not the Georgians, that Murry administered the most biting strokes of the lash. Indeed, he concentrated his severest criticism on J. C. Squire and the poets of the Squirearchy: Shanks, Freeman, and Turner. Though all the Neo-Georgians were guilty of emulation, Squire's verse alone 'would make an excellent subject for a critical investigation into false simplicity'. And from a line-by-line comparison of Squire's 'Rivers' to Walter de la Mare's 'Arabia' Murry brilliantly demonstrated not only that Squire had taken his central idea from de la Mare but that even the rhythms and metrical patterns were also derivative.

For the deterioration of Georgian poetry so amply evident in

Edward Marsh's first post-war volume, Murry, like most other critics, was willing to blame the times. Only through a disastrous decline in spiritual stamina and artistic standards, he observed, was such a volume as *Georgian Poetry* IV made possible. Its lassitude, enervation, and sickly imitation all argued that the Georgians, and most of the post-war world as well, had forgotten the most basic truths about poetry: that it is 'rooted in emotion', that 'it grows by the mastery of emotion', and that 'its significance finally depends upon the quality and comprehensiveness of the emotion'. Lacking both emotional vigour and fundamental brain-work, then, the verse in *Georgian Poetry* IV made application of serious critical standards absurd. 'The more stupid' of the contributors, Murry concluded, 'supply the matter for a good laugh; the more clever the stuff of a more recondite amazement.'[38]

By 1922, when *Georgian Poetry* V was published, it was universally conceded that the anthology had outlived its day. With the striking exceptions of D. H. Lawrence's 'Snake', some selections from Blunden's *The Shepherd* and *The Waggoner*, and several from V. Sackville-West's *Orchard and Vineyard*, *Georgian Poetry* V contained by and large the same kind of bloodless verse which had characterized volume IV. By 1922 it was if anything even clearer than it had been in 1919 that no amount of critical good will could justify an assertion that *Georgian Poetry* V represented the best accomplishment of English poetry during the previous three years. Even those critics normally most in sympathy with the aims and the tone of Edward Marsh's anthology were hard pressed to find enough noteworthy material in the fifth volume to fill the space allotted them for their reviews. The reviewer for the *Times Literary Supplement* could only introduce a more or less irrelevant comparison between the poetic forms used by the Georgians of volume V and those in use fifty years before, and question rather mildly whether the Georgians were perhaps not too greatly absorbed in 'the new love of detail' for its own sake.[39]

Edmund Gosse, writing in the *Sunday Times*, chided the Georgians for the lassitude which they displayed in *Georgian Poetry* V and attributed it to their 'determination to be anything rather than rhetorical'. Their misguided rejection of 'general ideas in favour of a pictorial representation of physical phenomena of life' has led them either to trivialities or to bathos, Gosse pointed out; often the Georgian poets 'are so determined to be simple that they succeed in being silly'. They have retreated from the high esteem that the poet of the nineteenth century felt for his art; their poetry is the poetry of minutiae. 'The broad outline, the radiating vistas of intellectual and moral life do not interest these young poets in the least. Their eyes are not lifted to the mountains, but are occupied in minute inspection of the ground. . . . No generation of writers . . . was ever more obsessed with the charm of nervous sensibility, cultivated for its own sake, and not shrinking even from an apparently prosaic diction in order to emphasise its presentation.'[40] Perhaps the most outspoken critic of *Georgian Poetry* v was Alec Waugh. The volume was characterized, he wrote, not only by lack of intensity but also by a 'distinctly tedious homogeneity of style and metre'. Nor did he confine his condemnation to the fifth volume alone. Quite correctly, he linked volumes IV and v together, asserting that the material in both of them was 'in the bulk uninteresting and undramatic. It limited the capacities of the universe to a number of natural objects, and to the poet who observed them. There is little if any recognition of the existence of other personalities'.[41]

Both in what he said and the manner in which he said it, Holbrook Jackson courageously did what one suspects most other reviewers would have preferred to do: he devoted precisely one short paragraph in *To-day* to a succinct dismissal of the volume. 'The fifth book of *Georgian Poetry*, despite the addition of seven writers who have not hitherto appeared in this collection, carries on a tradition of sameness. The quality is maintained but the freshness has departed—which means that E. M. has more or less completed his work as an anthologist. He has represented a poetic mode with fairness and accuracy, and it is not his fault that the particular vein has exhausted itself.'[42]

# IO

# The Failure of Imagination

What reasons can be adduced for the lack of vigour which so abundantly characterized *Georgian Poetry* IV and V, making inevitable the steady decline and final demise of the anthology? From the historical account of the series several reasons can readily be inferred. It is tempting, in the first place, to lay the blame upon Edward Marsh's poetic tastes. Such a course has been particularly attractive to those critics who define Georgian poetry as merely that poetry which appealed to Edward Marsh.[1] And though it too neatly oversimplifies a complex matter, there is obviously some truth in the argument. Marsh's taste, never precisely *avant-garde*, grew steadily more conservative in the post-war era.* As obscurity came increasingly into poetic fashion, Marsh was led to insist the more strenuously upon lucidity as the *sine qua non* for entrance into the post-war volumes of *Georgian Poetry*.

The charge of obscurity which he levelled at W. J. Turner in 1919—and which resulted in Turner's secession from *Georgian Poetry* V in 1922—is a case in point. And Marsh undertook disputes over poetic form with others of his Georgians as well, though none resulted in so serious a defection. In a rash moment in 1919 John Freeman confessed that he was 'getting tired of little lyric gasps' and advised Marsh that he was setting out to experiment with new forms. Alarmed, Marsh advised Freeman with some force to stick with the short lyric and, when his advice went unheeded, accused Freeman of 'throwing over form' altogether.[2]

---

* A tendency which even several of his original contributors to *GP* observed. Cf. Wilfrid Gibson, 'The "Georgian Poets", or Twenty Years After', *Bookman*, LXXXII (1932), 280.

Freeman defended himself on several occasions against the inflexibility of Marsh's taste. 'To throw over the brief lyric isn't suicide,' he replied to one of Marsh's preachments. 'Rather it is a withering than a rejection: leaves falling before fruit comes.'[3] Marsh was only partly reassured. 'I do hope you're not going to concentrate exclusively on content, and give form the go by,' he replied. 'I have no reason to think you will. . . . Except for a few odd people like Donne, I'm convinced that it is by form (not alone but as a *sine qua non*) that poets live.'[4]

It is also true that Marsh grew increasingly insistent upon the rightness of his own poetic judgments in the post-war years. He too seems to have shared in the mounting literary intolerance which accompanied intensification of the coterie spirit in post-war England. In a sense *Georgian Poetry* IV, unprovocative and well mannered as it was, was an act of defiance. In it Marsh seemed more stubbornly determined than ever before to raise his flag in the very teeth of hostile critical guns. With volume IV, he indulged his own tastes perhaps more extensively than in any other volume. Consequently, though none of the series was intended to be wholly representative, *Georgian Poetry* IV was the most narrowly conceived of them all. Gordon Bottomley was among the first of Marsh's contributors to recognize this difference. Soon after receiving his copy of the fourth volume he wrote Marsh:

> I don't know whether or not you intended it, or whether its aspect comes by you or by the time-spirit, but it seems to me to have drawn its being and nature from a different conception; in trying to register candidly its impression and effect on me, I can come nearest by saying that its three elder brothers strike me as being constituted on the lines of a national picture gallery, while this newest scion has rather the nature of one of the great private collections of the same calibre as the public ones. The former volumes have the feeling of having been chosen to satisfy connoisseurs of all schools, the present one to satisfy and exemplify the unresting and exacting taste of one of the great connoisseurs—so that, for the first time, I am eagerly enjoying the knowledge of your vision of poetry, and of what your own poetry would be like if you had chosen to write instead of to guide your age.[5]

In view of the almost universal critical condemnation of *Georgian Poetry* IV Bottomley's compliment to Marsh was a back-handed one, though surely he did not intend it so.

Marsh's second attempt to defend his principles in the face of post-war hostility was less indirect. No longer willing, by 1922, to ignore the sneering attacks upon his anthology, Marsh carried the battle to the enemy with an unusually lengthy preface to *Georgian Poetry* v. Characteristically, he attacked with the rapier, a weapon which he wielded with uncommon skill. 'When the fourth volume of this series was published three years ago,' he began, 'many of the critics who had up till then . . . been the dearest creatures in the world to me, took another turn. Not only did they very properly disapprove my choice of poems: they went on to write as if the Editor of *Georgian Poetry* were a kind of public functionary, like the President of the Royal Academy; and they asked . . . who was E. M. that he should bestow and withhold crowns and sceptres, and decide that this or that poet was or was not to count.' Nothing could have been further from his aim than to set himself up 'as a pundit, or a pontiff, or a Petronius Arbiter', Marsh alleged. An anthology is by nature exclusive, but *Georgian Poetry* did not seek to establish a poetic school or coterie; its aim was simply to place before the public eye 'a number of writers doing work which appeared . . . extremely good, but which was narrowly known'.

Moreover, Marsh entered his 'mild protest' against the commonly repeated charge that because *Georgian Poetry* 'had merely encouraged a small clique of mutually indistinguishable poetasters to abound in their own and each other's sense or nonsense', the poetic result had been only 'an insipid sameness'. 'It is only natural', he argued, 'that the poets of a generation should have points in common; but to my fond eye those who have graced these collections look as diverse as sheep to their shepherds, or the members of a Chinese family to their uncle.'

He saved his keenest thrust until last. To those critics who implied that in closing the pages of *Georgian Poetry* to 'modern' verse, Marsh was not only intensifying coterie warfare but was also being deliberately stiff-necked, his reply was simple and direct. 'Much admired modern work', he wrote, 'seems to me, in its lack of inspiration and its disregard of form, like gravy imitating lava.' But, he quickly added, 'Its upholders may retort that much of the work which I prefer seems to them, in its lack of inspiration and its comparative finish, like tapioca imitating pearls.' Edmund Blunden was no doubt right when he wrote Marsh, after reading the preface, 'The foreword to the *Georgians* is an act of vengeance which leaves you in possession. The enemy lies strewn about you, and all done with a rapier.'[6]

Marsh had effectively defended his anthologizing principles; he had again disavowed the assumption that *Georgian Poetry* was—or should have been—representative. The charge against his poetic taste, however, he could not so easily turn aside. Indeed, the preface to *Georgian Poetry* v was at once Marsh's admission that his tastes were out of date and his challenge to his adversaries to do their worst. Come what may, Edward Marsh would defend the lost cause of formal verse. Rather than submit to the powers of darkness, he would allow *Georgian Poetry* to die. Admiration for Marsh's integrity cannot be allowed to obscure the fact that his increasingly restricted tastes and his inflexible insistence upon the rightness of his own poetic judgments constitute significant reasons for the post-war senescence of *Georgian Poetry*.

Perhaps an even more considerable reason was the spiritual enervation of the post-war age itself. The tedious sameness of the verse in *Georgian Poetry* IV and V, as almost all the reviewers pointed out, occurred because emotions made taut by four years of horror had finally snapped; and being unable—or unwilling— to feel deeply, the post-war Georgian poets could scarcely have been expected to produce any but second-rate verse.[7] There was 'only one explanation for the preponderance in these last two collections of impersonal unemotional poetry', wrote Alec Waugh in 1924, 'namely that the poetry of personal passion and experience is no longer being produced with the rich abundance of the war and pre-war years'. Like the nation itself, many post-war poets were emotionally exhausted, and they recoiled from the strains of war either to simple poetry which extolled the 'calm beauties of the English countryside' or to the poetry of minutiae which required no sustained or strenuous emotional effort.[8]

Middleton Murry came to much the same conclusion. By 1920 he was willing to qualify his strictures against *Georgian Poetry* in one important respect. The 'false simplicity' and the complacency, or 'right-mindedness', for which he had belaboured *Georgian Poetry* IV in 1919 came about, he conceded one year later, not because the Georgians were consciously attempting to create a coterie but simply out of emotional fatigue. They were a reaction to the strains induced by war, a pitiful attempt to keep up poetic appear-

ances by assuming the outward pretence that nothing at all unusual had happened to the spirit of man from 1914 to 1918.
' "Right-mindedness",' he concluded, 'is, fundamentally, a clumsy
method of exorcising the devil that walketh at noonday; it is an
attempt to combat an insidious disease by assuming the outward
behaviour of a man in health.' Equally insidious, Murry added,
was the opposite disease, 'wrong-headedness', or the pessimistic,
despairing state of mind common to most of the more *avant-garde*
post-war poets. But both were caused by the same virus, both had
been nurtured by the war.[9]

Such analyses as Murry's and Waugh's, though essentially correct, seem just a shade too neat. Emotional exhaustion was not the
only attribute of the post-war years which helps account for the
insipid calm into which a large segment of English poetry sank
from 1918 to 1922. Another can perhaps be singled out in the
general drift towards conformity. The tendency of the poet towards corporate endeavour, his susceptibility to the coterie spirit,
and his consequent willingness to sacrifice a large measure of his
individual inspiration have already been noted and to some extent explained. But can the unusually strong appeal of the coterie
to the post-war poet be satisfactorily accounted for only by the
practical argument that the individual poet was forced to join a
coterie if he wanted to be published? Perhaps not, for such an
argument seems in part to beg the question.

War had made conformity both fashionable and habitual. It had
brought to many men of letters the necessity to conform to
majority opinions, even to reflect those opinions, to a degree
which most of them would have scorned as intolerable in peacetime. And the will to conform, the habit of acting in concert with
the group, enforced by four years of war, could scarcely have been
expected to disappear immediately at the onset of peace. 'There
was perhaps never a time', Douglas Goldring concluded as he
surveyed literary London after six months of peace, 'when our
scribes were more uniformly ingratiating and struggled more desperately to please. No pretty lady or earnest young curate has ever
approached some of the leading novelists and quill-drivers in the
fervour of their desire to make a good impression.' Again the
cause was the war: a time when 'the great mass of current literature
. . . cowered like a veritable Uriah Heep before public opinion,
rubbing its greasy hands with invisible soft soap'; when British

writers 'seemed to strive with almost one accord to reflect every popular prejudice and to echo every popular *banalité*'; and when there was 'scarcely to be found one "conscientious objector" who had the pluck to follow his own road, giving the herd—in passing —a sound clump over its collective *tête de mouton*'.[10] If the lifelessness of poetry in the immediate post-war years is to be attributed in part to the tendency of the British poet to seek out the security of a coterie, then surely the attractiveness of the post-war coterie is in turn to be explained partially by the peacetime survival of war-engendered habits of conformity, collective action, and the will to please.

Not all observers concurred in a pessimistic estimate of the temper of the age. J. C. Squire still fought a rear-guard action. From the citadel of the *London Mercury* he fired an occasional salvo intended to persuade literate Englishmen that the pre-war poetic revival was still in fact occurring. But his post-war bursts went off with all the impact of a wet firecracker. And by 1922 even Squire's comments were noticeably more guarded than they had been in the pre-war 'Solomon Eagle' days. He still stuck to his guns—the poetic revival had survived the war, he argued—but by 1922 he could only write ambiguously: 'we are far from thinking . . . that all our contemporary geese are swans, or that swans are very numerous. . . . But if we see no reason to believe that we are in the middle—though we may be at the beginning—of a great creative age, we certainly do not think that we are in the middle of a slump. No age has thought much of itself'.*

Contrary to such sanguine views, most critics agreed that the post-war imaginative paralysis boded ill for the future of poetry. The patience of even the *Times Literary Supplement* was finally taxed beyond endurance by the flaccidity of post-war verse. In a most uncharacteristic excursion into sarcasm it exclaimed: 'We have discovered the cause of world unrest. It is respectable minor poetry; poetry written without imagination at the call of cultivated emotions, rich in the righteousness of untroubled convention; poetry which tells us nothing but that a man is tired, or saw a sunset, or was mildly alarmed, or lived at Constantinople, and far from transporting us there, settles us more firmly in our chair in

* *London Mercury*, VII (1922), 2. See also a leading article in the *Athenaeum*, no. 4,637 (Jan. 1919), pp. 14–15, in which the writer argued that reasonable hopes for the future of poetry were possible if poetry were to consent to become more 'democratic', less esoteric, and less private.

an atmosphere of such chill indifference as invites the flames of revolution.'* Many observers were unwilling to dismiss the sorry state of verse in even such bitterly humorous tones. They agreed with another reviewer in the same journal who complained in a rather more serious vein: 'The crying fault of so many modern poems is that they do not move us strongly either to delight or disgust, that the material out of which they are made is not sufficiently dominated by its creator's idea, or illuminated by his passion, for us to forget the artifice in the art, the body in the spirit. Rather they suggest petty experiments in both matter and style, like the floral designs on Victorian china.'[11]

The listless temper of the age, then, and Edward Marsh's increasingly restricted tastes both partially explain the post-war decline of *Georgian Poetry*. But from out of the historical account of the anthology a third reason for the tepidity of the 1919 and 1922 volumes is perhaps even more clearly implied. The history of *Georgian Poetry* from 1917 to 1922 suggests that the Neo-Georgians were steadily gaining dominance over the anthology while the influence of the original Georgians was being continually whittled away, until, by 1922, it had almost reached the vanishing point. The Neo-Georgians' gain was *Georgian Poetry's* loss.

The Neo-Georgians who set the tone of *Georgian Poetry* IV and V were a very different breed of poets from Edward Marsh's original Georgians who had appeared in *Georgian Poetry* I and II. One of the most significant qualities of the first two volumes, for instance—and the one which most clearly distinguished the Georgians from their pre-war contemporaries—was poetic realism. Abercrombie, Bottomley, Masefield, Brooke, Gibson: all had taken their fling at realistic verse in 1912 and 1915, in several cases with controversial, if not entirely successful, results. And in 1917, in *Georgian Poetry* III, the young war poets—Graves, Sassoon, Nichols, Rosenberg—had in part followed the cue of their elder predecessors. Neo-Georgianism, exemplified in the Squire-Shanks-Freeman-Turner school, however, was precisely a reaction against Georgian realism. With the ascendency of the poets of the Squire-archy, as Herbert Palmer pointed out, 'the boisterous influence of

* *TLS*, 25th Nov. 1920, p. 772. One of the volumes which invited the *TLS's* stricture was Herbert Asquith's *A Village Sermon* (1920). Asquith had of course appeared in *GP* III in 1917, when objections to his inclusion on much the same grounds had been urged on E. M., by, among others, Edmund Gosse. See above, Chapter 7.

Masefield . . . and other ruddy poets was to be thoroughly checked'. In place of Georgian realism was to be substituted Turner's lush, tropic exoticism; in place of Masefield—'the most sunshiny of them all'—was to be substituted that veriest symbol of Neo-Georgianism: the moon. 'J. C. Squire's Moon! His own verse is hag-ridden by it; and it was on the banner of all the New Poetry. On the banner of all the new-comers—Shanks, Freeman, and W. J. Turner—casting its silvery beams across the whole landscape of Georgian verse.'* And what did this moon-worship mean for *Georgian Poetry*? It meant that in volumes IV and V the anthology had succumbed to the spiritual exhaustion of the age.

> It meant that passion was dying, that it was thought better that it should die, that emotions during the early part of the war had been keyed to too high a pitch, and that henceforth poets must seek strength in complete escape, in farther withdrawal from the turmoil of religion, of politics, of patriotism, of active life. The sun, the old life-giver, had gone corrupt; the moon, the new life-giver, was to be the symbol of the new serene order in the world of poetry, of art, of human life.
>
> Suppression! Resignation! Restraint!†

As it turned out, the Neo-Georgian moon lighted only the wide path to poetic oblivion.

Several of Marsh's contributors sensed the change of tone which had occurred in *Georgian Poetry* by 1919. Bottomley's comments on the difference in tone between volume IV and the first three volumes have been noted. Several younger poets were more out-spoken, particularly Robert Graves. While attempting to mitigate the sting of his comments with a wry joke or two, Graves deplored the lushness of Neo-Georgian verse. In its attempt to be vivid and colourful, he pointed out, much of the over-decorated verse in *Georgian Poetry* IV succeeded only in betraying the fact that the poets who wrote it suffered from an advanced case of spiritual anaemia.

* Palmer was not the only critic to remark the depressing recurrence of the moon, moonlight, and imagery connected with the moon in Squire's poetry. Middleton Murry also recognized it and, in fact, used it as the primary piece of evidence to convict Squire of poetic insincerity ('A Poet of the Moon', *Athenaeum*, no. 4,710 [6th Aug. 1920], p. 170).

† Palmer, *Post-Victorian Poetry*, pp. 182–97, and *passim*. Though the division of the Georgians into two schools (to which I have applied the names Georgian and Neo-Georgian) is Palmer's, he was not the first to notice the differences between pre- and post-war Georgian poetry. He was anticipated by Middleton Murry and several other contemporary reviewers in both the *TLS* and the *Athenaeum*.

'It's a very arborial book,' said Bob Nichols to me, and I remarked on the apparent instability of all the elms as contrasted with the enormous vitality of the nightingales. But that was only a joke and against ourselves really too.

. . . I wish the older blokes wouldn't borrow Turner's moon-washed apples and parrotty jungle and fishy conservatory. It upsets one so; I know Turner's scenario is fearfully good as written by himself and tempting for idea-less people to copy but that when they do it's a signal for someone with a more personal style to take over the torch. (This craving for exotic colour is a sign of anaemic old age; University dons always love red robes and their wives' purple hats. And in the vacation they revel in foul red sunsets on Brighton Esplanade. Compris?) If the tendency continues you'll have to go and publish in British North Borneo or Brett-Young's E. Africa on bamboo paper using ape-blood for printers' ink and crocodile for binding.[12]

The 'tendency' did continue. When *Georgian Poetry* v came under consideration, therefore, Graves made a suggestion which faced facts realistically and which Marsh might have done well to consider. 'Why not muzzle the critics' sweeping jibes by dividing the book historically into two parts?' Graves suggested. The first part would contain the work of the Georgians—'the old hands', as Graves called them—the second the work of the younger men, 'the ones who are now not more than 32 or 33—i.e., those who at the outbreak of the war eight years ago had not settled down seriously to write or formed their styles for good, in other words those who characters are entirely moulded by war-experience and after-the-war experience'. Such a division, Graves argued, would tend to spike the critics' guns by taking belated recognition of what had in fact already occurred: a split between the Georgians of the pre-war and those of the post-war tradition. It 'will make the book more sensible', he urged, 'and will account for the break-ing of the excellent Abercrombie-Hodgson-de la Mare-Davies-Brooke tradition of early Georgianism'. And he added a comment which Marsh might correctly have taken as evidence of a good deal of discontent among some of his younger contributors who were unaffiliated with the Squirearchy: 'It will be kinder both to old and young to put 'em in separate cages if the murmurings I hear are to be trusted.'

As Graves was aware, however, a division simply on the basis of age would not accurately reflect what had happened to *Georgian*

*Poetry* by 1922. There were not only two schools of poets to consider; there were three. Graves designated them metaphorically as the bull, the camel, and the ox. 'At present,' he told Marsh, 'you are ploughing with a Bull and a young camel.'

> By that token the Bull has begotten a rather ineffective Ox; which disgraces its very excellent sire and annoys the camel—its name is not Georgianism but Georgianismatism and it is against the inclusion of this occasional ox that the real hostility to recent volumes lies.
>
> Tortures wouldn't drag from me the names of this sham-Georgian school, but it is recognisable by its infernal cleverness and damnable dullness. Remember the end of the Yellow Book and forgive my impertinence . . . but take this view (about the ox) as expressing the secret opinions of that group of writers, Turner, Blunden, Nichols, Sassoon, Graves, etc., the camel which thrust its nose into the Arab's tent in 1916.[13]

For 'bull' read the Georgians of volumes I and II; for 'ox' read the Neo-Georgian moonlight school which had perverted the genuine Georgian tradition; and for 'camel' read that loosely knit group of young poets who, though contemporaries of the moonlight poets, were of a more virile stripe. It was the impotence of the ox which in large measure accounted for the enervation of *Georgian Poetry*, for with volumes IV and V the ox waxed fat in the pages of the anthology while the camel succeeded in getting very little more than his nose under the tent, and the bull, old and docile, was put out to pasture.

The failure of the Neo-Georgians was at bottom the failure of the poetic imagination. They were imaginatively bankrupt. Not that they had lost the ability to see; on the contrary, most of them were sensitive, perceptive recorders of the world of eye and ear. What they had surrendered was the ability to feel deeply and, perhaps more important, the ability to create out of what they saw, the power to transmute raw experience into art, to give shape, form, direction, and significance to the data of the senses. And so they slipped into impersonal, unimaginative, minor poetry.

At its worst the failure of imagination led some of the Neo-Georgians down the path of poetic insincerity. They became *poseurs*. For several of the post-war poets, as Harold Monro complained, appearance had become more important than reality; their 'desire to be thought a poet' was stronger than their 'love of poetry'.[14] The moonlight poets were so absorbed in the task of appearing superficially 'poetical' that they forgot a cardinal truth about poetry: it is based upon emotion deeply felt and imaginatively seized. Such critics as Monro and Graves, speaking from within the temple, were not the only observers to inveigh against Neo-Georgian Pharisaism. From outside the sacred precincts, too, there arose a chorus of voices, from 1919 through 1922, to deplore, to condemn, or to deride the patent insincerity of much Neo-Georgian verse. Aldous Huxley, T. S. Eliot, Osbert and Edith Sitwell, Middleton Murry: in varying tones they all pointed out the same basic deficiency in Neo-Georgian verse. Perhaps Murry may be permitted to sum up their comments, for he was more skilful than most in keeping the sneer from his voice but at the same time mincing no words. He chose a vulnerable point for one of his attacks, the title poem of J. C. Squire's *The Moon* (1920). Having analysed the poem at length, and having isolated several glaring weaknesses which arose, he pointed out, from Squire's attempts to copy the matter and the manner of other Neo-Georgians, Murry concluded with a perceptive one-sentence indictment: 'And when these weaknesses recur through the poem, the suspicion hardens into a certainty that it is not really a poem, because it did not have its origin in any compulsive emotion, but was the outcome of a desire to write poetry rather than the urgent need to express a perception.'[15] Murry had placed his finger precisely on a major weakness of several Neo-Georgian poets. They were, so to speak, faking poetry, playing mechanically by rote or by ear poetic chords which they did not feel. They had perhaps been shaken by experience—shaken too deeply, indeed—but their experience and their emotions were merely versified. Their perceptions had not been filtered through the alembic of the creative imagination to emerge as unique poetry.

Even at the best, when not the faintest suspicion of poetic insincerity can be allowed, the poverty of their imaginations often rendered the Neo-Georgians uncommonly ineffective poets. They were by no means lacking in poetic skills. Poets like Shanks and Freeman can scarcely be accused of technical ineptitude. But technical dexterity was no substitute for that one indispensable power which 'bodies forth / The forms of things unknown', permits the poet's pen to turn them to shapes, 'and gives to airy nothing / A local habitation and a name'. One recalls Edward Shanks's indictment of Mrs. Shove (who, though not strictly speaking a Neo-

Georgian, shared many of their shortcomings): she 'is like a house in which all the fittings for electric light are in position but which is not yet connected to the main. If something happened to her, I believe she might begin to write poetry'.[16] Shanks could not have prescribed a better remedy for 'Georgianismatism'; something had to 'happen' to the Neo-Georgians to turn them from versifiers into poets. Of course nothing did happen to them because, in the post-war world, they allowed nothing to happen. Too much had happened from 1914 to 1918. And so even at their best the Neo-Georgians often practised a poetry of shimmering mirages and half-lights, poetry dominated by that quality which in a painting one would call chiaroscuro.

Perhaps the foremost Neo-Georgian practitioner of such blood-less verse was W. J. Turner. No one can question Turner's sincerity. In his own genre he was unsurpassed; even Robert Graves, a poet of quite a different order, conceded that Turner's 'scenario is fearfully good'. But his genre was restricted, his aims severely limited, and his characteristic post-war poetry essentially unreal, remote, and fervourless.

> The stone-grey roses by the desert's rim
> Are soft-edged shadows on the moonlit sand,
> Grey are the broken walls of Khangavar,
> That haunt of nightingales, whose voices are
> Fountains that bubble in the dream-soft Moon.
>
> Shall the Gazelles with moonbeam pale bright feet
> Entering the vanished gardens sniff the air—
> Some scent may linger of that ancient time,
> Musician's song, or poet's passionate rhyme,
> The Princess dead, still wandering love-sick there.
>
> A Princess pale and cold as mountain snow,
> In cool, dark chambers sheltered from the sun,
> With long dark lashes and small delicate hands:
> All Persia sighed to kiss her small red mouth
> Until they buried her in shifting sand.
>
> And the Gazelles shall flit by in the Moon
> And never shake the frail Tree's lightest leaves,
> And moonlight roses perfume the pale Dawn
> Until the scarlet life that left her lips
> Gathers its shattered beauty in the sky.
>
> ('The Princess', *Georgian Poetry* IV, p. 185)

No matter what subject Turner chose to treat—and the seven poems Marsh chose for *Georgian Poetry* IV showed a remarkable diversity of subject matter—the tone remained essentially the same. With Turner one does not even inhabit a world where it seems always afternoon, but rather always evening. 'His voice comes to us' thin and spare, 'not out of the world we know, but out of some mirage of its own creation. . . . He brings to bear upon us a kind of aesthetic mesmerism.'[17] Turner's poetry was *par excellence* poetry of the moon. As one of his reviewers pointed out, in a typical Turner poem 'the passion . . . is subdued; the lighting very soft, the colour dim and rich. . . . It all seems very faint, old, and far-away. . . . There is very little brightness in Mr. Turner's rich old tapestry. On the other hand, the lighting is always rather that of moonlight than of sunlight; and the frequent mention of the moon is but just art'.[18] In a world which had barely emerged from the most frightful blood bath in history, a world of general strikes and continuing alarms of struggle and flight on an ever more darkling plain, Turner and the Neo-Georgians who followed his cue—Squire, Shanks, Freeman—had taken the road of retrenchment, of retreat into an hallucinatory world created by tired minds and over-taxed spirits.

It would be unwise to claim, however, that the failure of the post-war imagination was restricted to the Neo-Georgians alone. The old-line Georgians, too, faltered and failed; they slipped too comfortably into the undemanding Neo-Georgian temper. More specifically, having been temporarily deserted by their own muse, some of the Georgians began playing the sedulous ape to the Neo-Georgians. They seemed particularly attracted to Turner's 'moon-washed apples and parrotty jungle', as Robert Graves had complained to Edward Marsh.[19] In a poem the very title of which is revelatory, John Drinkwater demonstrated that Turner's muse was at least adaptable: given the only absolutely essential ingredient, moonlight, it could function as well in the Cotswolds as in the tropic jungle.

MOONLIT APPLES

At the top of the house the apples are laid in rows,
And the skylight lets the moonlight in, and those
Apples are deep-sea apples of green. There goes
A cloud on the moon in the autumn night.

A mouse in the wainscot scratches, and scratches, and then
There is no sound at the top of the house of men
Or mice; and the cloud is blown, and the moon again
    Dapples the apples with deep-sea light.

They are lying in rows there, under the gloomy beams;
On the sagging floor; they gather the silver streams
Out of the moon, those moonlit apples of dreams,
    And quiet is the steep stair under.

In the corridors under there is nothing but sleep.
And stiller than ever on orchard boughs they keep
Tryst with the moon, and deep is the silence, deep
    On moon-washed apples of wonder.

            (*Georgian Poetry* IV, p. 50)

In a poem completely at odds with his pre-war, realistic verse,
Wilfrid Gibson took a colourful look into the Neo-Georgian
'parrotty jungle':

        Somewhere, somewhen I've seen,
        But where or when I'll never know,
        Parrots of shrilly green
        With crests of shriller scarlet flying
        Out of black cedars as the sun was dying
        Against cold peaks of snow.

            ('The Parrots', *Georgian Poetry* IV, p. 74)

Even Harold Monro fell under the hypnotic spell of the Neo-
Georgian moon and nightingales in a poem which, for its insistence upon chiaroscuro and the contrast of light and darkness,
out-did even Turner.

    THE NIGHTINGALE NEAR THE HOUSE

    Here is the soundless cypress on the lawn:
    It listen, listens. Taller trees beyond
    Listen. The moon at the unruffled pond
        Stares. And you sing, you sing.

    That star-enchanted song falls through the air
    From lawn to lawn down terraces of sound,
    Darts in white arrows on the shadowed ground;
        And all the night you sing.

My dreams are flowers to which you are a bee
As all night long I listen, and my brain
Receives your song, then loses it again
    In moonlight on the lawn.

Now is your voice a marble high and white,
Then like a mist on fields of paradise,
Now is a raging fire, then is like ice,
    Then breaks, and it is dawn.

                    *(Georgian Poetry* IV, p. 103)

It is in the disastrous decline of the Georgian pastoral tradition, however, that one sees perhaps more clearly than in any other genre the failure of the post-war imagination. And again not all the deficiencies can be laid at the door of the Neo-Georgians alone; the Georgians, too, share at least some of the onus for allowing a once vital poetic mode to lapse into mere convention. Even in the hands of its most outstanding pre-war practitioner, W. H. Davies, the Georgian nature lyric had gone stale by 1920. The pre-war Davies had the rare gift of spontaneity, a quality which made his mode essentially inimitable. 'Nature poets, with their meticulous catalogues,' as Richard Church observed, 'can be bores. Davies, with his handful of references which he repeats over and again, is never a bore. On the contrary, he puts a sort of enchantment upon us. . . . The emotion is a kind of nostalgia, a hearkening back to the morning of life, of time, the lost realm of innocence, where everything is wonder, and nothing is knowledge.'[20]

But in some of his post-war efforts, Davies's spontaneity faltered, his imagination flagged. The early-morning freshness had departed. In one mood he began to seek the calm peace of the Neo-Georgian nightingale and moon:

    How many buds in this warm light
      Have burst out laughing into leaves!
    And shall a day like this be gone
      Before I seek the wood that holds
    The richest music known?

Too many times have nightingales
  Wasted their passion on my sleep,
And brought repentance soon:
  But this one night I'll seek the woods,
The nightingale, and moon.

('Wasted Hours', *Georgian Poetry* v, p. 41)

In another mood he turned, incongruously, to grim and bitter subjects, as if he were trying to exorcise 'the devil that walketh at noonday'. As early as 1917, he had published in one of the little magazines a most un-Davies-like lyric which amounted almost to a repudiation of his pre-war mood:

### CONFESSION

One hour in every hundred hours,
I sing of childhood, birds and flowers:
Who reads my character in song,
Will not see much in me that's wrong,
But in my ninety hours and nine
I would not tell what thoughts are mine:
They're not so pure as find their words
In songs of childhood, flowers and birds.[21]

And by the early 1920's the post-war pessimistic temper had so taken hold of Davies that he could write an incongruously macabre, Elizabethan-like lyric in which his central metaphor was a rotting corpse:

### DOWN UNDERGROUND

What work is going on down underground,
Without a sound—without the faintest sound!
The worms have found the place where Beauty lies,
And, entering into her two sparkling eyes,
Have dug their diamonds up; her soft breasts that
Had roses without thorns, are now laid flat;
They find a nest more comfortable there,
Than any bird could make, in her long hair;
Where they can teach their young, from thread to thread,
To leap on her white body, from her head.
This work is going on down underground,
Without a sound—without the faintest sound.[22]

Even though Edward Marsh saw to it that none of Davies's poems in *Georgian Poetry* iv and v dealt with cadavers, several of them nevertheless implied the change in tone which had come over the poet in the post-war years. His lyrics were no longer as insistent upon the joys of nature, the rainbow and the cuckoo's song, as upon the ironies, even the cruelties, of the natural world. An image of a robin with his head half pecked away would scarcely have occurred, one suspects, to the Davies of 1912. Yet that was the central image of a poem entitled 'The Truth', the last of Davies's lyrics to be published in the *Georgian Poetry* series and an ironic coda to his career as a nature poet:

> Since I have seen a bird one day,
> His head pecked more than half away;
> That hopped about, with but one eye,
> Ready to fight again, and die—
> Ofttimes since then their private lives
> Have spoilt that joy their music gives.
>
> So when I see this robin now,
> Like a red apple on a bough,
> And question why he sings so strong,
> For love, or for the love of song;
> Or sings, maybe, for that sweet rill
> Whose silver tongue is never still—
>
> Ah, now there comes this thought unkind,
> Born of the knowledge in my mind:
> He sings in triumph that last night
> He killed his father in a fight;
> And now he'll take his mother's blood—
> The last strong rival for his food.

*(Georgian Poetry* v, p. 42)

Surely Davies was as fully aware in 1912 as in 1922 that nature was red in tooth and claw, but in the euphoric pre-war years he could still suppress the knowledge of the head and surrender himself completely to the joy of the heart. By 1922, however, the poet had at least partially capitulated to bitter knowledge. In his post-war mood there seems a good deal of the Shropshire lad in W. H. Davies.

It is the Neo-Georgians, however, not the Georgians, who must bear most of the blame not only for the dreary failure of post-war nature poetry but also for the critical obloquy which that failure brought down upon the entire Georgian movement. In Neo-Georgian hands the once fresh, vital Georgian nature lyric became sentimental landscape verse or impersonal catalogue poetry. To be sure, the Georgians had furnished the models for the Neo-Georgians and, in several instances, had even shown the Neo-Georgians how to pervert them. As early as 1917 Marsh had published in *Georgian Poetry* III a particularly soporific catalogue poem of Harold Monro's extolling the joys of the simple rural life and entitled 'Weekend'. It began:

> The train! The twelve o'clock for paradise.
>> Hurry, or it will try to creep away.
> Out in the country every one is wise:
>> We can be only wise on Saturday.
> There you are waiting, little friendly house:
>> Those are your chimney-stacks with you between,
> Surrounded by old trees and strolling cows,
>> Staring through all your windows at the green.
> Your homely floor is creaking for our tread;
>> The smiling tea-pot with contented spout
> Thinks of the boiling water, and the bread
>> Longs for the butter. All their hands are out
>> To greet us, and the gentle blankets seem
>> Purring and crooning: 'Lie in us, and dream.'
>> *(Georgian Poetry* III, p. 82)

Following the lead of such perverted Georgianism as 'Weekend', the Neo-Georgians produced their own brand of banality. Indulging his fondness for cataloguing in a poem about birds, for example, J. C. Squire demonstrated perhaps more ornithological knowledge than poetic insight:

> Yes, daw and owl, curlew and crested hern,
> Kingfisher, mallard, water-rail and tern,
> Chaffinch and greenfinch, warbler, stonechat, ruff,
> Pied wagtail, robin, fly-catcher and chough,
> Missel-thrush, magpie, sparrow-hawk, and jay,
> Built, those far ages gone, in this year's way.
> And the first man who walked the cliffs of Rame,
> As I this year, looked down and saw the same
> Blotches of rusty red on ledge and cleft
> With grey-green spots on them, while right and left
> A dizzying tangle of gulls were floating and flying,
> Wheeling and crossing and darting, crying and crying,
> Circling and crying, over and over and over,
> Crying with swoop and hover and fall and recover.
> ('The Birds', *Georgian Poetry* IV, p. 176)

John Freeman indulged the Neo-Georgian penchant for cataloguing in a poem on the subject of flowers:

> I will ask primrose and violet to spend for you
> Their smell and hue,
> And the bold, trembling anemone awhile to spare
> Her flowers starry fair;
> Or the flushed wild apple and yet sweeter thorn
> Their sweetness to keep
> Longer than any fire-bosomed flower born
> Between midnight and midnight deep.
>
> And I will take celandine, nettle and parsley, white
> In its own green light,
> Or milkwort and sorrel, thyme, harebell and meadowsweet
> Lifting at your feet,
> And ivy-blossom beloved of soft bees; I will take
> The loveliest—
> The seeding grasses that bend with the winds, and shake
> Though the winds are at rest.
>
> ('I Will Ask', *Georgian Poetry* v, p. 65)

It is small wonder that the Neo-Georgians quickly attracted the richly deserved epithet 'weekend poets', by which derisive critics meant to connote the poetic insincerity which arises when town-born poets sentimentalize over rustic virtues. Small wonder, too, that *Georgian Poetry* IV and v should have been marked, as critic after critic observed, by a kind of vitiated pastoralism which was not only excessive and dull but also self-conscious and impersonal. 'It is these dreary catalogues of natural phenomena . . . which are most trying to the patience,' Osbert Sitwell complained in 1921; 'the last dead grisly remains of a once vital movement of poetry, they are as infinitely pathetic as the excavated final joint in the tail of some huge but extinct monster.' And though by 1921 it was too late by far, he attempted to give the Neo-Georgians some advice about poetic sincerity: 'It is not the facts in a poem that make it interesting, but the effect on the mind of their observer. . . . *Poetry* lies in the expression of an emotion, of whatever kind, however great or slight, but has no connection with the cause of that emotion. . . . By repeating the word "cuckoo" you do not make yourself the author of "Sumer is y-comin' in".'[23]

If he sensed the decline of the genuine pastoralism of his original Georgians, Edward Marsh could do little about it in 1919; no alternative to the Neo-Georgian landscape verse and catalogue poetry was at hand. By 1922, fortunately, Marsh could demonstrate to the world by at least one of his choices for *Georgian Poetry* v that good pastoral verse *could* be written in the post-war world: he had 'discovered' Edmund Blunden. As Christopher Hassall wrote, 'What was weak in the last two anthologies was pseudo-pastoral, but what was good, it should be noted, was none the less pastoral, *vide* the last of Marsh's discoveries, Edmund Blunden.'[24] But even Blunden's work, though it struck the authentic note again, was obviously too little and too late. The Neo-Georgian temper had won the day.

The appalling pastoral-cum-landscape poetry produced by the Neo-Georgians gave post-war critics abundant opportunity for bursts of withering scorn. More important, it afforded the evidence on which not only the Neo-Georgians but the Georgians, too, were condemned out of hand, and thus was set the tone of criticism of the Georgian movement for many years to come. In Christopher Hassall's phrase again, 'No critical distinctions were made—until recently—but all was damned as pastoral, in the sense of damnably pastoral, or what has been called "week-end verse".'[25]

Attacks on the nature cult in *Georgian Poetry* were not new. The pastoral poets of volumes I and II had absorbed their share of criticism even though their muse was infinitely fresher than that of the Neo-Georgians. As early as 1913 Richard Aldington had taken several of the pre-war Georgians to task for their *naiveté* in supposing that good poetry could be created out of the mere facts of botanical germination, florescence, and decay.[26] And T. S. Eliot had complained in 1917 that lacking a consistent philosophy of nature the Georgian nature poet was forced to keep his eye too exclusively upon the object itself. His verse was therefore thin and vague. 'Only in something harder can great passion be expressed,' Eliot warned; 'the vague is a more dangerous path for poetry than the arid.'[27]

After the war, when it became amply evident that Edward Marsh's anthology had been pushed too far down the path of Neo-Georgian pseudo-pastoralism ever again to recover, Aldous Huxley took up the argument where Eliot and Aldington had left off. One demands of nature poetry something beyond a mere record of agreeable sensations, Huxley reminded the Neo-Georgians in 1920. 'The mere enjoyment of country life is in itself quite uninteresting. We demand from a poet that he shall give to an emotion which we all feel some fresh significance, that he shall look on familiar sights with eyes that discover new and surprising beauties.'[28] The week-end poets were manifestly unable to meet such demands. At the heart of the matter was the failure of the Neo-Georgian imagination. 'To be a nature poet,' Huxley concluded,

> it is not enough to affirm vaguely that God made the country and man made the town, it is not enough to talk sympathetically about familiar rural objects, it is not enough to be vaguely poetical about mountains and trees; it is not even enough to speak of these things with the precision of real knowledge and love. To be a nature poet a man must have felt profoundly and intimately those particular emotions which nature can inspire, and must be able to express them in such a way that his reader feels them.[29]

To feel emotions 'profoundly and intimately'. If they had not lost the ability to feel, most Neo-Georgians and Georgians alike had lost the will to feel, to imagine, to mould and shape experience artistically. It was time, and past time, that *Georgian Poetry* be laid to rest. And so when Harold Monro wrote Marsh in 1925 inquiring of the possibility of yet one more, final volume of *Georgian Poetry*, alleging that the booksellers were 'clamouring' for one, that it would sell perhaps 5,000 copies, and that it would afford its editor 'a rare opportunity . . . to sum up and round off "the movement" . . . and to comment upon new directions', Marsh replied with an unmistakably decisive no.[30] The anthology had done its work, he wrote. 'We set out with the single object of stimulating public interest in contemporary poetry, and I shall always cherish the belief that the books had a great deal to do with the marked growth of that interest . . . within the thirteen years since we began.' But perhaps the reason which Marsh put second was even more to the point. By 1925 Edward Marsh was quite willing to concede what had in fact become increasingly clear from 1917 on: his taste was fundamentally and finally at variance with the new directions in which modern poetry had moved. His feeling towards the 'chief exponents' of modern verse, he admitted, was one only of 'tepid and purblind respect'.[31]

As much as to any other influence *Georgian Poetry* owed its demise simply to the relentless passing of time. That ambitious adjective 'Georgian' had been applied proudly by Marsh in 1912 to mean 'new', 'modern', 'energetic', but by 1922 it had come to connote only 'old-fashioned', 'outworn', or worse. Edward Marsh's anthology had played an important and, for a time, predominant part on the literary scene during a period which was for poetry probably the most momentous that the twentieth century has yet produced. *Georgian Poetry* had been published through twelve eventful years: through the first fervid flush of a poetic renaissance; through the powerful stimulus of the First World War; and through a subsequent period of emotional relapse, imaginative paralysis, and the sniping, petty coterie bickering which passed for literary activity in post-war London. But by 1925 time had inexorably decreed, and Edward Marsh had wisely bowed to the inevitable. *Georgian Poetry* was allowed to cross its Acheron. There were few to remark—and fewer to lament—its passing in the new world of Sweeney and Mrs. Porter. The time-spirit had dug the grave of *Georgian Poetry* abundantly deep, and the anthology was, as Edward Marsh said, 'hushed in grim repose'.

# Epilogue

'English poetry is now once again putting on a new strength and beauty. . . . We are at the beginning of another "Georgian period" which may rank in due time with the several great poetic ages of the past.' No more than five years after they were written, Edward Marsh's brave new words of 1912 had begun to ring hollow; by 1922 they had become bitterly ironic; and today they seem perhaps more incredible than ironic. Though a poetic renaissance did in fact occur from 1911 to about 1915, it is nonsense to attempt to rank the achievement of the Georgian age with that of 'the several great poetic ages of the past'—with that of the Elizabethan, say, or the Romantic. To be sure, as the Georgian poets took arms against the spirit of the *fin de siècle*, for a few short years English poetry succeeded in putting on new strength. That it also succeeded in putting on new beauty is perhaps more questionable. But if the Georgian age did not entirely live up to Marsh's too sanguine predictions for it, neither did it sink to the poetic nadir implied by much subsequent criticism. Some of the subsequent hostility is to be explained, I suspect, by the fact that many critics have misconceived what or whom they were describing by the word 'Georgian'.

The word is undeniably ambiguous. But the ambiguity is not dispelled by flying in the face of historical evidence and claiming, as did Herbert Palmer, for instance, that Edward Marsh was guided by no less than fourteen definite canons in selecting poetry for his anthology. Had Palmer looked closely at the specific works in Marsh's first three volumes, at least, he would have recognized major exceptions to every one of his canons. I see no reason why our reluctance to define 'Georgian' by a too dogmatic, rigorous set of poetic tenets should disturb, of all people, the modern critic, sceptical as he is about the validity of most literary labels. Is Keats a typical 'Romantic' poet, or are we to take Byron as the archetype? What is a 'Pre-Raphaelite' poet? Who is the most typically 'Victorian', Browning, Meredith, or James Thomson? And so with the Georgians. In what sense can we call D. H. Lawrence a Georgian and at the same time Walter de la Mare and John Masefield? If Wilfrid Gibson is a Georgian, can we include James Elroy Flecker in the same category? The fact is that Edward Marsh did not intend—in his first three volumes, at any rate—to establish a poetic coterie or deliberately to choose work which bore any particular 'ranch-brand' (as Robert Graves called it). Within the limits of his own taste of course, Marsh sought only to display the work of new, young poets, who, he thought, were not getting an adequate hearing. To be sure, as Marsh himself conceded, the new poets demonstrated what may be called a Georgian temper. They had, as Marsh wrote, 'certain points in common', several of which we have been able to identify: spiritual euphoria, a sense of vitality, anti-Victorianism, realism, and freedom of poetic diction. But most of these tendencies were not uniquely Georgian; they rather marked the Georgians, like the Imagists, Vorticists, and even Futurists, as scions of their age. Until 1917, at least, the Georgians were in no sense a formal school.

Again, assuming that the word 'Georgian' describes primarily a certain temper, or set of mind, and not (strictly speaking) a poetic school, we are still not using the word entirely accurately until we recognize that there were in effect two Georgian movements, not one. I have called them Georgian and Neo-Georgian; and I have suggested that although they share certain features—most notably, a predilection for pastoral verse—the differences between the two groups of poets are more striking than their similarities. In fact, the characteristic Georgian themes and techniques are so thoroughly distorted and attenuated in Neo-Georgian verse that the two groups come finally to differ more in kind than in degree. The Neo-Georgians achieved a glib competence in verse writing. Their poetry was what a more modern generation would call 'slick'. But they lacked the will, the emotional intensity, and the creative imagination by which alone the raw material of experience is moulded into art. Having lost their creative principle, they became too exclusively recorders.

In imputing to the Georgians the shortcomings of their Neo-Georgian successors, the critic often appears to be carrying coals to Newcastle. The Georgians have several deficiencies of their own which are sometimes a good deal more obvious than their virtues. Their shortcomings have also been a good deal more fully explored and publicized, thanks to the almost universally hostile criticism of the twenties. Subsequent critics of the Georgians, however, rang the changes by and large on the points made by several contemporary observers, notably T. S. Eliot, Middleton Murry, and Edith Sitwell. Eliot accused the Georgians—though only with volume III, it should be recalled—of too much 'pleasantness' of either the 'insidiously didactic, or Wordsworthian' variety, or the 'decorative, playful or solemn, minor-Keatsian' kind. Miss Sitwell charged them—though specifically exempting such poets as Davies, de la Mare, and Hodgson—with a too sentimental view of nature, a penchant for writing about 'dreamy, plaster-faced sheep with Alexandra fringes'. And though his remarks were directed more towards the Neo-Georgians than Georgians, Murry warned them against 'false simplicity' (the 'worship of trees and birds and contemporary poets in about equal proportions'), and the 'luminous haze' of a 'fundamental right-mindedness'. None of the charges can be entirely denied. Even at its best Georgian poetry suffers from a characteristic thinness. It shies away from both the profoundly intellectual and the profoundly emotional; the former tempted the Georgians too much to rhetoric, the latter too much to didacticism. But in their efforts to avoid seeming rhetorical the Georgians sometimes fell into the opposite trap of banality; in their efforts to escape didacticism they often wrote verse which presented the raw materials of experience but was not an imaginative elucidation of the meaning of experience. Their nature lyrics, the very genre in which they may be allowed to have excelled, frequently demonstrate this characteristic thinness. They attempted to preserve the Wordsworthian tradition divorced from the thoughtful aspects of Wordsworth. As both Eliot and Huxley pointed out, the Georgians tried to be nature poets without a philosophy of nature. And so despite their newness, the Georgians can be said in several respects to have come to rest in a comfortable poetic backwater, only faintly stirred by the mainstream of the emotions and themes of their age, apparently unaware, as Eliot complained, of the 'tragedies and ecstasies' of the 'adult, sophisticated, civilised mind' of the twentieth century.

To some observers the Georgians' virtues appear more debatable than their deficiencies. Nevertheless, it seems to me that not only according to the standards of their own age but also according to the standards of any age, *Georgian Poetry* I and II particularly contained some excellent verse. The Georgian poetic achievement is too severely limited to suit all tastes—as Sir Edmund Gosse remarked, the best Georgians were jewellers whereas the great Victorians were sculptors—but within their usually self-prescribed limits, some of the Georgians were uncommonly effective poets. Surely one should not have to apologize for an anthology containing such poems as Lawrence's 'Snapdragon' and 'Snake', Davies's 'Kingfisher', de la Mare's 'The Listeners' and 'The Mocking Fairy', Abercrombie's 'Sale of St. Thomas', and much of Blunden's pastoral verse.

Viewed solely in the context of their own age, however, the Georgians played a part in the revolution in technique which overtook English poetry from 1910 to 1920. How thoroughgoing a revolution it was can be too easily overlooked. Put in the simplest terms, English poetry entered the second decade with Watson and Phillips, and it emerged at the other end with *The Waste Land*. In the years between, Georgians, Imagists, Vorticists, Post-Impressionists, verslibrists, all played a part. With all the new schools of the time the Georgians too shared a common distaste for poetic verbiage; they tried to write without rant, bombast, or rhetorical flourish; and they insisted by and large upon a return to unstilted, unpretentious poetic diction. Centrists though they were, the major Georgians agreed with Ezra Pound: modern poetry must not 'try to seem forcible by rhetorical din, and luxurious riot'; it must have 'fewer painted adjectives impeding the shock and stroke of it'; it must be 'austere, direct, free from emotional slither'.

But the clearest evidence of the Georgian temper is to be found not in the technique but in the tone of Georgian poetry. The hallmark of the Georgian poet was his vitality, the sense of buoyancy and optimism which he carried over into his poetry. With the Georgians, English poetry regained for a few brief years the joy of living. Perhaps Rupert Brooke expressed it best: 'With such superb work to do, and with the wild adventure of it all, and with the other minutes . . . given to the enchantment of being even for a moment alive in a world of real matter (not that imitation gilt stuff one gets in Heaven) and actual people—I have no time now to be a pessimist.' The same sense of elation is apparent in almost every kind of Georgian utterance: in Davies's 'Good Morning, Life—and all / Things glad and beautiful'; in Lawrence's passionate cry of 'exultation after fear, the exultation in the vast freedom we have suddenly got'; in Abercrombie's perception of 'that terrific splendid fact, the fact *that we do exist*'; in Brooke's 'Breathless, we flung us on the windy hill'. The Georgians were characteristically breathless at their sudden beholding of the wonders of a 'world of real matter and actual people'.

What is more natural, then, than that the Georgians should have excelled in nature lyrics, in descriptions of England's farms and fields, moors and hedgerows? That was 'the world of real matter', in which they saw, with an early morning vision newly stimulated, a reflection of the spiritual vigour which they felt within themselves. What more natural, too, than that the Georgians should have scorned the poetic practices and attitudes of the Victorians and the cloistered aesthetes of the nineties? Hence Lawrence's strictures against 'the nihilists, the intellectual, hopeless people', Ibsen and Hardy, 'who represent the dream we are waking from'. Hence Monro's scorn of lean aesthetes 'in velvet coats and baggy trousers' and the 'poets and professors' who had tried to sequester poetry from life. From the Georgians' sense of vitality, too, arose perhaps their most characteristic trait: realism. What technique could have been more natural for the poet who attempted to convey his sense of joy or enchantment at being 'even for a moment alive' and sentient 'in a world of real matter and actual people'? Realism was also the device by which the Georgian poet frequently showed his disdain for odious Victorian sentimentalism; consequently, in works like 'Channel Passage' and 'King Lear's Wife' he sometimes overdid his rebellion. As Robert Bridges warned as early as 1912, the Georgian poet was likely to end up with too much of the raw experience of art but not enough art. In spite of his failures, however, the Georgian poet at least tried to see again with his own eyes and to feel with his own emotions.

Georgian vitality and optimism were short-lived. 'We have faith in the vastness of life's wealth,' wrote Lawrence in 1913. 'There is no winter that we fear.' But a year later the winter of the spirit descended. From the other side of the war, to a disillusioned and cynical generation, the Georgians' spiritual euphoria seemed only ironic, material for angry attacks and malicious jibes. And so the Georgians were all grouped indiscriminately together, labelled lark-lovers, and ignominiously dismissed from further consideration. Before we are tempted thus to damn out of hand, in all honesty we must recall that the Georgians were individual poets, not indistinguishable ciphers. And surely every poet is entitled to a separate hearing before condemnation. We must recall also that the too commonly accepted pattern of the Georgian as a lark-lover is a good deal too tidy to be true. Not a single Georgian poet entirely fits such a pattern. Pseudo-pastoralism, 'the "low-tension" verse, the false rusticity, the self-conscious charm conveyed in glib technique': if these are (in Christopher Hassall's phrase) the attributes which we ordinarily conjure up as 'Georgian', then an unprejudiced re-examination of at least the first three volumes of *Georgian Poetry* should suggest to us that it is time we reconsider our assumptions about what is and is not 'Georgian'. Moreover, the Georgians have too long been the victims of pure critical spleen. Vigour, optimism, energy, and vitality were the very qualities calculated to infuriate the critics of the cynical, jaded post-war generation. Many of their assaults were both unreasoning and unfair, for they too frequently boiled down to one fundamental proposition: the Georgian poet must be damned because he failed to foresee the disasters, spiritual and physical, which were to occur from 1914 to 1918. To condemn a poet for lack of insight is defensible. But to blame a poet for lack of foresight is absurd.

In their own place and time the Georgian poets were provocative; they were quite capable of raising passionate attackers and, in some cases, equally passionate defenders. But during the past three decades modern critics and literary historians have treated them by and large with a silence which is more eloquent, perhaps, than abuse. The past several years have afforded some evidence, however, that a re-evaluation of the Georgian achievement and of the significance of the Georgian movement has finally begun. At the very least, in the present climate of critical opinion it has once again become possible to discuss Georgian poetry with reasonable assurance that one will not be hooted down or laughed out of court. The late Christopher Hassall's edition of *The Prose of Rupert Brooke* (1956), his *Edward Marsh: A Biography* (1959), and his *Rupert Brooke: A Biography* (1964) go far towards righting some of the imbalance which has so long afflicted our criticism of the Georgians. Mr. Alan Pryce-Jones's recent anthology, *Georgian Poets* (The Pocket Poets, 1959), and Mr. James Reeves's more extensive collection, *Georgian Poetry* (Penguin, 1962), go even further.

None of these writers is interested in whitewashing the Georgians; none tries to exonerate them from certain obvious shortcomings. But none of them falls into the trap of the opposite extreme either; none adopts the contemptuous tone so familiar in the criticism of the twenties. Common to all of them are at least two basic assumptions: first, that it is time—and past time—that the Georgian poets be viewed in a historical perspective, in the perspective, that is, of their own age; and secondly, that in spite of certain deficiencies, the major figures in Edward Marsh's anthology wrote a good deal of serious poetry which should be evaluated seriously.

To this point have we come, then: because new facts and new documents have now become available, we can for the first time, undertake an assessment of the Georgian achievement in the light of solid historical evidence, not mere uninformed prejudice. Now that it has begun, how fast and how far the process of re-evaluating the Georgians can—or should—go depends upon how rapidly new evidence becomes available and perhaps also upon the vagaries of literary fashion. At this point it seems a reasonably certain prediction, however, that the last word on the place of the Georgians in the stream of English poetic history has by no means been said.

# References

In the following notes several abbreviations have been used. Among
the more important are the following:

  E. M.: Sir Edward Marsh
    *GP*: *Georgian Poetry*
  *MLC*: *The Marsh Letter Collection* (for complete identification see
         Acknowledgements, pp. 17–18, and Bibliography,
         pp. 279–80)
    *NS*: *The New Statesman*
    *PD*: *Poetry and Drama*
    *PR*: *Poetry Review*
   *SEL*: *Studies in English Literature* (a publication of the Imperial
         University, Tokyo)
   *TLS*: *The Times Literary Supplement*

## Chapter 1

1 Frank Swinnerton, *Background With Chorus: A Footnote to Changes
in English Literary Fashion Between 1901 and 1917* (London, 1956),
pp. 166–7.
2 Alan Pryce-Jones, ed., *Georgian Poets*, The Pocket Poets (London,
1959), p. 5.
3 Frank Swinnerton, *The Georgian Literary Scene* (London, 1935),
p. 265.
4 *Poetry of the Transition*, eds. Thomas Parrott and Willard Thorp
(New York, 1936), p. xxxiii.
5 J. Griffyth Fairfax, 'William Watson: The Poet of Public Affairs',
*PR*, I (1912), 163.

6 See, for example, Bennett's acknowledgement of his sources in the preface to *The Old Wives' Tale*.

7 Vivian de Sola Pinto, *Crisis in English Poetry* (London, 1951), p. 115.

8 Ibid., p. 116.

9 Ibid., p. 117.

10 Michael Roberts, *T. E. Hulme* (London, 1938), pp. 206–7.

11 Shane Leslie, *End of a Chapter* (London, 1916), pp. 222–3.

12 Edgar Jepson, *Memories of An Edwardian and Neo-Georgian* (London, 1937), p. 148.

13 Amy Cruse, *After the Victorians* (London, 1938), p. 220.

14 *The Letters of Henry James*, ed. Percy Lubbock (London, 1920), II, 273–4.

15 *TLS*, 11th Nov. 1920, p. 729.

16 de Sola Pinto, p. 119.

17 Edith Batho and Bonamy Dobrée, *The Victorians and After* (London, 1938), p. 73.

18 Edward Shanks, 'The "New" Poetry, 1911–1925', *Second Essays on Literature* (London, 1927), p. 111.

19 J. Middleton Murry, *Between Two Worlds* (London, 1935), pp. 239–40.

20 Harold Monro, *Some Contemporary Poets* (London, 1920), p. 21.

21 'The Georgian Renaissance', *Rhythm*, II (Mar. 1913), Literary Supplement, xvii–xx.

22 Henry James, 'Preface', *Letters from America*, by Rupert Brooke (London, 1916), p. xxx.

23 'John Drinkwater: An Appreciation', *PR*, I (1912), 169.

24 'The Poetic Revival', *Land and Water*, Christmas 1917, p. 63.

25 H. J. C. Grierson and J. C. Smith, *A Critical History of English Poetry* (London, 1947), p. 499.

26 Alun R. Jones, *The Life And Opinions of T. E. Hulme* (London, 1960), p. 35.

27 Quoted by Geoffrey Wagner, *Wyndham Lewis* (London, 1957), p. 196.

28 'The 'Nineties', *PR*, I (1912), 247.

29 Grierson and Smith, *A Critical History of English Poetry*, pp. 499–500.

30 Ford Madox Hueffer, *Thus to Revisit* (London, 1921), p. 174.

31 Laurence Binyon, *Tradition and Reaction in Modern Poetry*, English Association Pamphlet No. 63 (1926), pp. 5–6.

32 Laurence Binyon, 'The Return to Poetry', *Rhythm*, I, no. 4 (Spring 1912), 1–2.

33 Holbrook Jackson, 'A Plea for Revolt in Attitude', *Rhythm*, I, no. 3 (Winter 1911), 7.

34 Ford Madox Hueffer, 'Thus to Revisit', *English Review*, XXI (1920), 403.
35 Max Weber, *Cubist Poems* (London, 1914).
36 F. R. Leavis, *New Bearings in English Poetry* (London, 1950), p. 9.
37 Arthur M. Clark, *The Realistic Revolt in Modern Poetry* (Oxford, 1922), p. 11.
38 John Gould Fletcher, *Life Is My Song* (New York, 1937), p. 68.
39 Francis Bickley, 'Some Tendencies in Contemporary Poetry', *New Paths*, eds. C. W. Beaumont and M. T. H. Sadler (London, 1918), p. 2.
40 Edgar Jepson, *Memories of An Edwardian*, p. 150.
41 *The Letters of Ezra Pound: 1907–1941*, ed. D. D. Paige (London, 1951), p. 91.
42 Alan Pryce-Jones, ed., *Georgian Poets*, pp. 5–6.
43 *TLS*, 26th May 1921, p. 337.
44 Ibid.
45 Harold Monro, 'The Imagists Discussed', *Egoist*, II, no. 5 (1st May 1915), 78.
46 Robert Graves, *Hogarth Essays, No. 8*, p. 10.
47 Lascelles Abercrombie, 'Poetry and Contemporary Speech', *English Association Pamphlet No. 27* (1914), p. 11.
48 Alan Pryce-Jones, ed., *Georgian Poets*, p. 6.
49 A. M. Clark, *The Realistic Revolt*, p. 23.
50 Robert Graves, *Hogarth Essays, No. 8*, p. 9.
51 Ezra Pound, 'Prolegomena', *PR*, I (1912), 73 (italics mine).
52 *The Letters of Ezra Pound*, p. 50.
53 Ibid., p. 47.
54 'Prolegomena', *PR*, I (1912), 76.

# Chapter 2

1 Arthur Stringer, *The Red Wine of Youth* (New York, 1948), p. 57; *TLS*, 29th Aug. 1912, p. 337.
2 Harold Monro, *Some Contemporary Poets*, p. 23.
3 Edward Davison, *Some Modern Poets* (New York and London, 1928), p. 145.
4 Robert Lynd, *Old and New Masters* (London, 1919), p. 155.
5 Ibid., p. 150.
6 Harold Monro, *Some Contemporary Poets*, p. 23.
7 Edmund Blunden, 'Poetry of the Present Reign', *John O'London's Weekly*, 27th Apr. 1935, p. 111.
8 Harold Monro, *PD*, I (1913), 263.

9  Paris: Sansot, 1910.
10  *PD*, I (1913), 264.
11  Trans. Harold Monro, *PD*, I (1913), 263. The manifesto originally appeared in *Le Figaro*, 20th Feb. 1909.
12  *PD*, I (1913), 321–6.
13  Frank Swinnerton, *Background With Chorus*, p. 169.
14  *PD*, I (1913), 358.
15  Geoffrey Wagner, *Wyndham Lewis*, pp. 128–30.
16  *New Freewoman*, I, no. 12 (1st Dec. 1913), 226.
17  Edward Marsh, *A Number of People* (London, 1939), pp. 295–6.
18  Geoffrey Wagner, *Wyndham Lewis*, p. 130.
19  Richard Aldington, *Life for Life's Sake* (New York, 1941), p. 108. See also Charles Norman, *Ezra Pound* (New York, 1960), p. 148, for an amusing description of the same episode.
20  *Blast*, I (1914), 143–4.
21  *PD*, I (1913), 263.
22  *Egoist*, I, no. 1 (1st Jan. 1914), 8.
23  *NS*, II (1914), 349.
24  *Egoist*, IV, no. 1 (Jan. 1917), 6.
25  *Blast*, II (1915), 20, 48–50. In subsequent printing the title of the latter poem became 'Rhapsody *on* a Windy Night'.
26  'Our Contemporaries', *Blast*, II (1915), 21.
27  *Blast*, II (1915), 5.
28  *Blast*, I (1914), 143–4.
29  Ibid., p. 149.
30  *Blast*, II (1915), 147. See also Geoffrey Wagner, *Wyndham Lewis*, pp. 147–8.
31  John Gould Fletcher, *Life Is My Song*, p. 137.
32  *Blast*, I (1914), 30–42. The 'Manifesto' from which this passage was taken was signed by, among others, Lewis, Pound, Aldington, Gaudier-Brzeska, and Wadsworth.
33  *Blast*, I (1914), 11–28. Some of the names were deliberately mis-spelled (Wagner, *Wyndham Lewis*, p. 147).
34  *Blast*, I (1914), 45.
35  Ibid., p. 48.
36  Ibid., p. 49.
37  Ibid., p. 154. The subject is covered more comprehensively in Stanley K. Coffman, *Imagism* (Norman, Okla., 1951), pp. 204–7.
38  *Blast*, II (1915), 33–4.
39  John Gould Fletcher, *Life Is My Song*, pp. 62–3.
40  *Blast*, I (1914), 160.
41  Richard Aldington, *Life for Life's Sake*, p. 144.
42  Donald Gallup, *T. S. Eliot: A Bibliography* (London, 1952), p. 82.

43 Stanley K. Coffman, *Imagism*, pp. 196–7.
44 *New Freewoman*, I, no. 12 (1st Dec. 1913), 226.
45 Stanley K. Coffman, *Imagism*, p. 213.
46 'Parochialism in Art', *Egoist*, I, no. 23 (1st Dec. 1914), 443.
47 Quoted in Charles Norman, *Ezra Pound*, p. 95.
48 *Egoist*, I, no. 13 (1st July 1914), 247.
49 'The Imagists Discussed', *Egoist*, II, no. 5 (1st May 1915), 77–8.
50 Alun Jones, *T. E. Hulme*, p. 51.
51 Richard Aldington, *Life for Life's Sake*, p. 133.
52 For a fuller account of Murry's and Miss Mansfield's connection
   with *Rhythm* and *Blue Review*, see F. A. Lea, *The Life of John Middleton
   Murry* (London, 1959), pp. 27–38.
53 *Rhythm*, I, no. 1 (Summer 1911), 36.
54 *Rhythm*, I, no. 4 (Spring 1912), 34.
55 E.g. in *English Review*, XXXI (1920), 403–4.
56 *Rhythm*, I, no. 3 (Winter 1911), 36.
57 'The Meaning of Rhythm', *Rhythm*, II, no. 5 (June 1912), 18–20.
58 *Rhythm*, I, no. 3 (Winter 1911), 36.
59 *Rhythm*, I, no. 1 (Summer 1911), 10.
60 *Rhythm*, II, no. 2 (July 1912), 46, 49.
61 *Rhythm*, II, no. 5 (June 1912), 34.
62 *Rhythm*, II, no. 2 (July 1912), 38–9.
63 'A Plea for a Revolt in Attitude', *Rhythm*, I, no. 3 (Winter 1911),
   6–10.
64 'The Georgian Renaissance', *Rhythm*, II (Mar. 1913), Literary Supplement, xvii–xx.
65 'The Return to Poetry', *Rhythm*, I, no. 4 (Spring 1912), 1–2.
66 *Blue Review*, I, no. 1 (May 1913), 51, 55.

# Chapter 3

1 *PD*, I (1913), 265.
2 F. S. Flint, biographical preface to *The Collected Poems of Harold
   Monro*, ed. Alida Monro (London, 1933), p. vii.
3 F. S. Flint, preface to Monro, *Collected Poems*, p. viii.
4 Ibid., p. vi. This estimation is also agreed to by del Re (*SEL*, XII,
   327–9).
5 del Re, 'Georgian Reminiscences', *SEL*, XII, 325–6.
6 *TLS*, 11th Nov. 1920, p. 729.
7 F. S. Flint, preface to Monro, *Collected Poems*, pp. viii–ix.
8 *PD*, I, 265.
9 Ibid., p. 127.

10 *PR*, I (1912), 3, 499.
11 Ibid., p. 563. *The Poetical Gazette* and *The Journal of the Poetry Society* are variant titles of the same journal. Its full title was *The Poetical Gazette: The Official Journal of the Poetry Society.*
12 *PD*, I, 8–11. Most of the facts regarding Monro's struggle with the Poetry Society are taken from Monro's apologia found in this source. They are occasionally supplemented by information acquired during my interview with Mrs. Monro.
13 *PR*, I, 3.
14 Ibid., p. 4.
15 Ibid., p. 3.
16 Ibid., p. 277.
17 Ibid., p. 298.
18 Ibid., pp. 353–4.
19 Ibid., pp. 59–60.
20 Ibid., pp. 151–2.
21 Ibid., pp. 312–13.
22 Ibid., p. 62.
23 Anna Bunston de Bary, 'The Poetry of Christina Rossetti', *PR*, I, 203.
24 *PR*, I, 250.
25 Ibid., pp. 324–5.
26 Ibid., pp. 274–5.
27 Ibid., p. 498.
28 Ibid., pp. 202, 251, 295.
29 del Re, *SEL*, XII, 329.
30 Harold Monro to E. M., 12th May 1914, *MLC*.
31 *PD*, I, 7.
32 *PR*, I, 499 (italics supplied).
33 *PD*, I, 265.
34 John Drinkwater, *Discovery* (London, 1932), pp. 224–5.
35 *PD*, I, 128.
36 Ibid., p. 262.
37 Ibid., pp. 264–5.
38 Ibid., pp. 389–91.
39 Information was derived from my interview with Mrs. Monro.
40 The estimate of both the amount of funds expended and length of the period over which they were spent is Mrs. Monro's.
41 *PR*, I, 498.
42 Ibid. pp. 499–500.
43 Sir Osbert Sitwell, *Laughter in the Next Room* (London, 1949), p. 35.
44 Arthur Stringer, *Red Wine of Youth*, p. 91.
45 *PR*, I, 499.

46 Elizabeth S. Sergeant, *Robert Frost: The Trial by Existence* (New York, 1960), p. 120.
47 H. S. Ede, *A Life of Gaudier-Brzeska* (London, 1930), p. 131.
48 *PD*, I, 387.
49 Edward Marsh, *A Number of People*, p. 295.
50 Elizabeth Sergeant, *Robert Frost*, pp. 100–1.
51 Arthur Stringer, *Red Wine of Youth*, p. 131. For a slightly divergent account of the same episode, see Charles Norman, *Ezra Pound*, p. 152.
52 *PD*, I, 387.
53 Lascelles Abercrombie to E. M., 15th May 1914, and *passim*, MLC.
54 John Gould Fletcher, *Life Is My Song*, pp. 50–1.
55 James Stephens to E. M., 12th Dec. 1913, MLC.

# Chapter 4

1 Christopher Hassall, *Edward Marsh, Patron of the Arts: A Biography* (London, 1959), pp. 109–13, 178–9.
2 Brinsley Ford, 'Past and Present', *Eddie Marsh: Sketches for a Composite Literary Portrait*, comps. Christopher Hassall and Denis Mathews (London, 1953), p. 17.
3 John Rothenstein, *Eddie Marsh*, comps. Hassall and Mathews, p. 15.
4 Raymond Mortimer, ibid., p. 14.
5 Edward Marsh, *A Number of People*, p. 319.
6 Ibid., pp. 319–20.
7 Harold Monro to E. M., 6th Feb. 1912, MLC.
8 Lascelles Abercrombie to E. M., 19th Mar. [1914], MLC.
9 Edward Marsh, *A Number of People*, pp. 299–300.
10 Ibid., p. 300. Abercrombie lived at the time in Ryton, Dymock, Gloucestershire.
11 Wilfrid Gibson to E. M., 15th May 1915, MLC.
12 John Middleton Murry, *Between Two Worlds*, p. 237.
13 Wilfrid Gibson to E. M., 21st Mar. 1935, MLC.
14 Alan Pryce-Jones, ed., *Georgian Poets*, p. 8.
15 'Introduction', *Georgian Poetry*, ed. James Reeves. The Penguin Poets (London, 1962), p. xiv.
16 Edward Marsh, *A Number of People*, pp. 322–3.
17 Ibid., p. 32.
18 Sturge Moore to E. M., 14th Oct. 1912, MLC.
19 Sturge Moore to E. M., undated (but *c.* 20th Oct. 1912), MLC.
20 D. H. Lawrence to E. M., undated except 'Tuesday' (but postmarked '19.11.13'), MLC.

21 D. H. Lawrence to E. M., 17th Dec. 1913, *MLC* (italics supplied).
22 Christopher Hassall, *Edward Marsh*, p. 329.
23 Edward Marsh, *A Number of People*, p. 274.
24 Ibid., p. 276.
25 Ibid., Ch. XIII.
26 *Letters of Ezra Pound*, ed. Paige, p. 103.
27 del Re, *SEL*, XII, 461.
28 Reprinted in Arthur Stringer, *Red Wine of Youth*, pp. 97–8.
29 *PR*, I (1912), 178.
30 Edward Marsh, *A Number of People*, p. 277.
31 Arthur Stringer, *Red Wine of Youth*, pp. 101–2; Christopher Hassall, *Edward Marsh*, pp. 176–7.
32 Arthur Stringer, *Red Wine of Youth*, p. 102.

# Chapter 5

1 Edward Marsh, *A Number of People*, pp. 320–1.
2 Ibid., p. 321.
3 Christopher Hassall, *Edward Marsh*, p. 190.
4 Ibid., pp. 189–90.
5 Arthur Stringer, *Red Wine of Youth*, p. 129.
6 John Drinkwater, *Discovery*, pp. 228–9.
7 Christopher Hassall, *Edward Marsh*, pp. 190–1.
8 Frank Swinnerton, *The Georgian Literary Scene*, p. 267.
9 del Re, *SEL*, XII, 464.
10 Christopher Hassall, *Edward Marsh*, p. 194.
11 Sturge Moore to E. M., 26th Sept. 1912, *MLC*.
12 John Masefield to E. M., 27th Sept. 1912; W. H. Davies to E. M., 28th Sept. 1912; John Drinkwater to E. M., 29th Sept. 1912; Gordon Bottomley to E. M., 1st Oct. 1912, *MLC*; Christopher Hassall, *Edward Marsh*, p. 192.
13 W. H. Davies to E. M., 28th Sept. 1912, *MLC*.
14 D. H. Lawrence to E. M., 5th Oct. 1912, *MLC*.
15 Christopher Hassall, *Edward Marsh*, p. 193.
16 John Drinkwater to E. M., 29th Sept. 1912; Gordon Bottomley to E. M., 1st Oct. 1912, *MLC*.
17 John Masefield to E. M., 27th Sept. 1912, *MLC*.
18 Christopher Hassall, *Edward Marsh*, p. 195.
19 John Masefield to E. M., 30th Sept. 1912, *MLC*.
20 John Masefield to E. M., 12th July 1913; 20th Jan. 1914, *MLC*.
21 Arthur Stringer, *Red Wine of Youth*, p. 130.
22 Rupert Brooke to E. M., 9th Nov. 1912, *MLC*.

23 John Drinkwater, *Discovery*, p. 229.
24 E. M. to Rupert Brooke, 11th Nov. 1912, *MLC*.
25 John Drinkwater to E. M., 1st Dec. 1912, *MLC*.
26 Wilfrid Gibson to E. M., 14th Jan. 1913, *MLC* (misdated '1912').
27 Alfred Noyes to E. M., 19th Oct. [1912], *MLC*.
28 Maurice Hewlett to E. M., 10th Oct. [1912], *MLC*.
29 del Re, *SEL*, XII, 465.
30 Edward Marsh, *A Number of People*, p. 326.
31 Arthur Stringer, *Red Wine of Youth*, p. 129.
32 Harold Monro to E. M., 12th May 1914, *MLC*.
33 Harold Monro to E. M., 12th Dec. 1915, *MLC*.
34 *Chapbook*, vol. II (Jan. 1920), no. ii.
35 Harold Monro to E. M., 26th Nov. 1921, *MLC*.
36 Harold Monro to E. M., 30th June 1922, *MLC*.
37 Edward Marsh, *A Number of People*, p. 329.
38 F. R. Leavis, *New Bearings in English Poetry*, p. 62.
39 James Stephens to E. M., 14th July 1913, *MLC*.
40 John Drinkwater to E. M., 6th May 1913, *MLC*.
41 W. H. Davies to E. M., 12th July 1913, *MLC*.
42 D. H. Lawrence to E. M., 24th Jan. 1914, *MLC*.
43 W. H. Davies to E. M., 4th Mar. 1916, *MLC*.
44 Charles Norman, *Ezra Pound*, pp. 81, 107.
45 James Stephens to E. M., 14th July 1913, *MLC*.
46 Christopher Hassall, *Edward Marsh*, p. 203.
47 del Re, *SEL*, XIV, 38.
48 Sturge Moore to E. M., 21st Jan. 1914, *MLC*.
49 Christopher Hassall, *Edward Marsh*, pp. 268-9.
50 Harold Monro to E. M., 12th May 1914, *MLC*.
51 John Masefield to E. M., 20th July 1914, *MLC*.
52 John Masefield to E. M., 22nd July 1914, *MLC*.
53 Harold Monro to E. M., 19th Aug. 1914, *MLC*.
54 Lascelles Abercrombie to E. M., 24th Aug. 1914, *MLC*.
55 W. H. Davies to E. M., 25th Aug. 1914, *MLC*.
56 Wilfrid Gibson to E. M., 16th Aug. 1914, *MLC*.
57 Wilfrid Gibson to E. M., 23rd Aug. 1914, *MLC*.
58 *TLS*, 11th Jan. 1917, p. 20.
59 Harold Monro to E. M., 29th Sept. 1915, *MLC*.
60 Gordon Bottomley to E. M., 27th July 1915, *MLC*.
61 W. H. Davies to E. M., 31st Aug. 1915, *MLC*.
62 Harold Monro to E. M., 14th Oct. 1915, *MLC*.
63 James Stephens to E. M., 4th Mar. 1916, *MLC*.
64 Harold Monro to E. M., 21st Mar. 1916, *MLC*.
65 Gordon Bottomley to E. M., 23rd Jan. 1914, *MLC*.

# Chapter 6

1 Edward Marsh, 'Prefatory Note', *GP* II.
2 Edward Marsh, *A Number of People*, p. 322.
3 J. C. Squire, *London Mercury*, I (1919), 201.
4 'Introduction', *Georgian Poetry*, ed. James Reeves, pp. xi, xii.
5 'Introduction', *Georgian Poets*, ed. Alan Pryce-Jones, p. 7.
6 Herbert Palmer, *Post-Victorian Poetry* (London, 1938), p. 78.
7 Edward Marsh, *A Number of People*, p. 322.
8 del Re, *SEL*, XIV, 33-4.
9 Frank Swinnerton, *Background With Chorus*, p. 154.
10 'Introduction', *Georgian Poetry*, ed. James Reeves, p. xi.
11 J. C. Squire, 'The Poetic Revival', *Land and Water*, Christmas 1917, p. 64.
12 D. H. Lawrence, 'The Georgian Renaissance', *Rhythm*, vol. II (Mar. 1913), Literary Supplement, pp. xvii-xx.
13 J. C. Squire, 'Mr. W. H. Davies', *Land and Water*, 3rd Oct. 1918, p. 15.
14 del Re, *SEL*, XII, 465.
15 John Bailey, 'The Poetry of Robert Bridges', *Quarterly Review*, CCXIX (1913), 231-2.
16 S. P. B. Mais, 'Some Poets of Today', *Land and Water*, 30th Dec. 1915, pp. 15-17.
17 Ezra Pound, 'Prolegomena', *PR*, I (1912), 76.
18 Robert Bridges to E. M., 6th Feb. 1913, *MLC*.
19 *TLS*, 27th Feb. 1913, p. 81.
20 Ibid.
21 *PR*, I, 132.
22 Ibid., pp. 112-18.
23 Henry Newbolt, '*Georgian Poetry 1911-1912*', *PD*, I (1913), 52.
24 *TLS*, 27th Feb. 1913, p. 81.
25 Christopher Hassall, *Edward Marsh*, p. 684.
26 *London Mercury*, I (1919), 201.
27 D. H. Lawrence to E. M., 24th May 1914, *MLC*.
28 John Drinkwater to E. M., 27th Sept. 1915, *MLC*.
29 Gordon Bottomley to E. M., 3rd Oct. 1915, *MLC*.
30 Lascelles Abercrombie to E. M., 2nd Oct. [1915], *MLC*.
31 John Drinkwater to E. M., 1st Oct. 1915, *MLC*.
32 John Drinkwater to E. M., 27th Sept. 1915, *MLC*.
33 Gordon Bottomley to E. M., 28th Sept. and 10th Oct. 1915, *MLC*.
34 Christopher Hassall, *Edward Marsh*, pp. 268, 273.

35 Ibid., p. 277.
36 Gordon Bottomley to E. M., 30th Apr. 1914, *MLC*.
37 *TLS*, 9th Dec. 1915, p. 447.
38 *NS*, V (1915), 281.
39 Lascelles Abercrombie to E. M., 11th Dec. [1915], *MLC*.
40 Wilfrid Gibson to E. M., 29th Dec. 1915, *MLC*.
41 John Drinkwater to E. M., 29th Dec. 1915, *MLC*.
42 Gordon Bottomley to E. M., 8th Jan. 1916, *MLC*.
43 J. C. Squire to E. M., 13th Jan. 1916, *MLC*. See also Squire to E. M., 29th Dec. 1915, *MLC*. For a cogent modern defence of 'King Lear's Wife' see Christopher Hassall, *Edward Marsh*, p. 378.
44 Gordon Bottomley to E. M., 8th Jan. 1916, *MLC*.
45 John Drinkwater to E. M., 24th Dec. 1915, *MLC*.
46 Ibid.
47 Harold Monro to E. M., 17th Dec. 1915, *MLC*.

# Chapter 7

1 J. C. Squire, *Water-Music* (London, 1939), p. 131.
2 *The Times*, 26th Apr. 1915, p. 6.
3 Frank Swinnerton, *Background With Chorus*, p. 175.
4 *TLS*, 7th Jan. 1915, p. 4.
5 *PD*, II (1914), 250.
6 *TLS*, 1st July 1915, p. 217.
7 J. C. Squire, *NS*, VII (1916), 377.
8 Douglas Goldring, *Reputations* (London, 1920), p. 102.
9 Ibid., p. 112.
10 Robert Graves to E. M., 22nd May 1915, *MLC*.
11 Robert Graves to E. M., 10th Nov. 1915, *MLC*.
12 Robert Graves to E. M., 15th Mar. [1916?], *MLC*.
13 Siegfried Sassoon to E. M., 14th July [1915?], *MLC*.
14 Siegfried Sassoon to E. M., 10th Feb. [1916?], *MLC*.
15 Siegfried Sassoon to E. M., 16th Mar. [1916?], *MLC*.
16 Isaac Rosenberg to E. M., undated (but late 1915), *MLC*.
17 Isaac Rosenberg to E. M., undated (but *c.* Sept. 1916), *MLC*.
18 See letter from H. J. Creedy to E. M., War Office, 8th Jan. 1917, and letter from Rosenberg's C.O. (signature illegible) to E. M., 28th Jan. 1917, *MLC*.
19 Isaac Rosenberg to E. M., undated (postmarked 8th Feb. 1917), *MLC*.
20 Isaac Rosenberg to E. M., undated (but postmarked 25th Apr. 1917), *MLC*.

21 Isaac Rosenberg to E. M., undated (but postmarked 8th May 1917), *MLC*.
22 Isaac Rosenberg to E. M., undated [1916?], *MLC*.
23 J. C. Squire to E. M., undated (but *c*. June 1917), *MLC*.
24 Harold Monro to E. M., 22nd June 1917, *MLC*.
25 Harold Monro to E. M., 26th June 1917, *MLC*.
26 Lascelles Abercrombie to E. M., undated (but *c*. 20th June 1917), *MLC*.
27 Harold Monro to E. M., 26th–29th July 1917, *MLC*.
28 Harold Monro to E. M., 12th Aug. 1917, *MLC*.
29 Wilfrid Gibson to E. M., 1st Aug. 1917, *MLC*.
30 Wilfrid Gibson to E. M., 23rd Aug. 1917, *MLC*.
31 John Freeman to E. M., 5th Aug. 1917, *MLC*.
32 Harold Monro to E. M., 26th–29th July 1917, *MLC*.
33 Walter de la Mare to E. M., 3rd Sept. 1917, *MLC*.
34 Harold Monro to E. M., 27th Sept. 1917, *MLC*.
35 J. C. Squire to E. M., undated (but *c*. Aug. 1917), *MLC*.
36 W. J. Turner to E. M., 4th Aug. 1917, *MLC*.
37 J. C. Squire to E. M., undated (but *c*. Aug. 1917), *MLC*.
38 Maurice Baring to E. M., 13th Apr. 1917, *MLC*. In this letter I have supplied occasional punctuation and capitalization for the sake of clarity.
39 Maurice Baring to E. M., 4th July 1917, *MLC*.
40 Harold Monro to E. M., 26th–29th July 1917, *MLC*.
41 Edmund Gosse to E. M., 20th Aug. 1917, *MLC*.
42 *Athenaeum*, no. 4,626 (Feb. 1918), p. 103.
43 *To-day*, no. 11 (Jan. 1918), pp. 197–8.
44 *TLS*, 27th Dec. 1917, p. 646.
45 *Egoist*, V, no. 3 (Mar. 1918), 43–4. Eliot wrote this review under the pseudonym 'Apteryx'.
46 Maurice Baring to E. M., 14th Dec. 1917, *MLC*.
47 Edmund Gosse to E. M., 12th Dec. 1917, *MLC*.
48 *John Freeman's Letters*, eds. Gertrude Greeman and Sir John Squire (London, 1936), p. 65.
49 David Daiches, *Poetry and the Modern World* (Chicago, 1940), p. 58.
50 Ibid., p. 57.

# Chapter 8

1 Donald Gallup, *T. S. Eliot: A Bibliography*, p. 80.
2 T. S. Eliot, 'Reflections on Vers Libre', *NS*, VIII (1917), 518–19.
3 See especially J. C. Squire in *Land and Water*, 24th Jan. 1918.

4 D. H. Lawrence, 'Verse Free and Unfree', *Voices*, II, no. 4 (1919), 129–34. See above, Ch. 4.
5 Douglas Goldring, *The Nineteen Twenties* (London, 1945), p. 153. See also Douglas Goldring, *South Lodge*, pp. 124–5.
6 *TLS*, 4th Jan. 1917, p. 11.
7 *Egoist*, V, no. 3 (Mar. 1918), 44.
8 *TLS*, 30th Dec. 1920, p. 889.
9 Edith Sitwell, *Poetry and Criticism* (London, 1925), *passim*.
10 *Trio: Dissertations on Some Aspects of National Genius by Osbert, Edith, and Sacheverell Sitwell* (London, 1938), pp. 131–8. The book comprises six lectures, two by each of the three Sitwells, delivered in 1937 at the Univ. of London as the Northcliffe Lectures.
11 Edith Sitwell, *Aspects of Modern Poetry* (London, 1934), pp. 18–19.
12 *Art and Letters*, II, no. 1 (Winter 1918), 52.
13 *Art and Letters*, II, no. 2, n.s. (Spring 1919), 54.
14 Osbert Sitwell, 'Te Deum', *Art and Letters*, II, no. 1 (Winter 1918), 1–2.
15 *TLS*, 22nd May 1919, p. 274.
16 *Coterie*, nos. 6 and 7 (Christmas double no., Winter 1920–1), pp. 2–5.
17 *Criterion*, I, no. 1 (Oct. 1922), 50–64.
18 F. A. Lea, *The Life of John Middleton Murry*, pp. 68–9.
19 E.g. Thomas Moult to E. M., 11th Mar. 1919, *MLC*.
20 *Voices*, I, no. 4 (1919), 228.
21 *To-day*, no. 29 (July 1919), p. 161.
22 Later (1933) Sir John Squire.
23 Harold Monro, *Some Contemporary Poets*, p. 149.
24 Christopher Hassall, *Edward Marsh*, p. 420.
25 *NS*, II (7th Mar. 1914), 694.
26 *NS*, III (4th July 1914), 406. For Squire's equally acidulous comments on the second number of *Blast*, see *NS*, V (14th Aug. 1915), 449.
27 *London Mercury*, I (1920), 386–7. Note references to this periodical will hereafter be abbreviated to *Mercury*. For a more detailed account of Squire's power as the 'chief literary reputation maker' in pre-war days, see Frank Swinnerton, *Background With Chorus*, pp. 156–7.
28 Frank Swinnerton, *Background With Chorus*, p. 156.
29 *Mercury*, I (1919), 1–6.
30 Ibid., (1920), pp. 334–5.
31 *Mercury*, IV (1921), 432.
32 *Mercury*, III (1921), 441.
33 Ibid., (1920), p. 7.
34 Ibid., (1921), p. 359.
35 *Mercury*, I (1920), 388.

36 Herbert Palmer, *Post-Victorian Poetry*, p. 95.
37 *TLS*, 24th Nov. 1921, p. 771.
38 *Coterie*, no. 5 (Autumn 1920), pp. 59–60.
39 *Coterie*, no. 4 (Easter 1920), pp. 50–1.
40 E. V. Knox, *These Liberties*, pp. 129–30.
41 E. V. Knox, *Parodies Regained*, pp. 95–8.
42 Harold Monro, *Some Contemporary Poets*, p. 15.
43 Ibid., pp. 9–15.
44 Ibid., pp. 150–1.
45 E.g. Alec Waugh in *To-day*, no. 32 (Oct. 1919), p. 61.
46 Gerald Gould, 'Where Poetry Stands', *English Review*, XXXII (1921), 352.
47 Douglas Goldring, 'Modern Critical Prose', *Chapbook*, II (Feb. 1920), 12–13.
48 Bernard Lintot (pseud.), 'End Papers', *To-day*, no. 35 (Jan. 1920), pp. 197–200.

# Chapter 9

1 Harold Monro to E. M., 15th Apr. 1919; 25th Apr. 1919, *MLC*.
2 Harold Monro to E. M., 13th Dec. 1919, *MLC*.
3 Harold Monro to E. M., 30th Apr. 1921, *MLC*.
4 Harold Monro to E. M., 14th Aug. 1922, *MLC*.
5 Edmund Blunden to E. M., 28th Nov. 1922, *MLC*.
6 Edward Marsh, *A Number of People*, p. 329.
7 Thomas Moult to E. M., 18th May 1919; 17th July 1919, *MLC*.
8 E.g. J. R. Ackerley to E. M., 2nd June 1919, *MLC*.
9 Edward Shanks to E. M., 10th Apr. 1919, *MLC*.
10 Edmund Gosse to E. M., 11th Dec. 1919, *MLC*.
11 Thomas Moult to E. M., 1st Aug. 1922, *MLC*.
12 Thomas Moult to E. M., 7th Aug. 1922, *MLC*.
13 Robert Bridges to E. M., 9th June 1922, *MLC*.
14 Robert Bridges to E. M., 11th July 1922, *MLC*.
15 Robert Bridges to E. M., 6th Nov. 1922, *MLC* (italics supplied).
16 John Masefield to E. M., 12th July 1919; and undated postcard (but *c*. mid-July 1919), *MLC*.
17 Walter de la Mare to E. M., 18th Aug. 1919; 15th June 1922; and undated letter (but *c*. 25th June 1922), *MLC*.
18 Lascelles Abercrombie to E. M., 3rd July [1922], *MLC*.
19 Gordon Bottomley to E. M., 9th July 1922, *MLC*. See also Bottomley to E. M., 17th July 1922, in which Bottomley thanks E. M. for indulging his desire to be excluded from *GP* v.

20  Edward Shanks to E. M., 11th Apr. 1919, *MLC*.
21  Siegfried Sassoon to E. M., 16th July 1919, *MLC*.
22  Siegfried Sassoon to E. M., 11th July [1922], *MLC*.
23  W. J. Turner to E. M., undated (but *c.* mid-1919), *MLC*. See also Turner to E. M., 4th Jan. 1922, in which the poet defends his play *The Man Who Ate The Popomack* against Marsh's charge of obscurity.
24  W. J. Turner to E. M., 11th July 1922, *MLC*; Christopher Hassall, *Edward Marsh*, p. 495.
25  W. J. Turner to E. M., 14th July 1922, *MLC*.
26  *TLS*, 11th Dec. 1919, p. 738.
27  Amy Lowell, 'Weary Verse', *Poetry and Poets* (Boston, 1930), pp. 123–36.
28  *NS*, XIV (1919), 224–6.
29  Amy Lowell, *Poetry and Poets*, p. 125.
30  *TLS*, 11th Dec. 1919, p. 738.
31  *NS*, XIV (1919), 225.
32  *TLS*, 11th Dec. 1919, p. 738.
33  Amy Lowell, *Poetry and Poets*, p. 130.
34  *Egoist*, V, no. 3 (Mar. 1918), 43–4. See above, Ch. 7.
35  T. S. Eliot, 'A Note on Ezra Pound', *To-day*, no. 19 (Sept. 1918), pp. 3–4.
36  F. A. Lea, *The Life of John Middleton Murry*, pp. 68–9.
37  Christopher Hassall, *Edward Marsh*, p. 474.
38  J. Middleton Murry, *Athenaeum*, no. 4,675 (5th Dec. 1919), pp. 1,283–5; reprinted as 'The Present Condition of English Poetry' in Murry's *Aspects of Literature* (London, 1920), pp. 139–49.
39  *TLS*, 11th Jan. 1923, p. 24.
40  Edmund Gosse, 'Georgian Poetry', reprinted in *More Books on the Table* (London, 1923), pp. 231–4.
41  Alec Waugh, 'The Neo-Georgians', *Fortnightly Review*, CXV, n.s. (1924), 126–37.
42  Holbrook Jackson, *To-day*, no. 53 (Mar. 1923), p. 113.

# Chapter 10

1  E.g. William Y. Tindall, *Forces in Modern British Literature* (New York, 1947), p. 373.
2  Christopher Hassall, *Edward Marsh*, p. 464.
3  John Freeman to E. M., 1st Aug. 1920, *MLC*. See also letters from Freeman to E. M., 5th July 1920, and 30th July 1919, *MLC*.
4  Christopher Hassall, *Edward Marsh*, p. 465.
5  Gordon Bottomley to E. M., 29th Nov. 1919, *MLC*.

6 Edmund Blunden to E. M., 3rd Dec. 1922, *MLC*.

7 See above, Ch. 9.

8 Alec Waugh, 'The Neo-Georgians', *Fortnightly Review*, CXV, n.s. (1924), 129–30.

9 J. Middleton Murry, 'The Condition of English Literature', *Athenaeum*, no. 4,697 (7th May 1920), pp. 597–8.

10 Douglas Goldring, 'An Appreciation of D. H. Lawrence', *Art and Letters*, II, no. 2, n.s. (Spring 1919), 90.

11 *TLS*, 19th Jan. 1922, p. 38.

12 Robert Graves to E. M., 30th Nov. [1919], *MLC*.

13 Robert Graves to E. M., undated (but *c.* early 1922), *MLC*.

14 Harold Monro, *Some Contemporary Poets*, p. 15.

15 J. Middleton Murry, 'A Poet of the Moon', *Athenaeum*, no. 4,710 (6th Aug. 1920), pp. 169–70.

16 Edward Shanks to E. M., 10th Apr. 1919, *MLC*.

17 *TLS*, 16th Feb. 1922, p. 104.

18 *TLS*, 14th Apr. 1921, p. 241. The volume specifically at issue in this review was *Paris and Helen* (1921), but the critic's observations apply equally to much of the rest of Turner's verse.

19 Robert Graves to E. M., 30th Nov. [1919], *MLC*.

20 Richard Church, *Eight for Immortality* (London, 1914), p. 9.

21 W. H. Davies, 'Confession', *Form*, no. 2 (Apr. 1917), p. 18.

22 W. H. Davies, 'Down Underground', *The Golden Hind*, no. 3 (Apr. 1923), p. 3.

23 Osbert Sitwell, *Who Killed Cock Robin?* (London, 1921), pp. 7, 13, 27.

24 Christopher Hassall, ed., *The Prose of Rupert Brooke* (London, 1956), p. xlix.

25 Ibid., pp. xlix–l.

26 Aldington accomplished his purpose primarily by means of a satiric poem, 'To A Poet', *Egoist*, I, no. 9 (1st May 1914), 161.

27 *Egoist*, IV, no. 8 (Sept. 1917), 118–19.

28 *Athenaeum*, no. 4,701 (4th June 1920), p. 732.

29 *Athenaeum*, no. 4,717 (24th Sept. 1920), pp. 405–6.

30 Harold Monro to E. M., 8th June 1925, *MLC*.

31 Edward Marsh, *A Number of People*, pp. 329–30.

# Bibliography

The sources consulted for this volume fall into three general classifications: letters, periodicals, and individual books and periodical articles. The following list, though representing only a fraction of the sources examined, includes all items likely to be of substantial use to a student of the Georgian period. Some ephemeral reviews and editorial comments which have been referred to and documented in the text have been omitted here.

The major single source for this volume has been the Edward Marsh Letter Collection. That part of the Collection which I examined comprised letters to Sir Edward Marsh written by many of the major English poets and literary figures from approximately 1895 to 1950. The Collection also includes numerous letters—though I did not examine them in detail—from many prominent English social and political figures written over approximately the same span of years. When I consulted the Collection in 1954 and 1955, it was owned by Mr. Christopher Hassall. In 1957 it was sold by Mr. Hassall to the New York Public Library, where it has now become a part of the Berg Collection. With a few exceptions, such as the letters of D. H. Lawrence and Isaac Rosenberg, the correspondence in the Marsh Letter Collection is unpublished.

Out of a total of approximately 2,000 letters and postcards which I examined, the correspondence of the following persons proved to be the most useful and significant:

| | | |
|---|---|---|
| Lascelles Abercrombie | John Freeman | Thomas Moult |
| Laurence Binyon | Wilfrid W. Gibson | Isaac Rosenberg |
| Edmund Blunden | Sir Edmund Gosse | Siegfried Sassoon |
| Gordon Bottomley | Robert Graves | Edward Shanks |
| Robert Bridges | Ralph Hodgson | Edith Sitwell |
| Frances Cornford | D. H. Lawrence | Osbert Sitwell |
| W. H. Davies | Shane Leslie | Sacheverell Sitwell |

Walter de la Mare  John Masefield   J. C. Squire
John Drinkwater   J. Middleton Murry James Stephens
James Elroy Flecker  Harold Monro   W. J. Turner

Of the periodicals and the little magazines of the Georgian age which
I consulted, the following are the most significant:

*Art and Letters*     *Flying Fame*     *The New Statesman*
*The Athenaeum*     *Pamphlets*     *The Owl*
*Blast*         *Form*       *Poetry and Drama*
*The Blue Review*    *The Fortnightly*   *Poetry Review*
*Calendar:*        *Review*      *The Quarterly*
 *A Quarterly*     *The Golden Hind*   *Review*
 *Review*       *John O'London's*  *Rhythm*
*The Chapbook:*     *Weekly*      *Root and Branch*
 *A Monthly*     *Land and Water*   *The Times Literary*
 *Miscellany*     *The London Mercury*  *Supplement*
*Coterie*       *The New Age*    *To-day*
*The Egoist*      *The New Freewoman*  *Voices*
*The English Review*   *New Numbers*

The following books and periodical articles are the most useful. The
place of publication is London unless otherwise specified.

Abercrombie, Lascelles. 'The Function of Poetry in Drama', *Poetry
 Review*, I (1912), 107–8.
 *The Idea of Great Poetry.* 1925.
 'John Drinkwater: An Appreciation', *Poetry Review*, I (1912), 168–70.
 'Poetry and Contemporary Speech', *English Association Pamphlet No.
 27.* 1914.
Aldington, Richard. *Egoist*, I, no. 13 (1st July 1914), 247.
 *Life for Life's Sake.* New York, 1941.
 *New Freewoman*, I, no. 12 (1st Dec. 1913), 226.
 'Parochialism in Art', *Egoist*, I, no. 23 (1st Dec. 1914), 443.
Bailey, John. *Poetry and the Commonplace.* Oxford, 1920.
 'The Poetry of Robert Bridges', *Quarterly Review*, CCXIX (1913),
 231–55.
Baring, Maurice. *Punch and Judy and Other Essays.* 1924.
Batho, Edith, and Bonamy Dobrée. *The Victorians and After, 1830–
 1914.* 1938.
Beaumont, C. W., and M. T. H. Sadler, eds. *New Paths, 1917–1918.*
 1918.
Benson, A. C. *Escape and Other Essays.* 1915.
Beresford, J. D., and others. *Tradition and Experiment in Present-Day
 Literature.* 1929.

Binyon, Laurence. 'The Return to Poetry', *Rhythm*, I (Spring 1912), 1–2.
> *Tradition and Reaction in Modern Poetry*: English Association Pamphlet
> No. 63. 1926.
Blunden, Edmund. 'Poetry of the Present Reign', *John O'London's Weekly*, 27th Apr. 1935, pp. 111–14.
> *Undertones of War*. 1928.
Brererton, Frederick, comp. *An Anthology of War Poems*. 1930.
Brooke, Rupert. *Collected Poems*. 1918.
> *Letters From America*. 1916.
> *New Statesman*, III (1914), 638–40.
Bullough, Geoffrey. *The Trend of Modern Poetry*, 3 ed. 1949.
Burdett, Osbert. *Memory and Imagination*. 1935.
*Catholic Anthology*. Ezra Pound, comp. 1915.
Chesterton, G. K. *Come to Think of It*. 1930.
Church, Richard. *Eight for Immortality*. 1941.
Clark, Arthur M. *The Realistic Revolt in Modern Poetry*. Oxford, 1922.
Coffman, Stanley K. *Imagism: A Chapter for the History of Modern Poetry*.
> Norman, Okla., 1951.
Collins, H. P. *Modern Poetry*. 1925.
Cournos, John. *Autobiography*. New York, 1935.
> *Egoist*, IV, no. 1 (Jan. 1917), 6–7.
Croft-Cooke, Rupert. *How to Get More out of Life*. 1938.
Cruse, Amy. *After the Victorians*. 1938.
Cunliffe, J. W. *English Literature During the Last Half Century*, 2 ed.
> London, 1923.
Daiches, David. *Poetry and the Modern World*. Chicago, 1940.
Davison, Edward L. *Some Modern Poets and Other Essays*. New York,
> 1928.
de la Mare, Walter. *Rupert Brooke and the Intellectual Imagination*. 1919.
Delattre, Floris. 'La Poésie Anglaise', *Revue Germanique*, no. 4 (July–
> Aug. 1912), pp. 433–57.
> *La Poésie Anglaise d'Aujourd'hui*. Paris, 1921.
De Sola Pinto, Vivian. *Crisis in English Poetry, 1880–1940*. 1951.
Drew, Elizabeth, and John L. Sweeney. *Directions in Modern Poetry*.
> New York, 1940.
Drinkwater, John. *Discovery, the Second Book of an Autobiography*. 1932.
> *Inheritance, the First Book of an Autobiography*. 1931.
> *Rupert Brooke: An Essay*. 1916.
> 'Tradition and Technique', *Poetry Review*, I (1912), 296–300.
Ede, H. S. *A Life of Gaudier-Brzeska*. 1930.
*Egoist*, II, no. 5 (1st May 1915). 'Special Imagist Number'.
Eliot, T. S. ('Apteryx'). *Egoist*, V, no. 3 (Mar. 1918), 43–4.
> 'A Note on Ezra Pound', *To-day*, no. 19 (Sept. 1918), pp. 3–4.

'Reflections on Contemporary Poetry', *Egoist*, IV, no. 8 (Sept. 1917), 118–19.

'Reflections on Vers Libre', *New Statesman*, VIII (1917), 518–19.

Aldous Huxley, and F. S. Flint. 'Three Critical Essays on Modern Poetry', *Chapbook*, no. 9, 1920.

Ellis, G. U. *Twilight on Parnassus: A Survey of Post-War Fiction and Pre-War Criticism*. 1939.

Evans, Sir Benjamin Ifor. *English Literature Between the Wars*. 1948.

Fairchild, Hoxie Neale. *Religious Trends in English Poetry*. Vol. IV. New York, 1957.

Fairfax, J. Griffyth. 'William Watson: The Poet of Public Affairs', *Poetry Review*, I (1912), 160–3.

Flecker, James Elroy. *Collected Prose*. 1920.

Fletcher, John Gould. *Life Is My Song*. New York, 1937.

Flint, F. S. 'The History of Imagism', *Egoist*, II, no. 5 (1st May 1915), 70–1.

Ford (Hueffer), Ford Madox. *Return to Yesterday*. 1931.

   *Thus to Revisit*. 1921.

Freeman, Gertrude, and Sir John Squire, eds. *John Freeman's Letters*. 1936.

Gallup, Donald. *T. S. Eliot: A Bibliography*. 1952.

Gawsworth, John. *Ten Contemporaries: Notes Toward Their Definitive Bibliographies*. 1932.

Gibson, Wilfrid. 'The "Georgian Poets", or Twenty Years After', *Bookman*, LXXXII (1932), 82, 280–2.

Goldring, Douglas. 'An Appreciation of D. H. Lawrence', *Art and Letters*, II, no. 2, n.s. (Spring 1919), 89–99.

   'English Literature and the Revolution', *Coterie*, no. 3 (Dec. 1919), pp. 69–73.

   'Modern Critical Prose', *Chapbook*, II (Feb. 1920), 7–14.

   *The Nineteen Twenties*. 1945.

   *Reputations*. 1920.

   *South Lodge*. 1943.

Gosse, Sir Edmund. 'Georgian Poetry', *More Books on the Table*. 1923, pp. 227–35.

Gould, Gerald. 'Where Poetry Stands', *English Review*, XXXII (1921), 347–52.

Graves, Robert. *The Common Asphodel*. 1949.

   *Contemporary Techniques of Poetry: A Political Analogy*. Hogarth Essays, No. 8. 1925.

   'The Future of English Poetry', *Fortnightly Review*, CXIX (1926), 289–302, 443–53.

   and Laura Riding. *A Pamphlet Against Anthologies*. 1928.

   and Laura Riding. *A Survey of Modernist Poetry*. 1927.

Grierson, H. J. C., and J. C. Smith. *A Critical History of English Poetry*. 1947.

Grigson, Geoffrey. 'Notes on Contemporary Poetry', *Bookman*, LXXXII (1932), 287–9.

Hassall, Christopher. *Edward Marsh, Patron of the Arts: A Biography*. 1959.

— ed. *The Prose of Rupert Brooke*. 1956.

— and Denis Mathews, comps. *Eddie Marsh: Sketches for a Composite Literary Portrait of Sir Edward Marsh, K.C.V.O., C.B., C.M.G.* 1953.

Haythorne, W. 'Georgian', *Contemporary Review*, CXXVI (1924), 222–8.

Hodgson, Geraldine. *Criticism at a Venture*. 1919.

Hughes, Glenn. *Imagism and the Imagists: A Study in Modern Poetry*. Stanford, Calif., 1931.

Huxley, Aldous. *Athenaeum*, no. 4,701, 4th June 1920, p. 732.

— *Athenaeum*, no. 4,717, 24th Sept. 1920, pp. 405–6.

— ed. *The Letters of D. H. Lawrence*. 1932.

Jackson, Holbrook. 'A Plea for Revolt in Attitude', *Rhythm*, I (Winter 1911), 6–10.

— *To-day*, no. 11 (Jan. 1918), pp. 197–8.

— *To-day*, no. 53 (Mar. 1923), pp. 113–14.

Jepson, Edgar. *Memories of an Edwardian and Neo-Georgian*. 1937.

Johnstone, John K. *The Bloomsbury Group*. New York, 1954.

Jones, Alun R. *The Life and Opinions of T. E. Hulme*. Boston, 1960.

Keynes, Geoffrey, ed. *The Poetical Works of Rupert Brooke*. 1946.

Knox, E. V. *Parodies Regained*. 1921.

— *These Liberties*. 1923.

Lawrence, D. H. 'The Georgian Renaissance', *Rhythm*, II (Mar. 1913), Literary Supplement, xvii–xx.

— *The Collected Letters of D. H. Lawrence*. Harry T. Moore, ed. 2 vols. New York, 1962.

— *The Letters of D. H. Lawrence*. Aldous Huxley, ed. New York, 1932.

— 'Verse Free and Unfree', *Voices*, no. 4 (1919), pp. 129–34.

Lea, F. A. *The Life of John Middleton Murry*. 1959.

Leavis, F. R. *New Bearings in English Poetry*. 1950 ed.

Leslie, Shane. *The End of A Chapter*. 1916.

Lewis, Wyndham. *Egoist*, I, no. 1 (1st Jan. 1914), 8–9.

— 'Long Live the Vortex!', *Blast*, I (1914), 7–8.

— and others. 'Manifesto', *Blast*, I (1914), 30–42.

— 'The Melodrama of Modernity', *Blast*, I (1914), 143–4.

'Lintot, Bernard' (pseud.). 'End Papers', *To-day*, no. 35 (Jan. 1920), pp. 197–200.

Lowell, Amy. 'Weary Verse', *Poetry and Poets*. New York, 1930, pp. 123–36.

Lynd, Robert. *Old and New Masters*. New York, 1919.

Mackenzie, Compton. *Literature In My Time*. 1933.

MacNeice, Louis. 'Poetry Today' in Geoffrey Grigson, ed., *Arts Today*. 1935, pp. 25–67.

Mais, S. P. B. 'Some Poets of Today', *Land and Water*, 30th Dec. 1915, pp. 15–17.

Mansfield, Katherine, and J. M. Murry. 'Seriousness in Art', *Rhythm*, II (July 1912), 46–7.

Marinetti, Filippo. 'New Futurist Manifesto', Arundel del Re, trans., *Poetry and Drama*, I (1913), 319–26.

Marsh, Sir Edward. *A Number of People*. London, 1939.

    ed. *Georgian Poetry, 1911–1912; 1913–1915; 1916–1917; 1918–1919; 1920–1922.* 1912, 1915, 1917, 1919, 1922.

    'Rupert Brooke's *Poems*', *Poetry Review*, I (1912), 178–81.

Maugham, Somerset. 'Proofreading as an Avocation', *Publishers' Weekly*, CXXXVI (1939), 136.

Megroz, R. L. *Modern English Poetry, 1882–1932.* 1933.

    *Walter de la Mare: A Biographical and Critical Study.* 1924.

Monro, Alida, ed. *The Collected Poems of Harold Monro.* 1933.

    ed. *Recent Poetry, 1923–1933.* 1933.

Monro, Harold. 'Freedom', *Poetry Review*, I (1912), 59–60.

    'The Imagists Discussed', *Egoist*, II, no. 5 (1st May 1915), 77–80.

    'The 'Nineties', *Poetry Review*, I (1912), 247–8.

    *Poetry and Drama*, I (1913), 263–4.

    *Some Contemporary Poets.* 1920.

Moore, T. Sturge. *Some Soldier Poets.* 1919.

M[orton], J. B. *Georgeous Poetry, 1911–1920.* 1920.

Muir, Edwin. *Transition: Essays on Contemporary Literature.* 1926.

Murry, J. Middleton. 'Art and Philosophy', *Rhythm*, I (Summer 1911), 9–12.

    *Aspects of Literature.* 1920.

    *Athenaeum*, no. 4,646, 16th May 1919, pp. 325–6.

    *Athenaeum*, no. 4,675, 5th Dec. 1919, pp. 1,283–5.

    *Between Two Worlds.* 1935.

    'The Condition of English Literature', *Athenaeum*, no. 4,697, 7th May 1920, pp. 597–8.

    and Katherine Mansfield. 'The Meaning of Rhythm', *Rhythm*, II (June 1912), 18–20.

    and Katherine Mansfield. 'Seriousness in Art', *Rhythm*, II (July 1912), 46–7.

'A Poet of the Moon', *Athenaeum*, no. 4,710, 6th Aug. 1920, pp. 169–70.

'Who Is the Man?', *Rhythm*, II (July 1912), 37–9.

Newbolt, Henry. '*Georgian Poetry 1911–1912*', *Poetry and Drama*, I (1913), 45–52.

*A New Study of English Poetry.* 1917.

Nichols, Robert, comp. *An Anthology of War Poetry, 1914–1918.* 1943.

Norman, Charles. *Ezra Pound.* New York, 1960.

Noyes, Alfred. *Two Worlds for Memory.* 1953.

Palazzeschi, Aldo. 'Futurist Manifesto', Arundel del Re, trans., *New Statesman*, II (1914), 625–6.

Palmer, Herbert. *Post-Victorian Poetry.* 1938.

Parrott, T. M., and Willard Thorp, eds. *Poetry of the Transition: 1850–1914.* New York, 1936.

*Poetry and Drama*, I (Sept. 1913). 'Special Futurist Number'.

Pope-Hennessey, J. 'Eddie Marsh', *Spectator*, CLXXXIX (1952), 623.

Pound, Ezra. *The Letters of Ezra Pound, 1907–1941.* D. D. Paige, ed. 1951.

*Poetry*, I, no. 4 (Jan. 1913), 123–7.

'Prolegomena', *Poetry Review*, I (1912), 72–6.

Powell, Charles. *The Poets in the Nursery.* 1920.

Pryce-Jones, Alan, ed. *Georgian Poets.* The Pocket Poets. 1959.

del Re, Arundel. 'Georgian Reminiscences', *Studies in English Literature*, XII (1932), 322–31, 460–71; XIV (1934), 27–42.

Reeves, James, ed. *Georgian Poetry.* The Penguin Poets. 1962.

Reviews, unsigned:

Brooke, *Poems. Times Literary Supplement*, 29th Aug. 1912, p. 337.

*Coterie. Times Literary Supplement*, 22nd May 1919, p. 274.

*Georgian Poetry* I. *Times Literary Supplement*, 27th Feb. 1913, pp. 81–2.

*Georgian Poetry* II. *Times Literary Supplement*, 9th Dec. 1915, p. 447.

*Georgian Poetry* III. *Times Literary Supplement*, 27th Dec. 1917, p. 646.

*Georgian Poetry* IV. *London Mercury*, I (1919), 201–5.

*Georgian Poetry* IV. *New Statesman*, XIV (1919), 224–6.

*Georgian Poetry* IV. 'Georgian Poetry: New Style', *Times Literary Supplement*, 11th Dec. 1919, p. 738.

*Georgian Poetry* V. *Times Literary Supplement*, 11th Jan. 1923, p. 24.

Matinetti, *Zang Toum Toum. Times Literary Supplement*, 7th May 1914, p. 219.

'The Poems of Ralph Hodgson', *Times Literary Supplement*, 7th Oct. 1915, p. 342.

Squire, *Selections From the Modern Poets. Times Literary Supplement*, 26th May 1921, p. 337.

*Wheels. Times Literary Supplement*, 4th Jan. 1917, p. 11.

*Wheels. Times Literary Supplement*, 30th Dec. 1920, p. 889.

Rhys, Ernest. *Everyman Remembers*. 1931.

Riding, Laura. *Contemporaries and Snobs*. 1928.

  and Robert Graves. *A Pamphlet Against Anthologies*. 1928.

  and Robert Graves. *A Survey of Modernist Poetry*. 1927.

Roberts, Michael. *T. E. Hulme*. 1938.

Rosenberg, Isaac. *The Collected Works of Isaac Rosenberg: Poetry, Prose, Letters and Some Drawings*. Gordon Bottomley and Denys Harding, eds. 1937.

Rothenstein, Sir William. *Men and Memories: Recollections of William Rothenstein, 1900–1922*. 1931.

Sassoon, Siegfried. 'Englische Lyrik Seit 1914', *Die Literatur*, XXVII (1925), 201–6.

Scott-James, R. A. *Fifty Years of English Literature, 1900–1950*. 1951.

Sergeant, Elizabeth S. *Robert Frost: The Trial by Existence*. New York. 1960.

Shanks, Edward. *New Statesman*, X (1917), 280–1.

  *Second Essays on Literature*. 1927.

Sitwell, Edith. *Aspects of Modern Poetry*. 1934.

  *Poetry and Criticism*. 1925.

  and Osbert and Sacheverell Sitwell. *Trio: Dissertations on Some Aspects of National Genius*. 1938.

Sitwell, Sir Osbert. *Great Morning*. 1948.

  *Laughter in the Next Room*. 1949.

  *Left Hand, Right Hand*. 1945.

  *Who Killed Cock Robin? Remarks on Poetry and its Criticism*. 1921.

Squire, Sir John C. *London Mercury*, I (1920), 386–8.

  'Mr. W. H. Davies', *Land and Water*, 3rd Oct. 1918, p. 15.

  ('Solomon Eagle'). *New Statesman*, II (1914), 349.

  ('Solomon Eagle'). *New Statesman*, III (1914), 406.

  ('Solomon Eagle'). *New Statesman*, V (1915), 281.

  ('Solomon Eagle'). *New Statesman*, VII (1916), 377.

  ('Solomon Eagle'). *New Statesman*, IX (1917), 594.

  'The Poetic Revival', *Land and Water*, Christmas 1917, pp. 63–4.

  *Reflections and Memories*. 1935.

  'Rupert Brooke', *New Statesman*, V (1915), 85–6.

  *Tricks of the Trade*. 1917.

  *Water-Music*. 1939.

Stringer, Arthur. *The Red Wine of Youth*. New York, 1948.

Strong, L. A. G. 'English Poetry Since Brooke', *Nineteenth Century*, CXVI (1934), 460–8.

Sturgeon, Mary E. *Studies of Contemporary Poets*. New ed., 1920.

Swinnerton, Frank. *Background With Chorus: A Footnote to Changes in English Literary Fashion Between 1901 and 1917.* 1956.
  'Coteries', *Athenaeum*, no. 4,675, 5th Dec. 1919, pp. 1,281–2.
  'General Literature', *Blue Review*, I (May 1913), 51–5.
  *The Georgian Literary Scene*, cf. p. 263, n. 3, London ed., 1935.
Tindall, William York. *Forces in Modern British Literature.* New York, 1947.
Vines, Sherard. *One Hundred Years of English Literature.* 1950.
Wagner, Geoffrey. *Wyndham Lewis.* New Haven, Conn., 1957.
Ward, Alfred C. *Twentieth Century Literature: 1901–1940.* 11 ed., 1951.
Waugh, Alec. 'The Neo-Georgians', *Fortnightly Review*, CXV, n.s. (1924), 126–37.
Weber, Max. *Cubist Poems.* 1914.
West, Rebecca. *New Freewoman*, I, no. 5 (15th Aug. 1913), 86.
Williams, Harold. *Modern English Writers.* 1918.

# Index

*See p. 263 for abbreviations used*

288

Marsden, Dora, 69
Marsh, Sir Edward: 101–17
—— life: Letter Collection, 17, 279–80;
knighted, 101; education, 101–2; early
literary associations, 102–3; civil
service, 102; art collector, 103, 106;
patron of poets, 104–7, 151–8, 167, 171
—— editor of *G.P.*: aims for, 27–8, 118–
9, 130–1, 257; relationship with
Monro, 104, 119, 127, 175, 177–8; and
*G.P.* I, 118–29; and *G.P.* II, 130–5,
136–8, 154–9; and *G.P.* III, 166–7,
174–80, 187; and *G.P.* IV and V, 222–
8, 234–7, 241–3; on possible *G.P.* VI,
254. *See further under Georgian Poetry*
series
—— poetic standards: 107–12, 176–80,
234–7; and poetic renascence, 27–8,
80, 101–2, 104, 126–7, 140; and realism, 55, 114–17, 153–4, 156–7, 176;
and Poetry Bookshop, 59–60, 97; on
'modern' poetry, 103–4, 108–9, 210,
225–6, 227–8, 234–7; as anthologist,
107–8, 176–80, 187, 224–5; on poetic
drama, 153
—— relationship with poets, 104–7,
151–8, 167, 171
—— relationship with Brooke: influence of Brooke's *Poems*, 104; friendship with Brooke, 104, 112–17;
Brooke's influence on, 113, 116–17; on
Brooke's realism, 114–16; *Memoir* of
Brooke, 113. For correspondence
between Brooke and E.M., *see under*
Brooke, Rupert
—— letters from: Abercrombie, 99,
105, 132, 133, 151–2, 155–6, 175, 227;
Baring, 179; Blunden, 223, 236;
Bottomley, 134, 135, 152, 152–3, 156,
157, 176, 227, 235; Bridges, 141, 225,
225–6; Brooke, 105–6, 124; Davies,
122, 129, 133; de la Mare, 129, 177–8,
226; Drinkwater, 128–9, 151, 152,
156, 157, 158; Freeman, 177, 234, 235;
Gibson, 124–5, 133, 156, 176; Gosse,
180, 183, 224–5; Graves, 168, 169,
184, 242, 242–3; Hewlett, 126;
Lawrence, 110–11, 112, 122, 129, 151;
Masefield, 122, 123, 132; Milne, 125;
Monro, 60, 104, 127, 132–3, 134, 175,
178, 179, 222, 222–3, 223, 254;
Moore, 109, 110, 131; Murry, 107;
Pound, 122; Richmond, 125; Rosenberg, 171, 172, 173; Sassoon, 169,
169–70, 170–1, 227; Shanks, 181,
224; Squire, 156–7, 163–4, 178, 181;
Stephens, 99–100, 128, 130, 135;
Turner, 228. For subject matter of
letters, *see under* individual writers

Masefield, John: as poetic realist, 34, 47,
51–5, 147, 157; and *G.P.* I, 121,
122–3, 128; and *G.P.* II, 132; as 'Georgian', 139–30; Baring on, 183; and
*G.P.* IV, 226; Neo-Georgian reaction
against, 240–1; mentioned, 103, 136,
195, 204, 257; *Biography*, 123, 139–40
(quoted), 147 (quoted); *Dauber*, 55;
*Story of a Roundhouse*, 55; *Widow in the
Bye Street*, 55, 122
—— letters to E.M.: on *G.P.* I, 122, 123;
on *G.P.* II, 133
—— 'The Everlasting Mercy', 37, 51–5,
104, 116, 122, 184; quoted, 52, 53–4
Mayakovsky, Vladimir, 62, 141
Meredith, George, 30, 257
Mew, Charlotte, 177–8, 224
Meynell, Alice, 104
Meynell, Francis, 103–4
Middleton, Richard, 90
Miles, Susan, 197
Millay, Edna St. Vincent, 191
Milne, A. A.: letter to E.M.: on *G.P.* I,
125
Monro, Alida Klementaski, 80
Monro, Harold: 80–100 *passim*
—— life: political views, 35, 82; early
years 80–3; Mrs. Monro, 80; war
service, 190
—— as editor: *Poetry Review*, 84–9; and
Poetry Society, 84–5; *Poetry and
Drama*, 89–92; *Chapbook*, 190–1
—— as publisher: at Poetry Bookshop,
80, 93, 94–5, 99–100; of *G.P.* I, 119,
120, 121, 126, 127; of *G.P.* II, 131,
133, 134–5, 158; of *G.P.* III, 175,
177–8; of *G.P.* IV and V, 222–3, 224;
possible *G.P.* VI, 254
—— and Poetry Bookshop: 93–100,
190; association with *G.P.*, 72, 130;
inception of, 93; aims of 94–5; loca-
tion, 95–6; poets in residence, 96–7;
public poetry readings, 97–9; post-
war influence, 190
—— influence of: as popularizer of
poetry, 80–1, 83–4, 88–9, 90–1, 97; in
pre-war poetic circles, 80, 85–6, 97,
98, 100; as publisher of new poets,
94–5, 99–100, 191; relationship with
E.M., 104, 119, 121; position in post-
war poetic circles, 98, 99, 190–1, 202,
205
—— poetic principles: and pre-war
vitality, 38, 82, 83, 220; on 'Everlasting Mercy', 52, 55; and Futurism,
61, 85, 91–3; and Imagism, 73, 91;
poetic credo, 83, 85–7, 95, 97–8; as
reviewer, 87–8, 90; and literary coteries, 98, 219–20, 243